RIVERINE

RIVERINE

A Memoir from Anywhere but Here

ANGELA PALM

GRAYWOLF PRESS

This publication is made possible, in part, by the voters of Minnesota through a Minnesota State Arts Board Operating Support grant, thanks to a legislative appropriation from the arts and cultural heritage fund, and through grants from the National Endowment for the Arts and the Wells Fargo Foundation Minnesota. Significant support has also been provided by Target, the McKnight Foundation, the Amazon Literary Partnership, and other generous contributions from foundations, corporations, and individuals. To these organizations and individuals we offer our heartfelt thanks.

Published by Graywolf Press
250 Third Avenue North, Suite 600
Minneapolis, Minnesota 55401

All rights reserved.

www.graywolfpress.org

Published in the United States of America

ISBN 978-1-55597-746-7

2 4 6 8 9 7 5 3 1
First Graywolf Printing, 2016

Library of Congress Control Number: 2015953721

Cover design: Kimberly Glyder Design

Cover art: shaunl / Getty Images

For Corey, who was there, and Mike, who is here

CONTENTS

RIVERINE

PART I

MAP OF HOME

Every map is a fiction.

—D. J. WALDIE

I used to spend hours poring over the state road map, perplexed by the way towns and cities were annotated. Here was a small pink dot called Hebron, its name typed neatly in a little sans serif font. I moved my finger across light yellow paper, then across a wavy blue line until it touched the next pink dot. This one was called DeMotte. This was where I lived. In the pink dot called DeMotte in the map of Indiana. But our address was Hebron, Indiana, and not DeMotte, Indiana. Knowing little of governance and less of mapping, I rested my eyes curiously on the yellow paper—what was between the two pink-dot towns? A vast patch of nothing? How could we reside in both towns, yet seemingly in neither at the same time? Where did one town start and the other end? Was there an unnamed part between the two that was up for grabs? I wanted to conquer that yellow land and write myself all over it: this part, this swath of land right here, belongs to a girl.

I obsessed about this empty space. I turned it round and round in my head, mulling over its possibility. At school, I was learning about the laws of physics—a primary introduction to an invisible governance that was as old as time. I became aware of moving forward in time, bound by the laws of the universe. This, too, I obsessed about. It changed the way I saw everything around me, including Corey, the boy next door whose bedroom window faced mine. He moved mechanically, rhythmically, through time and space. At eight years old, I had imagined mapping myself onto his skin, clinging to the idea of a future between me and my eleven-year-old friend that did not exist. I followed him closer than his own shadow. Little girl, second skin. He did not mind.

The yellow space on the map could be an isolated system, I thought, enclosed and separate with a nuclear interior—like a thermodynamic system, where all the energy is contained and nothing gets out. I was well acquainted with the sensation of exterior isolation and interior energy, of the power in that juxtaposition. We lived many miles away from most of the kids I went to school with in DeMotte. I lacked a true set of friends, our home far from the subdivisions where kids from school played together. Instead, I took to books and art, to sketching still life pictures with charcoal and singing loudly in the rain. Though I watched Corey in his window as if he were a television show, he was a real friend, materializing beyond the frame as hands that gripped mine and swung me in circles, as feet to kick a ball to, as ears to listen to me talk and sing. As proof that we existed beyond our windows. But mostly, solitary pursuits replaced social ones and a cacophony of ideas swirled inside me, while DeMotte's social hubbub remained distant and encamped within a town I didn't feel much a part of. Further isolation stemmed from the fact that the town center, several miles from where our houses were located, was comprised of the affluent Dutch, who had settled and built homes, farms, and churches there many decades earlier. The DeMotte Dutch were a close-knit bunch: tall and blond with smart little noses, nearly interchangeable last names, and conservative values and politics. In this town, you were either Dutch or you weren't. Other backgrounds weren't given attention.

Most of the kids we lived near were poorer than us. Some of

them were the kind of poor that amounted to dirty hands, hunger, unwashed and ill-fitting clothes, and no coats at the school bus stop in the thick of winter. Many were the kind of kids who either bullied or were bullied by others. My brother, Marcus, and I were well fed and clean clothed. While our food wasn't fancy, it was abundant. A measurable amount of parental love was available to us. Our clothes were from the clearance racks at Montgomery Ward, which my mother felt was an extravagance—it was more than she'd had, and certainly more than my father had had. And it wasn't much to complain about. The clothes were usually one season removed from fashionable, but they were new and our very own. Despite these differences, all of us living by the river were the kind of kids who sometimes had money for the ice cream truck and sometimes did not. We were the kind of kids who sometimes looked on, frozen in our tracks as the truck rolled by, a plea hanging between us as a slowed-down, creaking version of "Home on the Range" cut through the air.

Something about our neighborhood had caused my parents to set physical boundaries of roaming allowance that did not extend much farther than our backyard. The road, barely wide enough for two cars to pass, had no sidewalks, and there were many drunks, as we called them, who often drove recklessly down our shared street. If you were playing on the road and a car came, you didn't simply step aside. You ran out of the way. There were also near vagabonds, supposedly unsavory individuals who stayed a spell in one of the makeshift pole barns or partially dilapidated trailers and then moved on. These were factors in our boundaries, though I didn't yet know how or why.

The area to which we were restricted had once formed the bed of the Kankakee River and often flooded. Every few years, when the human-made part of the river swelled and reclaimed its old course, our home became an island. Periods of flood became epic adventures, because our house was constructed in the exact place where the river ought to have been. Where it once *had* been. Floods gave us the opportunity to go back to a time when sustenance came from the land, as did fear and injury. We learned from our neighbors, who were active Revolutionary War reenactors and rendezvousers, how to suck the thin pink trills of grapevine when we were thirsty. We practiced spearing fish on gigantic carp, the mud-veined fish that seemed to rise up from the bloated overflow like Loch Ness monsters, with the point of an arrow. Leaning over the edge of a canoe, we would look the mythical beasts right in the eye. Then, *wham,* we hit them straight through the spine, justifying their deaths by the fact that they were inedible and served literally no useful purpose on Earth.

One day I asked my mother about the space between the pink dots. "Look at the map. Dot here. Dot there. No middle."

What was in the yellow? Could we go there and find out?

My mother was a good sport, letting my child's mind discover these small curiosities according to its own will. We got into the car and drove past two houses. The first was Corey's house. The second house belonged to my aunt Carleen, who was my mother's younger sister. We turned right, passing the River, the bar and restaurant that sat fifteen feet from the riverbank. I would someday get a job there— a rite of passage in this neighborhood that I looked forward to. We then drove across the bridge that spanned the actual river, the mighty Kankakee, as we moved along the path I'd traced on the map with my finger. Then we stopped. I'd been holding my breath.

We hadn't driven far at all.

"This is it," she said. "This is the part between the two towns."

Through the back window of our van, I could still see our house. On the other side of our newly constructed fence, smoke rose from a narrow pipe that stuck out of the top of Wild Bill's workshop, where he was undoubtedly tinkering with a metal forge, clanking red-hot iron with a small mallet, a tobacco pipe hanging from his lower lip and a green beret set askew on the top of his graying head. We thought he resembled a renegade Bilbo Baggins, the adopted uncle of all the neighborhood kids reincarnated from our favorite story, from which he read to us in his cabin as we chewed homemade sourdough pretzels by the fire. Another trail of smoke seeped from the top of his tepee, which he lived in a few months of the year, though he had a perfectly functional house. From where I sat with my mother, I could also see Penny's rusted mailbox, felled and flattened by the side of the road, left there in protest against the man who'd run out on her or as a reminder of him and how she would never take him back again. Brightly colored azaleas bloomed around its metal carcass, growing up and around its remaining parts, demanding that passersby take note of its irony. A little farther in the distance, a blue tarp extended from the front of Earl's trailer, rigged up on steel poles staked into the ground. The trailer's door hung wide open.

The laws of thermodynamics, I would learn, deal with the concept of entropy—a measure of a system's disorder and uncertainty. Entropy cannot decrease within any isolated system. It only shifts, like all matter, changing shape and colliding with itself. Diluting, diffusing, evaporating, and folding back onto itself. In our perfect history, junk particles from the big bang eventually become Lake Michigan, the Sahara, a field of tulips in Holland. What wonder is the order in disorder. What beauty. What certainty. A more specific definition of entropy considers the energy within the closed thermodynamic system. This energy serves as a yardstick for the disorder, where entropy is directly proportional to the energy's heat and inversely proportional to its temperature. In our closed system, the river was the heat and the water table was the thermometer. It was a system that seemed desperate to break the boundaries of physics.

"We live in the middle?" I asked my mother.

"Technically," she said. "Our address is in one town, and our phone number is in the other. Pay taxes to one, and go to school in the other. It's like not living in either town. Or like living in both at once."

"So nobody wants us."

I looked around, stunned by my new perspective. Most of what I saw was familiar—driveways and houses I'd seen before. These were signs of home, but I felt spat out like bad milk. And yet, I was looking at it in a new way—seeing it for the first time with the scrutiny of a stranger. It occurred to me then that this part of the map was unlike either of the pink-dotted towns. Children I went to school with did not live like us, shooting handmade weapons into the woods and wearing deerskin costumes. They were not learning Morse code or the words to Revolutionary War folk songs.

> *Soldier, soldier won't you marry me,*
> *With your musket, fife and drum?*
> *Oh, no, sweet maid I cannot marry ye,*
> *For I have no coat to put on.*

In the songs we sang, I always pictured myself as the girl waiting to be married off to a soldier or a carpenter or a sailor like some certain destiny, packaged, but unaddressed, for a future delivery date. When I was asked what I wanted to be when I grew up, I never knew how to answer. "What do you think I should be?" I would reply.

When I sketched with charcoal, I anticipated the sensation of blurring the crisp black lines into something softer, more fluid and wet-washed. When I painted with watercolors, I most often favored textures that were salt spattered or misted with water. I was engaged in an ongoing corruption of medium, and every undertaking was an exercise in thinning and thickening substances of expression until they were perfectly muddled. "Here is the fringey edge where elements meet and realms mingle, where time and eternity spatter each other with foam," Annie Dillard writes in *Holy the*

Firm. Dillard has an intimate relationship with land that shifts, with water that rises around people who can only watch and try to understand what they're seeing. Fringe investigation was the science of my neighborhood and of my art.

Along the banks of the Kankakee, where water met the land and foam blurred the line between solid and liquid states, Wild Bill lived in a tepee. *But why?* I wondered. And from that *why,* other *whys* flowed. Why did the ice cream truck driver look relieved when we shrugged our shoulders as he drove by? Why had the river been moved? Why had anyone built a whole neighborhood in an old riverbed that flooded half the time and stunk like rot and heat all the time? More important, why did they stay there? Why did some people seem a part of the land more than others, more entwined with it?

Filled with this new view, I knew that I was neither sort, but instead some half-breed spawn of both worlds and alien to both. A bookish fishergirl who longed for the social opportunities of a cookie-cutter subdivision. When I looked more closely, I saw that Penny's mailbox might well have been blue at one time. One day in the distant past, Penny and her man had bought a little house with a nice blue mailbox. They had planted flowers that emerged newly green from the soil each April. Once, hope had filled the emptied valley of the river's bends.

"You shouldn't look at it that way," my mother said, and drove the car a little farther down the road. I looked out the back window at the river behind us, the river that, over time, would thrill me, claim me, disappoint me, and save me. It wasn't a wavy blue line like its cartographic representation, but brown with muddy water that ran quickly westward. It gave me the sense that the water was the only thing that would ever get out of this place. And it was in a hurry to do so.

We were isolated by our coordinates, by the *where* of us. Where we lived was rural, in the broadest and most specific senses. Isolation was a measure of that fact. Our address was Rural Route 101. The in-between space on the map was a real place that had been there all along. Not unclaimed, not up for grabs, but completely inhabited by the parts of the two towns that were beyond "town limits." Address over here, phone number over there, missing from the map. Energy contained. Separate. Because we were beyond limits, isolated and insular, rural and unclaimed, we became unassuming outlaws of sorts. We were both on the map and off it at the same time. We were the entropy of the two towns, the junk particles of the nucleus with its own status. But even so, there was a pulse that connected us, a bloodline of sorts. In our in-between-towns land, population forty, there were nights of whiskey-fueled fireside revel, when everyone sang sea shanties and knuckled washboard rhythms beneath full moons. There were archery lessons and tomahawk throws and jewelry-making lessons. There were gourd paintings and firecrackers and canoe races. There was a band of kids who swung from the thick vines that draped our very own Sherwood Forest.

Decades later, I would find that it's in places like these that I am truly comfortable—in the square half inch of yellow paper between pink dots. The in between here and there, where damp moss grows and people sometimes live in tepees. Where a boy turns his bedroom light on and off to send an SOS signal across a small patch of grass to a lone girl who sits on a rock with a book and cannot save anyone. Where hologram children play forever and eat electric blue Popsicles and never wash their hands and sometimes spear fish with arrows. Where things stay a little bit broken. On maps, you notice, they never put a line. Between countries and states and counties, yes, but not in the yellow space between bright pink dots. But sometimes the yellow is green. Sometimes it is white. Sometimes it is brown river water, rising above the flat line of the land to prop up the identity of a tiny village.

When I came back to this spot twenty years later to see what had become of the riverbed, to see what ghosts would rise from its eroded banks, it was all still there. The road had a new name, the one-way arrow of time expanding here as it was anywhere else on Earth, but the defining entropy of the place was the same. There was no aftermath through which I could proceed as story, as I'd hoped for—no obvious tale waiting to be told. There was only stasis and the recapitulation of a contained present tense, moving toward a future that bears scars of the past. I glimpsed Earl, older now than ever, still adding scrap-made structures that outcropped around his aging trailer. Corey's parents remained, though their little white dog was no longer yapping on the front steps and Corey himself was in a prison hours away from the river. The blue house with the accidental magenta door, where I'd lived for fourteen years, was still there, the way my father had left it when we moved. The people, the *who* of the place, still bore the unmistakable marks of rural folk— that telltale dichotomy of endurance and neglect, active and passive states happening at once.

If there was a fixed point from which every other happening here flowed, it was when the river was recoursed, its snaking dregs drawn taut in the 1800s. Beyond that, there is no single human crisis, no single lens, from which this place can be understood. "We begin with the trouble," Kyle Minor writes in *Praying Drunk*, "but where does the trouble begin?" In my story, the uncle does not blow his brains out. He threatens to, but it never happens. And where is the story in that? "Nothing is going to happen in this book," writes Dillard. "There is only a little violence here and there in the language, at the corner where eternity clips time." Violence clips the corners of my past, and language sets me free.

But there is more than that. Flowers bloom and drown. Dogs

die. A friend kills. The sediment is dredged for valuable metals. The water rises and recedes. Everyone hangs on, waiting for a god to deliver a life preserver or else not. A girl becomes a woman, nearly normal. Not quite. The girl, our girl, makes it out of the riverbed, but she carries traces of brown water in her lungs and sediment in her pockets so she knows the river is still there, despite all her moving on.

AN ARSENAL OF SAND

Notice the sand which is somehow both inside you and beneath you.
—LORRAIN DORAN, *Phrasebook for the Pleiades*

On Sundays during the summer of the 1991 flood, men and their cigarette smoke circled our card table, which my father had made himself with wood left over from the ongoing remodeling he did to our home. Sundays were roll-your-owns; hand-carved pipes stuffed with tobacco; squishy, pocket-sized packs of Camels; piles of Jays potato chips on the green felt tabletop next to piles of quarters and dollar bills; and cans of bronze-rimmed Stroh's that my dad let me sip when my mom wasn't watching.

School was about to let out. Unlike the more haphazard schedule the summer months would bring, the rhythms of my school-year days began and ended with my neighbor, Corey. In the morning, we met at the bus stop and he let me get on first. At night, after his bedroom light went out, I put his wristwatch to my ear and let its quiet tick-tock lull me to sleep. He had given it to me one night when he had stayed over. I'd been scared about a storm and held his hand to my cheek as I lay in bed. "You can have it," he said as I fell asleep. When the water began to rise at the start of the summer, I started wearing it all day.

I always wanted a reason for the floods. I thought that they might be a sign from God, that perhaps we were suffering a punishment for the sins of our forebears or for sins of our own. During a flood, the end of times seemed to barrel toward our small enclave of riverfolk, while land beyond the floodplain was unaffected. During a third-grade field trip, I had learned about the over 800 Potawatomi who in 1839 had been marched at gunpoint from their land in northern Indiana southwest to Kansas. Our class had visited the nearby historic marshes containing the ruined ancient burial grounds of the Potawatomi and their lucrative trapping territory, and I came to believe that times of flood were the Potawatomi's revenge. President Andrew Jackson's Indian Removal Act of 1830 had instituted the right of the American government to negotiate land exchanges with Native American groups via treaties. Under the act, lands held east of the Mississippi by Native American tribes could be confiscated in exchange for undisclosed lands in the "west," sight unseen. Tribes that refused to negotiate, which included the Potawatomi under the leadership of the unwavering Chief Menominee, were often forcefully removed. The Potawatomi's violent extraction from their homeland in the Kankakee Marsh, though by comparison it was not as massive or as deadly as the more widely noted Cherokee Trail of Tears, was known as the Trail of Death.

The farmers had been gauging heavy rains for a week. They then made phone calls to those who lived in the old riverbed, or along the new river's banks, depending on your terminology, to report on the probability of a flood. That gave the residents two or three days to prepare for the water, which the farmers had determined would surely rise. After the necessary phone calls were made, the news burning up the wires, two dozen anxious men—my usually gregarious neighbors—set their faces to stone and hauled load after load of sandbags to dam the weak banks of the young river. Their sons and daughters—including Marcus and I—watched from their porches. Someday, we would be the ones to haul the sand. We needed to know how it was done.

The men labored silently in a long line, passing the weighty bags from man to man to man like a crew of sailors loading a ship with provisions. The last man in the line threw the bag on top of the last bag until the stack was man-high. They prepared the riverbed itself first, adding height and breadth to the banks; then the crew filled the eroded hollows between the houses of the little riverside hamlet that we called home. After that was done, they helped each other secure their own homes until every home was ready to receive the rising water.

Most folks could see the river from their porches. Everyone could smell it. When a flood was coming, an ancient stench of mud and fish and scum hung in the air—the scent of the river amplified, swollen and ready to burst. The flood itself, though, the water's tipping point, always arrived in the middle of the night.

When this one came, our phone rang around midnight on Friday. My dad put on his waders and sloshed over to his pickup truck. He pulled two more sandbags from the bed of the truck and hoisted one onto each shoulder, looking like Atlas in the moonlight to my wide eyes, and then he put them on top of the line of bags near our front door. For good measure, I guessed. Though I had the feeling that if the water got that high, sandbags wouldn't much matter.

In a question-and-answer session after reading aloud his story "On the San Juan," Ron Carlson addressed the topic of water shortage in the American Southwest in a way that only a writer can— with personification: "You get the sense that the heat wants to hurt you." It was all he really needed to say. He was talking about the violence of nature. Violence like the hot, slapping hand of the sun. Violence like cracked earth and scorched vegetation, of prolonged thirst and hunger. I thought of the Kankakee and its opposite problem. I thought of the river that taunted us each year as it crept up and spilled over its human-made boundaries toward our homes. I thought of drowning, a swifter aggression than drought.

A flood was a call to the strongest and ablest among our tribe of riverfolk, but it never stopped anything important. Not school, not work. Definitely not poker games.

The beer had been stocked early that week. On Saturday, families tended their properties for most of the day. They secured their porch furniture with chains and ropes, waiting out the rise, periodically lowering the end of a two-by-four into the water to see how much it had gained on them. Half inch by half inch. On Sunday, a couple of the men came to our house by canoe and tied it to the handrail with a mud-caked yellow rope. The other men trekked through the marsh in waist-high rubber waders, hauled themselves over the sandbag barricade, and stripped down to their clothes on the porch, which had become a peninsula, surrounded by the river's water. Once inside the house, they pulled apples and boxes of raisins from their overall pockets for me and my brother, smiling as if nothing were out of the ordinary. They handed over the treats on their way to the card table, while my mom hung their waders on metal hooks and lay towels on the linoleum beneath them to catch the brown water. The men took their seats, the same ones they hunkered into each week. My dad sat right across from Uncle Tom; Slims sat to my dad's left, Slick to his right. They began to smoke.

"Shoo-ee, young lady. You see how high that water is?" Uncle Tom said through his near-toothless smile, rubbing his flannel-covered chest with grease-stained hands. He was from a little piece down the road. Though he wasn't my real uncle, he'd have made a good one. Kind as you'd want. Much kinder than Ralph, who was cold and brusque with children. A drinker like my pops, but a different type.

Slick leaned toward me and held out his palm. "Blow on this quarter." A fella called Slick had gotten such a moniker for good reason.

I blew. That was for luck. *I hope Slick does good, but I hope Daddy does better,* I thought, my fingers crossed under my leg.

Then it was one up, one down. Bring in, ante up. The dull clank of quarters kept time over the game as the men flicked the edges of their cards with dirty fingernails and hummed to themselves. Five different tunes were going at once, none of them a recognizable melody.

I chomped apple after apple down to the core while I watched the game, juice and seeds running down my chin. My dad let me sit on his lap and watch them play, even though by his word I was too old for it at nine years old, so long as I promised not to mention which cards I saw and kept a straight face. What you couldn't do when you were playing poker was conflate the language or give yourself away. You couldn't bid when you meant to call. You couldn't fake anything. Even if you were bluffing, you had to mean it, believe it yourself. And I got real good at bluffing. Even better than my dad. In the mirror, I learned not to trust my own expressions. I could look like nothing, when I felt everything. When our dog died, my brother cried while my face stayed ordinary. Dimples and bright, dry eyes. I found myself smiling at my father all the more, bidding his favor in spite of my own aching heart while my brother crouched by his knee and sulked. When Corey walked into the room, I pretended my insides weren't ablaze. When the river flooded, I played cards with the men and it was no trouble at all.

The Kankakee River's course was significantly restructured throughout the first half of the nineteenth century. The river had once crept through one of the largest wetlands in the United States, the Great Kankakee Swamp. The swamp spread for over 5,300 square miles of dense marshland, the river jutting through it, until the Swamp Land Act of 1850 was passed. Before the Swamp Land Act and the Indian Removal Act, the Kankakee had been an important waterway for the Potawatomi and early European settlers, who trapped riverine creatures and traded their fur. Over the course of the next several decades, the Swamp Act straightened the bends of the river, one of many measures taken to drain the mega-marsh in order to turn the Indiana soil into mineral-rich farmland. In the mid–nineteenth century, Americans had begun to populate the heartland. Its rivers aided in transporting the goods produced by an impending regional industrial boom—including grains, iron ore, coal, and lumber. By the end of the nineteenth century, the new Kankakee River no longer meandered, but rather cut somewhat adroitly across Indiana and Illinois. Its new path was fortified with drainage ditches, leaching even more of the marsh's excess water outward in rigid grid patterns that fed the new farmland. The drainage system fed what was left over westward to join with the Iroquois River, eventually emptying into the Illinois River. Though I could never believe the river had looked any other way but straight, every few years the water proved me wrong and the river reclaimed its natural course, filling in its original sediment bed behind our house and throughout our neighborhood as if the very ground itself had called it back home.

Like rivers, people are always folding back on themselves, and then straightening again. Contradicting themselves. Pulling off a bluff even as they try to begin anew, and then collapsing back onto the past. Acts are passed, then are repealed by government bodies. Human progress is a bendable substance. It moves half inch by half inch. But water must go somewhere; the laws of science rarely bend.

I raked in the pile with my sticky hands when my dad won the pot. I got to count the stack, and he peeled off ones every so often and gave them to me and said, "Good work, baby girl." It was early afternoon, and he was still generous with his kindness. Then I folded the bills and put my cut of the winnings into my pocket, where the ones dampened and tore a little at the edges.

For card games, my dad wore his tattered carpenters' union T-shirt and his lucky blue trucker's cap, his curly brown hair peeking out at odd angles around his neck. On the front of the hat, a voluptuous cartoon woman stood next to a caption and looked sideways over her shoulder, blond hair tumbling midway down her back. The caption read "Tight butts drive me nuts!"

I shuffled the extra deck as the game went on, warming it up in case they needed it. I wanted badly to be useful to the men and be noticed by them—especially by my father, but also by Corey. Sometimes Marcus, Corey, and I would play our own poker game, gambling Chips Ahoy! cookies and Doritos. We were always practicing at being adults.

The men laughed their gravelly laughs and took another drink from their cans of beer. I didn't know what made the cap lucky, but I wanted to look like the woman with the tight butt. I wanted to drive a man nuts, to form curves in the right places. I was waiting for mine, and I wanted to know what to do with them when they arrived. Driving a man nuts had to be better than being someone's ol' lady, which is what my dad called my mom when he was at the poker table. The old lady, his old lady, our old lady. Like something owned. My mom brought cold beers and more food. She stayed in the kitchen, wearing a sweat suit that was a decade old, as the game progressed and the men grew drunker. She clanked pots and pans so hard you'd have thought she was trying to break something.

In poker, you didn't get to hang back and stew about what to do. That's what I liked about it. I did enough of that already, and this was a lively game that forced motion. A poker player led with thought-out action—you didn't just think, and you didn't just act.

You decided, you faced the consequences, then you got another go at it. Maybe you got lucky the next time. Maybe you broke even the whole time. But you kept perfecting your game and your bluff, thinking and acting, until the two were one.

As the game went on, the piles of money grew higher and lower as the pot shifted. I listened to the men's stories about how high the water was and who was stranded this time. Bruce from the other side of the river was making stew that everyone was welcome to, even though he'd lost his cat Buckles and his car was flooded. Penny from down the way was all alone. Some of the men helped make sure her place was taken care of, trading off hours of work for beer or fresh-baked peanut butter cookies.

The men around the poker table told and retold stories of prior floods, ones I had never seen, the water higher each time they spoke of it.

"Three feet that year we canoed the whole way down a road with them bottles of Wild Turkey," said Slims. "Floated 'em over to some right thirsty folks on Frisbees. Shoulda seen their faces light up. You'd think they'd seen Jesus walk on water."

"Five feet," said Slick, shaking his head. "And one year Willie had his motorboat out, too. You never seen a supper delivered like that."

"Nah, six feet deep if it was an inch." Uncle Tom was the biggest tale-teller of them all, once he got enough beers down. Who knew what was true? But telling the stories brought them together more than it kept them apart. It balanced the loss, which they rarely inventoried. And I liked listening, weaving myself into their history, belonging with them to something bigger than me in my own head.

When the phone rang, my mom brought it in from the kitchen—stretching the thirty-foot cord until it almost snapped. Sometimes she'd do that so you were stuck talking in front of her while she waited for you to hand it back. The phone was her territory. She handed it to my dad and then folded her arms, the sleeves of her sweatshirt pushed up to her elbows, exposing tan wrists and forearms.

My dad mumbled what sounded like an agreement and then handed the phone back. "Looks like some sandbags aren't holdin'. Said I'd give it a look after we call it a night here."

My mom nodded and walked away, the cord snagging on her way to the kitchen. She slammed the phone back onto the hook so hard it rang back at her. Everyone looked up from the poker table expectantly for a moment, then returned to the game.

My river was not the only river moved for the convenience of humans. An act of government can move a mountain if it wants to. It can move buildings and communities of people. It can build a bridge that connects two slips of land or, as in the case of Alaska's Bridge to Nowhere, it can connect one strip of land to absolutely nothing. An act of government can move a river. It sounds simple and swift when it is boiled down to words: "Move the river." But speed and ease are feats not readily scaled to a body of water. How vast the human need must be to unbend a current.

In his essay "Rivering," Dinty W. Moore discusses one such river, the Hockhocking in Ohio, which was also strategically rerouted to suit human purposes. "The engineers managed a rather graceful curve in the new riverbed," he writes, "but it doesn't feel natural. It can't be mistaken for the unpredictable, sometimes elegant, sometimes abrupt, always idiosyncratic way that a river actually cuts through a landscape." Without a current propelling it and banks to guide it, a river is only water. Moore draws a parallel between determining what's crucial to include in a narrative's undercurrent and the way that rivers are directed and controlled—both by their natural paths and by the ones that have been carved by people. The boundaries must be tempered, or else the water will burst forth and drown us all.

· · ·

Later that night, well after the men had made their way through the water and back to their homes, I sneaked out of my bedroom to the card table and put a cigarette butt in my mouth. My brother was asleep, and my parents squabbled about something in the distance. Stir crazy was what we called it. Stuck inside, stirring around each other until someone went crazy. Usually, my dad.

The refrigerator door opened and closed. I heard a can pop open, and I tried to count back how many times I'd heard that pop since the card game had started. Back and back, all day. Double digits, easily.

I pretended to smoke and said *full house* in a low voice, making it into a one-syllable word like the men did. "F'ous, boys. Read 'em and weep." Puff.

I heard a cracking sound then, and yelling. A familiar routine. Everything got loud for a few minutes, then the door slammed and the house was quiet again. These episodes tended to rattle my brother more than me. He'd wail and intervene in a heated argument, offering himself as a shield for either party, or as a bargaining chip. I'd retreat to my bedroom and wait for the talk that never came: we're getting a divorce. If I ever cried, I did it in the shower, which made it only half true.

In the morning, there was a hole the size of a dinner plate in the wall near the kitchen. My dad was already gone to work.

"What happened?" I pulled my long hair into a high ponytail.

"Your dad wanted to order a pizza. I told him we couldn't get one," said my mom. She was wearing different sweats—her going-out sweats. They were less embarrassing than her staying-in sweats, but I still hated them. Maybe she didn't know my dad liked women to look like the one on his hat—tight jeans and tight butts and small waists that cinched neatly beneath their breasts. "That was his answer." She nodded at the hole that had been punched through the wall. She said it as if it were true, unflinching, as if she dared me to believe otherwise.

I stood at the fridge and nodded, alternating bites of Pop-Tarts with drinks of milk from the jug. Anger in our family was like the water: it had to go somewhere. Rise up, sink down, or burst everywhere at once.

My mom hammered a nail into the drywall above the hole. She took six plastic pears out of a basket on the kitchen table. She shoved the pears into a random drawer and hung the basket over the hole. "The bus won't come because of the flood," she said in a flat voice. Her anger was the sinking kind.

But the bus would come. I knew it would. It just wouldn't come right up to the house. It wasn't the first flood we'd been through. When it flooded, we were supposed to get a ride out to where the water was lower, where the dead-end road met with the road that led toward town. But I guessed my mother was proving a point about the pizza, so I didn't argue. I wanted to go to school. I would miss seeing Corey that morning, but I wanted to get to where the water wasn't and where my chest didn't burn like it was trapped under a heavy rock when I tried to breathe. I needed to run around some, fill my shoes with playground rocks until home seemed a vague memory, like someplace I had read about in a book and then remembered only circumstantially, or in summary. *Oh, the place with the hole in the wall, yes, I remember it now.*

I put Corey's watch on my wrist, and it slipped down to my hand, even on the smallest setting. But I was determined to wear it. It smelled like him, and, what was more, it softened the distance between us. I wore my dad's oversized cement boots to get to the van, which was parked in the garage, where it had stayed relatively protected from the water due to the slight incline. As I waited for my mother to come out of the house, I stabbed my pocketknife into a sandbag. I wanted the sand to spill out like blood, like air from a punctured lung or helium from a popped balloon. I wanted to do harm to this bag. Inflict my ire quietly upon it. I'd make a sinkhole in the barrier, a slow leak that would float me away from this place forever. But it didn't work. The whitish-gray material that secured the sand within was dense and fibrous, and it resisted the dull blade. I worked it through with a few more jabs and wiggles, dragging it lengthwise until a small gash formed. The sand inside was packed so tightly that nothing happened at all.

When my mother walked into the garage, I stashed the knife between two of the sandbags, and we set off for school. My brother sat in the bench row seat behind me, none the wiser about the hole in the kitchen wall or about the hole I'd made in our arsenal of sand. I envied his disinclination to question the world around us, to grow weary of it. His mind didn't wake up with "Why?" in it like mine did.

My mother drove slowly along the river road, easing the front end of the blue and silver van into the water, and I watched the water filling in behind us where the vehicle had briefly parted it. I watched her face want to cry and then stop itself. Seeing this was too much for me to bear. I knew my anger would one day grow large enough to battle my father's, even if my mother's would not. I could not help her out of this, but how I wanted to try. Our eyes met in the rearview mirror. "You look pretty," I said. Prettier than the girl on the hat with the tight butt. Pretty enough not to settle for being someone's old lady, perpetually subservient and wearing sweatpants in the kitchen. When I thought I might cry, I called up my poker face. I shifted my gaze to the mailboxes that popped from the water like spring flowers. To chain-link fences half-covered in water. The roads beyond ours weren't flooded, only the parts where the river had once been. I thought of our little house plunked down right in the middle of one of those ghost bends, and the way the bottom two feet of siding were rotting away after too many floods. From the window of the van, I saw a farmer standing in thigh-deep water in the middle of his bean field. He seemed to be having a long think about what to do. I watched him as long as I could, waiting for him to raise his fist to all that water, but he never did.

THIS MOVABLE STATE

I

The year after a flood wiped out half the crops in the nearby fields, it was not uncommon for drought to have its way. From our front yard, the world was small and immediate, humid and hazy. One summer of intense heat, new fixtures within the boundaries of my range moved the days along: a dog, my father's new job, biking on the road for the length of a few neighbors' yards. On any given day, our new dog, a collie named Fido, would sleep on the porch. Her long toenails clacked against the deck when she rearranged herself in the sun, and a gigantic, cancerous tumor hung from her belly when she stood. I could peer into the living room window, where, if my father was working close to home, the television would be on and he would be napping in front of it after a long day of hoisting wooden planks and metal piping and of arranging them into towering structures. I would hear Offspring or Pearl Jam or Metallica blaring from Corey's bedroom window. When I climbed onto the roof, I would hear Wild Bill singing "Rolling Down to Old Maui" in an Irish brogue, a deep tenor, as he fiddled with an engine that wasn't likely ever to start. Across the street, cars came and went from the restaurant, holding families who gathered to celebrate birthdays, anniversaries, and graduations. I watched them carry wrapped gifts inside. Later, they would come out carrying doggy bags. Aunt Carleen's house, two houses down the road from ours, was usually quiet, and from my perch I would see its long, rectangular roof glinting sunlight back at me.

My father had begun traveling for work to New York and Delaware and Pennsylvania, building scaffolding around some of the country's oldest buildings so that they could be restored and repaired. He was gone for weeks at a time throughout a six-year stint, and we saw him less. He sent us photographs of himself a few hundred feet up in the air, a blurred father. I would kiss my index finger and press it onto the snapshot or newspaper clipping about the project. I wrote him letters on my mother's legal pads: *Dear Dad, I wish we could come visit you at work, but Mom says we don't have enough money. I love you. When are you coming home?* "Put a smile on," my mother would say. "It could be worse."

She meant he could be dead, like her dad was. We were lucky we had a father at all. There were always a few minutes when he returned home from work trips when everything was right—we rushed to hug him, and he seemed genuinely happy to see us. He'd give us T-shirts from the states he'd visited. He would play a card game with us for half an hour. He would speak to us at dinner. But it only lasted a little while. Soon, he would be brooding and fiery again. One wrong word at supper would devolve into an hour of screaming. Soon, he would eat supper in front of the television instead of facing us at the table, or he would spend his time working on another home improvement project. Soon, I would cower in my room again with my books, certain I was adopted. I suppose we were all surviving.

At the same time, though, our lives were improving. I went to a horseback riding camp for a week. We got an above-ground swimming pool and a new archery set, and we inherited Fido from an estate. My mother met all kinds of sad people at her job as a probate paralegal. Everyone she worked with had recently lost a loved one and was coming into some money or fighting over the settlement of an estate—who got the carriage house, who got the horses, who got the doilies, who got the oil lamp that didn't work. She said it got so bad sometimes that some of them would have fought over garbage. If it weren't for her, some of the grief-stricken might still have been standing there, keys in hand, surrounded by aftermath, mouths agape. She was good at helping them figure out what to do with it all. She was good at holding their hands and crying with them. Good at reminding the ones who argued of what was important. I think it was a role she liked filling. She liked to handle the big estates and say the words *millions of dollars.* Sometimes clients gave her one of their newly acquired possessions as thanks for helping them decide what to do with housefuls of inherited things. She helped them understand their new tax situation and lent a hand as they cleared through the clutter and shuffled through the ordeal of loss. Often they gave antiques or pieces of china. The dog was the only living creature she ever received. Per our inheritance, Fido came with a lifetime supply of premium dog food, paid health care, and a doghouse the size of a lawn shed. I could tell how well this dog had been loved by the way she expected love from us. On the day she came home to us, she extended her paw to me and smiled, teaching me how to love her before I'd had a chance to decide for myself whether I wanted to. I tried to give her a better name, something I could warm up to more easily than *Fido;* she pointed her snout to the sky and looked away until I came to my senses.

I also had a new cousin named Dawn, who had come to us that summer in the manner of the collie. Dawn and her father, Tully, had moved in with Aunt Carleen. The new family of three now lived in the nearby brown-and-white trailer, which was lucky for me because now I had another place to escape to. Their home sat in the center of a vast corner lot, a good place for racing or playing red rover. From our roof, I saw their entire property. The plastic Big Wheels tricycle that used to be mine rested on its side in the middle of the gravel driveway. A howling mutt chained out back slowly wrapped himself around a tree, then unwrapped and ran as far as his tether would let him. Red and yellow flowers sprouted in bright clumps, lighting up a gingerbread lawn. If I squinted, the trailer could have been a milk carton, coated with frosting and lined with graham crackers. Its scraggy shrubs, green gumdrops.

At school, I was learning about the parts of a cell. I obsessed over the idea of the perfect miniature within the perfect miniature: the idea of an atom, for example. Atoms atop atoms, eventually human. Or petal. Or tree. Or dog. The perfection of design within each thing I touched was a well of wonder that I couldn't help plunging into. From the roof, I imagined myself round and suspended in the thick liquid of my atomic world, electrically charged, ready to connect to like atoms. Water to water. Open hand to open hand. I sat on the roof, burning my bare feet on the tarry shingles, and I saw the whole of my world—everything within the cell membrane. I made myself dizzy looking round and round, tracing the circuit of this tiny kingdom until I was sick. I would have liked to go much farther than its borders. I would have liked to visit the kids farther down the road or spend all day with kids from school. I would have liked to visit anyone at all who would let me. My legs could run forever, but there was nowhere to go.

One day, Corey, my brother, and I went fishing at the creek that fed the river, scooping up crawdads with our bare hands and coaxing minnows into the soft traps of our palms. We caught a bluegill with a piece of corn on a hook. As we began the walk home with our catch, my heart stopped. There was pressure in my chest and I couldn't breathe or walk. Corey carried me home like a tiny bride, immobile in his arms, while my brother carried our fish back in a coffee can. By the time we reached the house, I was okay. We added the fish and the crawdad to our tank, which already held two black-and-white-striped angelfish—one male, one female. I told my mother about my heart, but she didn't believe me. "You're fine," she said. "It's growing pains." But when it kept happening, she took me to a doctor. He used a sonogram machine to show me nothing whatsoever was wrong. But I remembered: everything in me had frozen.

II

Aunt Carleen managed a Cracker Barrel, and Uncle Tully worked at Pizza Hut. Aunt Carleen would tell us the story about the time she met Tom Cruise when she was working at a restaurant in Miami. Uncle Tully brought us kids whatever extras he could manage—the pepperoni savior of our too-long afternoons, a god among children who ate from Green Giant cans and packages of ramen noodles. Sometimes their car ran and sometimes it didn't. One of Tully's dark brown eyes shot sideways, which made me try extra hard to look him in the eyes when we talked. He was comical—our very own cartoon character come to life. He wore cut-off, sleeveless T-shirts and did Tasmanian Devil impersonations, his tongue flaying the air wildly, lapping up our laughter—mine, my brother's, and Mandi's, when she visited. Dawn was harder to coax a smile out of. Tully would get down on the floor to play Sorry! or old maid with us, on his hands and knees, not like most adults, who waited for kids to get bored with them and go find something else to do. Not like my father, who only rarely engaged us in play. We laughed and Dawn sulked, skittish and turned almost entirely inward.

Dawn was Tully's daughter from another relationship. Three years old and she did not yet speak. The girl was like a new kitten. Startled, wet eyes and small mouth noises. No violence to speak of, just the smack of early maternal abandonment. Shy to enjoy play, a tentative batting at the thing called *ball*. I'd been paired with her as a role model. A supposedly natural situation: the older cousin who might inspire progress through the language known only by children. I had no idea what to do with her.

Behind Aunt Carleen's house was a wide, stout pine tree that I liked to climb. I liked to lie down on its thick branches, grip the boughs with my hands, then pull them away slowly to feel the stick of sap. It gave me a magnetic, spidery feeling. Touching the rest of the world with hands that held parts of it fast to my body. I'd rather do this than play with Dawn. I understood her silence as a sign that she didn't like me, selfishly denying that her silence was a reaction to her own troubled life.

Once, Tully surprised me with a jar of sand. It could have been anyone who received it, but it was I who walked in that day. It was summer and I had been hauling myself back and forth on my bike along the little stretch of road where we were allowed to play, hoping for something interesting to happen. I wandered over to bum a push-up pop, but instead he handed me the jar of sand. "There's a rock inside. Find it without taking the lid off."

I knew this trick—it kept kids busy. Our Papa Lou, my grandmother's fifth husband, had occupied us with 52 Pickup, a game of distraction. No strategy at all. I held the jar with both hands, tipped it upside down, and peered in as I'd done with my morning cereal in search of the prize. "What color is the stone?" *Let's make it a game,* I thought. *More than a trick.* I wanted to know what to look for, wanted to visually categorize it.

"Doesn't matter," he said.

But it mattered to me. *Stone* sounded more elegant than *rock*. *Pebble* was more fragile. I wanted to know its dimensions and qualities. What to compare it to. What I might begin to feel about it. What it might come to represent. I spun the jar clockwise, then counterclockwise. It took almost ten minutes to find it: a smooth, white stone. It was definitely not a rock, which would have been jagged and irregularly shaped. Then it disappeared, as quickly as it had surfaced. When it was gone again, merely a jar of sand again, I quickly forgot the stone's size: a failure of memory or of seeing. Gigantic or small? Marble-sized or gumball? How white the white? Egg white or paper white? Whiteout white or whitewash white? Smoke or clouds?

"Meditation is the same thing: a stone in a jar of sand."

The word *meditation* sat on my tongue like a cube of salt, simple and addictive. It held the promise of a long suck life. He offered to teach me how.

He placed the jar on the table. We sat on the living room floor of Aunt Carleen's mobile home, Indian style, our knees and palms sweating. He told me to close my eyes and picture the white stone. I tried, but instead I wondered what his wandering eye did when it was closed, whether it changed the darkness into alphabet soup or split it like a speedboat, pushing one part north and another part south, a clip of rough water smudging the centerline. How did it change his meditation? How black was the curtain of that closed side eye? How white was his stone? The mystery of other people's minds was endless. Did Dawn think words even though she didn't say them? Did my mother really not believe that my heart had stopped? Did my father have any thoughts at all after all the screaming matches? There was, from a young age, already a disconnect between the way I processed experiences and the way others conducted themselves, the way I was critical of my surroundings and the way others seemed to float through them without taking note of anything.

Tully told me to be very quiet, as though he could hear the roar of my mind, and to listen for silence. When I tried, I found the silence right away and was proud of myself for being such a peaceful and meditative person. I was a natural, I thought, enlightened by birth. He told me to listen longer: that silence was a stone in a jar of sand and that finding the silence, the stone, was a meditative practice. I tried again, eyes closed, visualizing the jar and the manipulations I'd performed to bring the stone into view. This time, a few moments after I reentered the silence I thought I'd found the first time, there came a barrage of sounds I hadn't noticed at first. A car barreling down the road outside created a Doppler wave of noise. A housefly buzzed against a window screen. My uncle's breath hissed in and out. My own breath made its own slight sound, and the soft rush of blood to my head pulsed. The window air conditioner hummed in the bedroom down the hall. The kitchen faucet plunked drops of water into a sink. My uncle's pager vibrated itself right off the coffee table, landing on the carpet with a muted thud. Nothing was as I had perceived it to be. What I had thought to be true was false, entirely. The lesson was this: what my mind wanted, my mind could create. I heard "silence" by ignoring the blur of everyday noise. But silence was a whole concept. It required purity. It was like truth in a literal sense, which any fallacy rendered tainted. It was fleeting and easily corruptible.

Meditation, I would discover in time, brought its practitioner to the halfway point—creating a bubble between silence and noise, consciousness and unconsciousness, that lent itself to the quality of noiselessness if not the thing itself. Frequent meditators found the stone in the sand more easily. They didn't even have to look for it. They had stones for eyes.

Break down a subjective feeling into constituent parts: language fails, and you resort to cause and effect, relational equations that help make sense of things by putting words to them. Eventually, it can feel like blame—all this connecting of who did what and why and to what outcome. I felt sad because; I was happy because. One thing acted on another, and a third thing resulted. My heart had stopped and I was certain there was a cause for that sensation, but what was it? No one could pinpoint it with a machine. Did that mean it wasn't real? Then, I never gave the kitten milk. I never held her. I never said, "Here, see how I hold your hand. Feel this. Know this." I would have done it for another person. This one, I couldn't explain.

Why I failed Dawn, I don't know. She looked at me with those eyes. I looked away. I climbed a tree instead, and the tree made me feel better. I was busy breathing my way through heart failure and could not help her. We could neither of us save each other from this place, and no one knew we were in need of saving. When I began to wonder if I was even real, whether my feet were planted on Earth and my blood was pumping, I opened the door of meditation, of altered consciousness, and I walked through to keep myself from going insane, from falling over, exhausted from the limitations of my tiny world and tinier existence. At points in my life, I would keep choosing trees over people. I would keep escaping through the boughs of pines, sap-handed and daydreaming. Higher and higher, as if some kind of answer lay waiting at the upper limit of the world. Meditation would become a way out, a quicker exit to the sky, a way to soften a seized heart, a way of remembering what the mind can do.

Ten years later, the kitten became a cat. Dawn stole my graduation money. She stole my underwear. She packed a bag full of my things, whatever was around, as though she were me leaving in the middle of the night. Where was she going with all that? It was a better idea than climbing trees, so what could I say? When she was caught, she had no explanation. We sat with our mothers, all four of us aghast. Startled, wet eyes and small mouth sounds. But I was already long gone in my mind. I let her keep the clothes. They meant nothing to me.

III

A recent *Time* magazine fold-out diagram of the big bang shows the expansion of the universe alongside the trajectory of time. Wider and wider it grows along the x-axis. I cannot look at it too closely, for it shocks the body to consider the brevity of a life in the context of the endless universe. Max Tegmark, a quantum physicist at MIT, is working on a hypothesis about consciousness as a state of matter that can process information. His theory asserts that consciousness might have emerged alongside time. The scientific community generally accepts that consciousness, like all matter, cannot be broken down into smaller pieces. Perhaps this is why language fails. It alone could never do the accounting for thought or for the choices we make. Perhaps consciousness is the supportive tissue upon which language is constructed. Blame is a scaffolding. Fault is another. Time heals both, moving along at the same pace as thought.

Tegmark's hypothesis says that consciousness, the state of matter termed "perceptronium," requires "a certain amount of independence in which the information dynamics is determined from within rather than externally." Meditation requires even more than using one's own awareness to recognize internally the pretense of external surroundings. It requires training one's mind, its perceptronium, to dismantle the reality contained within the pretense and to make it into something useful and enjoyable by peeling back the layers of perceived reality. That takes practice. It would seem that, if Tegmark is correct, meditation could be tangible proof of consciousness. The fourth state of matter manifest.

IV

After my aunt and uncle moved out of the trailer, another family moved in. Two parents, a daughter. There were more dogs. There was more yelling from this set; I'd hear them in the mornings from our house. The woman screamed, a door slammed, the man screamed. Sometimes I heard crying, loud sobs. A need that no one within earshot could fulfill and so no one even tried. It would go on that way for hours. Breakfast through lunch. Sometimes I wanted to live that loudly.

The new family had big black guns and knives with handles wrapped in leather. The father was only five feet tall, covered in tattoos. Smaller than me at age eleven. I tried to see his eyes once. I wanted them to be kind. They were not. Even a girl looked to him like the enemy. He mowed the lawn shirtless, weapons strapped to his bare body. He was ready for a war that never came, his capacity for violence stitched onto his skin. Waiting.

The mother towered over the small man, at least a foot taller. She was massive and fleshy. The daughter looked like her mother. Over tight stretch pants, she wore large T-shirts featuring gigantic faces of kittens and puppies and Tweety Bird, a false sense of softness atop her body. On the school bus she held her friends like dolls. She offered overt acts of care: one hundred hair brushes, licks from her own Blow Pop, long back rubs to anyone who would endure them. I curled into a ball in the green seats, counting telephone poles until they let me off, fingers checking my own pulse. Still alive.

V

In a truly meditative state, the cousin of dreams, the mind lingers in a pleasing purgatory between consciousness and unconsciousness in a space that might be visually represented by the intersection of a Venn diagram. Outside the crosspatch are the tools we use to manipulate the sensation of feeling and understand the dreams. Language, experience. Whatever happened in a day. We move the matter around, sand in a sandbox. Children at play. Families rotating through the same house over time. Wisdom, a sieve. Sometimes, a glimpse of stone.

I have wondered which part is most real—the conscious or the unconscious. Whether the place itself is the thing that stays, or its effects on a person. One is concrete and one is embedded in the brain, in memory. Does the dog fit into its new family, molding itself to its ways, or does the dog's life before that dictate the new family? Fido brought her old home with her. She ordered us to abide by its rules and we obeyed. That she was in a new place, a new home, changed nothing about her previous experience. What she had known as a pup stuck, though we could not see it in the air.

Dawn's abandonment as a toddler had stuck. It affected her development for years, though it was not palpable. Speaking would come slowly for her. I would not be the last woman she stole from, her subconscious need to reinstate loss stronger than her control over right and wrong. I have taken meditation everywhere and sprinkled its soft gray middle across the land like salt. The place stays, and the people go. They take the experience of the place with them in their perceptronium. Thought could be *a state of matter*, resilient as water or stardust, moving in parallel with the passing of time.

VI

When I walked by the trailer twenty years later, on a visit back to the road I grew up on, I tried not to look too closely at what it had become. The home had outlived the manufacturer's guarantee. A smattering of litter covered the ground around it like a light rain that would not soak in, caught by twigs and corners and sharp edges, arranged almost artfully. Exposed cinder blocks propped up the trailer, its aluminum stairs shakily supporting the daily comings and goings of a family of three and plenty of neighborhood kids.

Other families had come and gone. A TV tray was climbing the stairs. Eyes on the road, I tried not to look inside the windows. I walked on, stopping to look up at Corey's old window. In my pocket, I carried my stone, which had long since been removed from the jar. Curiosity will kill this cat. I could nearly feel the sap beneath my fingernails, transferred from tree bark to skin long ago.

Matter cannot be created or destroyed: the sap was somewhere, the families were somewhere, Corey was somewhere. The memories still existed. Though I discovered meditation here, my first way out of that riverbed, I could not knock on the door of any of these houses. I would not be let inside. I could only return in my mind. If I thought of Corey long enough, meditated on the day he'd carried me home that first time my heart failed, my body would follow and leave a gap in the present.

DIY FOR THE FAITHLESS

When Magic Precedes Belief

Early memory: It is dark. My father, a welder at Merit Steel, walks into our trailer and sits down on a bench near the shiny aluminum door. Our carpeting is brown and the floor in this room slopes when I crawl toward the window, beneath which brightly colored balls collect during daytime play, as though one end of the home tilts toward the center of the earth. Sometimes I dream of falling through this floor into a cracked-open world exposing a belly full of snakes. My father looks very tired, and his face is reddened and rugged. White strips of tape secure two white patches of gauze over his eyes: never look directly at the flame, unprotected. He wears a navy blue T-shirt and stained, faded blue jeans. He smells like oil and scorched metal. He bends to remove his work boots, which are made of brown leather and tied with yellow industrial-grade laces. I comfort him. I make sure he knows he will be all right. I don't know how I accomplish this, but I do. I don't know how I know that his work is difficult and dangerous, but I know. What I don't know is that my father is only twenty-three years old, trying to avoid falling into a snake pit of his own. He has come so far already. The home he grew up in did not have running water or a bathroom.

Early memory: I have my own bedroom in a real house, and the walls are painted a soft peach color. There are no pictures on the wall, only the paint. I have a small bed and a pink blanket beneath a high canopy, the shabby quarters of a poor princess. My window is trimmed in white. Outside my white square of window stands a large sycamore tree that sways in the nighttime wind. When I'm scared, I watch the boy in the window across from mine to help me fall asleep. He is my bedtime story, and he keeps the monsters away. I watch him laugh and jump off his bed when he is alone. I watch his brothers beat up on him. I watch his mother scold him. We are both so powerless. I believe that someday he'll save me and we'll disappear, wriggling free from this place like little Houdinis. It takes me forever to fall asleep when my boy in the window is gone. One night, a shadow approaches and then comes close to my window screen. A man's head, looking in. I wake my mother and she calls our neighbor, Wild Bill, our street's self-appointed patrolman, but they never find a man to go with the shadow.

Early memory: My imagination reigns for a time and books become reality. When I am seven, our crabgrass yard is my Secret Garden, or I am Matilda, smarter than her parents already, or I am the Little Princess, secret heir to another life, or I walk through mirrors into upside-down lands. I push a glass of milk across the table without touching it. I bend a spoon with my blue eyes. During a tour of an antique jail, I see a stuffed white dog stand up and walk across the small cell. "Is that so?" my grandmother says, looking at the dog, then at me. Then his friend the stuffed raccoon follows him. "I see what you mean," she says. I recall a favorite line from *Macbeth*, though I've never read Shakespeare, and quote it out loud: "My dull brain . . . wrought with things forgotten." I have someone else's memories in my head. A blue jay lands on my hand and talks to me in blue jay, and my papa says, "Don't talk to blue jays. They're mean." I wear Indian beads on my fingers. I point my toes and float above my house, above the river, so high. Everything is possible.

Blood, 11

Heaven would be something different for everyone. It would be each person's unique earthly happiness, manifesting in different ways. My heaven had wide sidewalks made of pure gold and castles made of milk chocolate with gold-plated widows that stretched toward another sky, another heaven, another layer in the great beyond. All day, and it was always daytime, God played a chocolate piano that had no white keys, and the music fell onto white-clad angels moved to monastic silence, like chocolate rain.

Over spring break of fifth grade, I started my period. I was the only girl in my class who had gotten it, and I was both ashamed and prideful. It did not go the way of the pancake ovaries and uterus with a smiling mother, sensitive and informative and helpful, helming the spatula, like we saw in the video at school. Instead, I was camping near the swamp with Corey and Marcus when it happened. A canoe's ride away from home, I was surrounded by birds that we'd maimed with overcocked BB guns. Instead, my mother was nowhere to be found and I had to sneak the cordless phone from the living room, leaves still nestled in my matted hair, while my father watched television after work. I was not allowed to use the telephone unless I stayed in the room with my father and he approved the person I was calling. When I told him I wanted to call my mom, he demanded to know why. "Because," I told him, which wasn't enough. We went around and around like that until I was sobbing, pressed into a corner, and I finally told him the reason: blood. With that, we were both defeated, and I was permitted to leave the room. After I called my mom at work, hiding in the bathroom, she bought me a new denim dress that buttoned to the neck and still screamed "girl," and my father looked awkward and angry. He would stay that way for years.

A few weeks later, when I still believed in my chocolate heaven, my parents decided I would take a bus to the Baptist church in the next town over every Sunday. While my father mowed the lawn with his shirt off and my mother napped or washed the dishes, I would go to church. My brother got to stay home, presumably because he was a boy. It could have been that they knew I'd been looking at the *Playboy* magazines in our bathroom, wedged beneath the stack of mismatched towels at my eye level. But no one mentioned that, and in any case, no one removed the magazines.

Once I was unloaded from the creaking bus and brought inside the aluminum-sided structure that was the church, strangers asked me if I was ready to be saved. This preceded the asking of my name and the shaking of hands, which was bad manners. From what I needed to be saved, I wasn't sure. I wondered if my mother knew about that, but I said, "I am."

A teary-eyed woman ushered me into a semicircle of souls volunteered for saving, all adolescent girls like me. Together, we formed an arc around another woman with curly hair and thick thighs. There were plenty of fat girls in church, I noticed. My father had told me that if I got fat, no one would marry me. The width of my hips concerned a shocking number of people, and I sensed that I was growing too quickly for their liking. In fifth grade, I was five feet, five inches tall and 103 pounds and already a B-cup. The other girls my age still looked like children; the boys snapped my bra and called me names. I was an island of growth and hormones.

"Do you accept Jesus as your savior?" the woman asked.

"Yes."

"Will you let Him into your heart?"

"Yes."

"Will you live your life for Him and sing His praises?"

The singing was the only thing I enjoyed about the church— that and the fact that it gave me something to do, another place that permitted me to leave the compound of our home. I loved school but found the work boring, always done with tests well before my classmates. Church was more fun than school—it offered music and stories. I could get behind the energy of their music if I closed my eyes. I could make myself believe any story they told me if it meant someone, even an invisible someone, would love me back. I knew this because singing to Jesus, a total stranger professing love to me and anyone else who would take it, made me cry.

I wondered whether anyone ever said no, no. I cannot carry a tune, in fact. I will have to take a pass on the singing of praises; save that for so-and-so. I wished that my cousin Mandi were with me, but she was four towns away at another church because her parents were getting a divorce. And four towns in the country was something of a drive. Mandi would have made it all seem fun by drawing fancy hats on the Apostles in the workbook pages that followed the saving of souls.

At home, I looked at myself in the mirror. I was on Satan surveillance. The Baptists warned me that this lower-case "he" would upper-case "Get Inside" any way he could. Their fear followed me home. I breathed through my nose sparingly and squeezed my legs together at the crotch, plugging up all the openings I could think of as often as I could remember. *Can he shape-change and slither up into my heart through my vagina?* I wasn't sure, but I didn't trust him.

I opened one of the *Playboy* issues in our bathroom. Across a two-page spread, a man bent a woman over the hood of a red Corvette. The woman had platinum blond hair and wore a bandanna around her neck. She looked slightly frightened and slightly excited, as if it wasn't what she wanted exactly but she was beginning to enjoy it anyway. The man had a small Afro and a huge, erect penis that was aimed at the woman's rear end. This was how I imagined the devil would take me.

I stayed on guard all day and later that night. I looked for Satan in my fingertips and in my underwear, I looked for him in the grocery store, I looked for him in my closet while the others slept. I knew that he could make an offer on my soul at any moment. There was one thing I would trade it for: Corey to love me back.

That following night, Corey babysat me and my brother. I did not understand how, although I could bleed and bear children, I could not be left unattended while my parents went to a party. The three of us played truth or dare. We ate ketchup and peanut butter sandwiches and mouthfuls of toothpaste to prove we weren't chicken. We admitted our fears and confessed our lies. It was me who left Marcus's bike in the rain. Corey was afraid of spiders. Marcus had broken our walkie-talkies. Later, Marcus and I pretended to have gone to bed, but we were still playing the game. My next dare was to kiss Corey. I crept down the hallway and into the living room, where he sat on the floor in front of the fireplace. His legs were bent, one arm wrapped around them, the other holding the fire poker. He didn't look up, though he must have heard me. I leaned in quick, my white nightgown swishing around my legs, and pecked him gently on the jaw. He reached forward and stirred the fire. It crackled and hissed. I ran away and climbed into bed, jittery, tearful, and feeling completely invisible.

I hid my own soul deep down in my spine to keep it from the Devil. If Corey didn't want it, Satan couldn't have it. I folded my hands in prayer. I was passed over, blood safe. Saved. I would go to a chocolate heaven. I waited for a vague notion of death that would take me there and fell asleep obsessing about my own funeral. Who would come? What would they wear? Would anyone cry? Would Corey?

Covenants, 13

Our Papa Lou had died, and no one was saying much about it. He was there for Christmas, and then he went to Florida with his cancer and didn't come back. We thought they knew this was coming, but nobody would say. And anyway, we had another grandpa whom we liked almost as much and had known longer than this one.

"Don't be sad, girls," our mothers said to Mandi and me. "He's watching you all the time."

"Like Danny Boy?" I asked. We'd gotten Danny Boy after Fido died of cancer. We could not keep dogs alive. Danny Boy had been hit by a car. My mother said it was an old Ford pickup that hit him, a white one like the neighbor drove from home to work to the bar and home again each day.

"Exactly like that."

I likened dead Papa Lou to Jesus and Santa, to Danny Boy and Fido. This bothered me because I preferred to pee alone, and now there were two invisible persons, one invisible God, and two dead dogs following me into the bathroom. It was getting crowded. I said to dead Papa Lou, as I'd said to the others, "Close your eyes when I have to go." But how did I know he was listening?

Our mothers took us to the beach at Lake Michigan to cheer us up, although we were not very much in need of cheering. We felt cheated because we did not get to see the body. He went to ash, and into a jar. Then he went all across the Florida Keys, where he'd lived out the last of his cancer with my grandma.

"Our girls," my mom said in her patented sad voice. She would have made an excellent professional mourner in another culture, another time; the roiling emotions to which she could not put words she easily refracted through the pain of others. Mandi and I wore the matching bathing suits they bought us, yellow one-pieces with pink flowers that rode up our backsides. Mandi preferred dragon-flies to flowers and I wanted a blue two-piece, but we had no choice. Through us, they would recreate the childhood they were robbed of by their own parents' failures, even as we suffocated in it. We would be made in their likeness if it killed us all.

"It's like looking at ourselves," said Mandi's mom, my aunt Eileen.

The sisters cried twin sets of tears, and we rolled our eyes.

"Get a therapist," we joked under our breath.

My mother had brought a little paperback book by Danielle Steel and Aunt Eileen had brought a gigantic Bible, but they didn't read. Books were decoration with these women. Instead, they watched us from behind their oversized sunglasses.

We looked absurd in our children's swimsuits, but it was better than being at home, where there was nothing to do but watch the corn grow and poke the cats that slept in the windowsills. We began the rituals: arranging towels, removing sandals, nailing down our lightweight things with heavy things. That was where our routines diverged. Mandi ran headfirst into the water, without flinching when she reached the rocky parts that bit the balls of your feet. She dove in, eyes open, hair tangled against her face and neck. I lingered in the sand, hoping the water was not too cold, and tied my hair back into a safe ponytail. I inched my way in carefully. Toes, then ankles, then calves. I did not trust water to stay put.

Our mothers decided from behind their sunglasses that we would have a Girls' Night. My father was going out again and Mandi's parents were divorced. Our fathers had met in basic training fifteen years earlier and had never gotten too far out of one another's sight until now. Marrying sisters seemed to be insurance against their separating. But with the divorce, loyalties had split.

Later, when we were done with painted fingernails and mud masks, Mandi and I said we were tired and filched the Ouija board game from under my mattress. We locked my door. Our mothers watched black-and-white films upstairs, ruminating over the bright spots of their collective past, that handful of stardust they so cherished. Reliving the few happy memories they shared. They took turns crying over Jimmy Stewart because he looked like Grandpa

McCann, whom we never met and whom they barely knew. There had been so many fathers that his true fatherness got watered down. He was reduced to three qualities: abusive drunk, Greyhound bus driver, dead in a bathtub from a heart attack at forty-one. Every story we heard about him could be categorized as one of the three. *Is that all a life came down to?* I wondered. I thought of Papa Lou. Funny, gentler than anyone else in our family, kept a small farm full of animals that we loved to tend. I had already reduced his life to that. I wondered if someday I would be like my mother and aunt: remembering my past in a dozen stories, six good, six bad, told and retold at Thanksgiving dinners. A glossed-over life. The day-to-day of it foggy.

Mandi and I stayed up that night cavorting with spirits. We were confounded by Milton Bradley's genius. They had either packed souls into the flimsy board or aroused a desire in our minds strong enough to make us subconsciously move the pointer with our energized fingers. We didn't care which was true. We asked to talk to Kurt Cobain, who had recently committed suicide. We asked for Janis Joplin and Jimi Hendrix. It never occurred to us to talk to Papa Lou or Grandpa McCann.

But the rock stars were busy.

"Who am I going to marry?" I asked next.

The board pointed to C, then to E.

I knew one person with those initials: Corey. But I said, "Ew. Clint Eastwood? He's old."

"I'm never getting married," Mandi said.

"Fine, I still am."

Perfection of Grace, 14

By age thirteen, I had been to a dozen different churches or more. At one point, our town was featured in *The Guinness Book of World*

Records for having the most churches per capita; there were plenty available options. New ones seemed to open every week, and I attended many of them with friends, via a bus or van that would pick me up from my house, or with another relative. I had been to the First Dutch Reform Church and the Second Dutch Reform Church. I had been to Grace Fellowship, which met in the gymnasium of my elementary school. I had been to the Virgie Christian Church, a tiny white chapel with narrow wooden pews. I went to the Nazareth Presbyterian Church for vacation Bible school, where I memorized the Lord's Prayer. Everywhere, families entered, gathered, prayed, and exited together. I wondered what it was like, to be together and smiling with your family. To be dressed nicely together, to have had a breakfast of eggs and grits, share jovial chatter and then go to a movie. To have that be regular and not a once-a-year event.

One Sunday I went with Mandi to the Church of the Nazarene. Her mother—a true believer—had been church hopping as I had been, and this one wasn't as far away. I did not know what *Nazarene* meant, but I imagined cloaked monks and secret, cobbled paths, knife rituals and possibly some sex. I was mistaken.

The Church of the Nazarene was made of wood, painted a deep brick red that flaked and chipped away in a strong wind. A large ramp wrapped around a small staircase that led to the unadorned door. I took the long way up. This church had very few windows, and inside it smelled permanently of sugar cookies, the weeks and weeks of postsermon refreshments having permeated the makeshift walls and thin carpets that lined the building's interior. I was uncomfortable because we were late. The girls' worship class had already started, and I didn't want them to stare at me. I was Sarah, plain and tall, a newcomer in an established community. The girls would be mean. They would think my dress was ugly. My mother made me wear it, and she dressed me like a spinster, ensuring as much of my neck and chest and arms was covered as was possible. Since the age of eleven, I had begun to feel the attention of boys and men upon me, their gazes warm and penetrating as the sun. Even in churches.

"This is my cousin, Angela," Mandi said to the group. We stood there, an alarming spectrum of traits spread across our faces in one matrilineal stroke: toothy, trusting smiles paired with suspicious eyes. We waited for the question.

"Cousins? You look like sisters."

We shrugged. We never had a good answer for this.

The class's leader invited us into their circle. We sat. A Bible was passed around the circle, lap to lap. We took turns reading lines from the book of Matthew.

When it was my turn, I read, "If a blind man leads a blind man, both will fall into a pit." I passed the book to the blond girl on my right. I wanted to be as blond as the women in my father's magazines, and I didn't like her because she was blond by nature and because she looked at my dress disapprovingly. I wanted to say *my mother made me wear this,* but I kept quiet. I wanted to say *this streak of gold in my hair is for real,* but the truth was I squeezed lemon juice onto it and sat in full sunlight so it would lighten even though it sometimes got so hot that I nearly passed out.

I felt an urge to walk out of the room when they started singing. I almost acted on it, and then I looked to Mandi for her approval. She was not singing. She only moved her lips to the words, so I moved my lips, too.

Omniscience, 14

Besides Mandi, I had a best friend, Valerie. We bought necklaces that announced our friendship in two halves of a heart that when pressed together fit like a zipper down the center. After a few weeks at the Church of the Nazarene, I went with her family to Saint Cecilia's on Sunday mornings. This church had very high ceilings, which I think was on purpose—meant to make the patrons feel small and unworthy of a god so large and a religion so hierarchical.

I never stayed at one church for long. Some I attended only once. Others I attended for weeks or months. I was a religion junkie, arbitrarily adopting any beliefs I encountered—Baptist, Presbyterian, Dutch Reform, Methodist. But in rural Indiana, they were all variations on the same concept—patriarchal, restrictive, and full of people who looked and acted more or less the same. I remained outside their communities, even as I attempted, albeit halfheartedly, to integrate into them. I'd been told my grandmother became a Buddhist, temporarily, while she was living on the South Side of Chicago, and this knowledge pulled at me, a kind of tether between us. Mostly, I went to churches with other people's families while my family stayed at home. Intermittently my mother would redouble her efforts to instill in us "Christian values" by going to church with me and my brother. The slogan she adopted and would use for years to come was a ubiquitous salvation whose principles of honesty, abstinence, and obedience reflected the core of my parents' parenting style. As a consequence of those principles, I was forced to lie to get through life as a mildly sinful human. I feared punishment, and operated largely in an effort to avoid it. I learned much later that negative punishment of children—both corporal and noncorporal—was detrimental to their psychological development. I had been subjected to both. Spending weekends at Valerie's house afforded me more freedom than I'd ever known. When we walked outside the house into the backyard to swim, we didn't have to ask permission. When we rode her brother's moped around the subdivision, no one raised an eyebrow. When we had male friends come over to watch a movie with us, it was no big deal. I was relieved to be normal, neutral, innocent until proven guilty.

"We would be so ashamed if you got into trouble," my mother would say. I never heard her say the word *pregnant*, but that's what she meant—their ultimate fear. It didn't matter what the circumstances were—going to the Pizza Hut with kids from school, going to Friday-night football games. When I did go, one or both of my parents went, too, and my father watched me closely, sometimes making accusations that were not true, insisting he saw me kissing some boy or another. But I could go to church and I could go to Valerie's house, no questions asked. No tagalong, suspicious parent.

While I visited churches, Corey visited boys' homes and juvenile detention centers. His behavior had started to change. He was becoming a troublemaker—getting kicked out of school, being arrested for petty delinquency, running away from home. But he was no different from me. One night I told him over our walkie-talkies that a girl at school was hitting me and harassing me at lunch for no reason. He asked who it was, and I told him. He said he'd take care of it. She never bothered me again. Still, he came over to see us less. Often his window stayed dark at night. I didn't know where he was, how to reach him, or when he'd be back. But then as suddenly as he'd left, he'd show up one day, smiling and dribbling a basketball, and everything would be back to normal.

My father would not attend church. "I believe in God," he once told me, "but I'll never go to church." The thought of my father praying to any god, even privately, was unfathomable.

"Can't you do it for Mom?" If it would make her feel loved, somehow make our family seem more united, then I wished it for her.

"No," he said. End of discussion.

I prayed the same prayers to the same mysterious god at these churches, ignoring the rules of their various belief systems. The differences between them were unclear to me. Showing up to pray, to feel something, was the extent of my commitment. I was there because I wanted something back, not because it was right or good.

I prayed for a mother who could find more worth in herself than my father would lead her to believe she possessed. Once, I thought a prayer had come true. My mother emerged from her bedroom dressed for an office holiday party wearing a black dress. She had swept her hair up into a neat bun, put on makeup, and traded her glasses for contacts. She glowed. She was making an entrance, and I rooted for her silently as if she were in the running for homecoming queen. She presented herself to my father, smiling. He told her she looked like a fat geisha, and sent my mother spinning back into herself. Down and out. Another time, when she enrolled in night classes at the nearest Purdue extension campus, I thought it had happened. "I won't have a wife that makes more money than me," he said. Between his discouraging her and her being unable to comprehend algebra, she stopped. At all of the churches, I prayed for a father who was not so harsh, a father who replied, "Yes, dear?" when I said, "Dad, Dad. Dad, I have something to say," instead of staring at the television or banging away with a hammer until I simply gave up and went away. I prayed for a brother who was not pressed flat by my father's big thumbs, who was not knocked upside the head and brought to tears for every tiny infraction of my parents' impossible standards. I prayed for a home where yelling wasn't the main means of communication. I prayed for my parents to divorce—an end to a constant state of what felt to me like disorder and tension. I prayed for Corey to stay home, to look straight at me, count my freckles, touch an index finger to the chicken pox scar above my right eyebrow, and say, "What's this from?" I prayed for him to keep looking. I did not pray for myself specifically because I didn't have words for what it was I needed or wanted. In my mind I was already gone from our home, and I had taken Corey and Marcus with me to the future.

There was less music in the Catholic church than in others I'd visited. What I liked most about Catholicism was the forced kindness between the parish's members, an instant community of positivity. "Peace be with you," I said with a shy smile to the middle-aged woman in front of me at my friend's church. Her hands were thin and frail, and I didn't want to let go. I wanted her to know that I meant it. I wanted her to see that I was earnest. I tried to look empathetic, tried to absorb some of her problems, whatever they might be. But Catholics didn't want to win you over the way that Baptists did, or even the way that Methodists did. They didn't want you nearly as badly. No one recruited visitors to join the Catholic faith. Their faith required far more than a spirit of volunteerism. The woman shrank away from me and turned to spread the peace elsewhere.

The ritual responses became familiar quickly, rolling off my tongue like cotton clouds puffed into the air. I uttered them as though I'd been saying them for years, and this was a comfort even though I knew it was a lie. Which brings me to the topic of confession. In Catholicism, non-Catholics are prohibited from partaking in many of the faith's perks, including confession. This turned out to be a real disappointment, even more so than being prohibited from taking communion, when you have to sit in the pew while the rest of the faithful in your row sashay by you to line up for the Eucharist. Stark exclusion from this particular religious perk felt like the equivalent of a dunce cap. "Dunskey," my father called us at home. He had endless ways of noting our stupidity. I said it over and over to myself while I waited for the rest of my aisle to return. *Dunskey, dunskey.* Almost rhymed with *drunksky, skunksky.*

My Catholic friend and I had been writing poetry. We filled the widely lined pages of black-and-white composition tablets. We revised and rewrote, drawing flowers and clouds around the final drafts with crayons. These poems were mostly abstract constructions of our overwhelming feelings. Often, we brought ourselves to laughter and tears within the space of a minute. We wrote about grievances against the authorities of school and home. We wrote about grievances of the heart. This boy did not call, this boy liked another girl. This one said he would see us at the basketball game, but where was he? Woe was us. The poems were totems of our coming of age, a record of our existence. *We were here,* we wrote in black ink. We wanted badly to matter, but there was nothing artful about our words.

There was a transgression I wanted to confess, but no one in the Catholic church would hear it. One Sunday, I said I had to use the bathroom. I lingered outside the confession box, looking into the screened grate. I could hear the monotone call and responses in the church's cathedral. The voices echoed down the hall. A week earlier, I had been filling another composition tablet with depressing pop song lyrics in my room when someone hooted at me. I went to the window and Corey was there with two other neighborhood boys, Brandon and Micah. I tried to play it cool, but I was giddy that he'd come to see me without my asking him over. The three of them were all older than me and, while they never spoke to me at school, they doted on me in their own boyish ways or teased me almost sweetly when we were in our own territory—the Kankakee swamp, river rat country. Occasionally we would play Hackey Sack on the porch or video games in our living room or eat an entire bag of Doritos while laughing at nothing. They usually ran off when my dad's truck hauled onto our road after work because I wasn't allowed to be alone with them, or any boy, for that matter. But this time, I was alone and the three of them were outside, sitting on the little hill outside my window, right below Corey's bedroom window. They were drunk—their eyes were bright and their smiles were soft and playful. The sun was nearly sunk and my parents were gone later than usual. "Take it off," one of them called. Then a sharp, short whistle.

The idea must have come from Corey. Neither of the other boys would have spoken to me like that without his lead or approval. For a while, I had noticed his light snapping off as soon as I closed my bedroom door at night, wrapped in a towel after showering. It was surprising that parents who were paranoid about my exposed body had not thought to install blinds on my bedroom window. I wasn't sure that Corey had been watching me, but I would take my time getting dressed, sitting naked on my bed to brush my hair and put on lotion. Had he seen? He'd never said anything.

I looked down at my clothes. I was wearing a gray White Sox T-shirt featuring Snoopy dressed in a team uniform with faded khaki shorts. "Very funny," I called back.

My light was on and it was almost dark. I had watched Corey in his room at this time of night many times before, lifting weights and pacing back and forth, growing his muscles and his manhood. So I knew they could see me well even though it was getting hard for me to distinguish them as anything but voices in the night. "Come on," one said impatiently.

Awkward as it felt, I craved their attention—from Corey especially, whom I adored secretly and from afar. Things were changing between us. I could tell by the way that he gripped my thighs when he carried me on his back and by the way that he could no longer look me in the eyes when we were near one another. We orbited ever closer to some unnamed center. A gravity had begun. We were happy when we were together, an easy fit, even if we were unsure of what to do or say. I couldn't remember a day of my life when I hadn't known him, or imagine a future that didn't include him.

I moved my arm slightly and leaned forward, discreetly looking down my own shirt. I was wearing a black bra with a red plaid print that wrapped around the cups. My underwear even matched. I took this to be evidence of serendipity. Of God's approval. A prayer crossed my mind—I beseeched the dead to look away. I was tired of being watched by angels. Some things weren't meant for them to witness.

"We're getting bored," Brandon said. "Take something off." They did sound bored, but they also sounded hopeful. Still, their boredom felt like my personal failure. I wanted to apologize for disappointing them.

Instead of turning off my light and rising above the situation that was unfolding, I decided that this could be an opportunity to become more womanly, more like the women I had seen in *Playboy*. It was a chance to ensure that Corey would look at me and see me as I wanted him to—as more than his friend, more than a playmate he had nearly outgrown. If two more boys had to witness the invitation, so be it. It would be worth it. I took off my T-shirt, my back to the window, and then turned around to face them. One of them whistled louder, but I'd run out of courage. I stood there for a few seconds, willing myself to do something else. But what?

"Is that it?" one of them called. I knew they had actual *Playboy*s they could be enjoying.

That's not it, I thought, determined to do something more. To reveal a body part that would keep them there outside the window. The night grew thick and blue, full of stars. I stood in my bra and shorts, lights on, and looked around my room. I pretended to scratch at a mosquito bite on my leg. I shifted my weight from one leg to the other, never looking directly at the window, never smiling. I was bluffing. It was only meant for Corey, not these other boys. Three hidden faces laughed in unison. "My grandma puts on a better show than that," one said. After a few minutes, I heard nothing. I was alone in my bedroom, half-undressed. My bottom lip quivered. They were gone.

I wanted to offer my confession to the Catholics and their dusty little confession closet, but no one let me. No one even asked if I would like the opportunity to confess. "Hello?" I said to the door. Nothing. I wondered if Papa was still watching me, if the dead dogs were still following me. I wondered if they were paying attention when I took off my shirt and failed to entertain the three boys. And if a god was watching us all the time, why did people have to say out loud everything they had done wrong?

Bread and Wine, 14

After Catholicism ignored me, I went to the Methodist church in town. If I stayed at this church for a year, I would become an official member and a blue name tag would hang on the welcome board each Sunday, and each Sunday I would pin my name tag with my very own name to my sweater. After a while I might be asked to be responsible for something important, like handing out napkins during refreshment hour. To exhibit enthusiasm for this church and to show my commitment, I signed up for community events that they hosted—car washes and working at Wednesday dinners. At Wednesday dinners, anyone could eat a hot, home-cooked meal with seconds and dessert for three dollars. At first I couldn't figure out why anyone would want home-cooked food when everyone knew eating out was so much better. It seemed like a crappy combination. You had to go out and pay, but you ate bad food. But after a few weeks, I decided I'd rather eat than help in the kitchen. As it turned out, the food tasted amazing and came from Family Recipes. My family had no Family Recipes. We ate overcooked pork chops with no seasoning or boiled hot dogs and canned vegetables or went to McDonald's. Even our potatoes came canned, or else in flakes. I was angrier than ever because my mother had never cooked manicotti.

Astral Projection, 15

The religious roulette ended after the Methodist dinners stopped. It ended up being one more community that was inaccessible to a fifteen-year-old without a whole family alongside her. Books, though, had never shut me out or made me feel like I didn't belong. When I gave up churches, Mandi and I started asking our mothers to take us to the nearest bookstore to hang out on Sunday afternoons. We read for hours at Barnes & Noble—the closest bookstore to my parents' house, a forty-minute drive away. We became interested in alternative religions and purchased instructive books on dream interpretation, palm reading, and astral projection. After studying up on astral projection, we decided to try it ourselves. We locked my bedroom door and dimmed the lights. The book said to lie *supine,* but I confused the term with *lupine,* imagining my eyes as two bright, sunward-reaching flowers. A diagram on page four of the book helped me correct my error. In addition to the bookstore trips, I had also checked out nearly every book on the single shelf reserved for texts on non-Christian religions in our school library. I had read the Tao and the Bhagavad Gita and books on Buddhism. I put the flowers to rest and lay on my back, trying to focus on the imagined apple that hovers eight inches above my mind's eye. The book suggested an apple as the focal point for novice astral travelers, and I was one for following directions. I didn't like red apples, so it was a yellow apple I used to tempt my soul to emerge from its hiding place and rise up, up. I would position it on my bed, where it would look down at me freely, unencumbered by my body and the clothes my mother made me wear. I tried to coax it from where it rested, dormant but simmering with energy, at the bottom of my spine. I asked it to slowly boil and bubble up my vertebrae, *hop pop hop pop,* to come out of my face, transform into a mutant hand, and take the apple. Hold it, bite it, gag me with it, whatever it took to get it *out.* It was like trying to pick a dandelion that weighed a thousand pounds. Mandi lay three feet from me in the same position, palms to the unknowable god we had both abandoned. There was no second Jesus coming for us. Mandi now had a stepdad at her mom's house and a slew of young women at her dad's house, and I was suffocating in my life. We would not keep praying for other people to learn how to change, to see us as people with our own thoughts and feelings. Mandi's apple was red because that was the kind her mother bought. We disagreed on those aspects of project-ing. Maybe that was why it wasn't working. We relied too much on what was familiar.

Mandi tried to stifle a laugh, but it came out her nose, which was perfect. I was beginning to hate my nose. It was too round by several millimeters. I compared my face to the shapes in magazines. I could not find a match, so I clamped my nostrils together at night with one of my mother's clothespins. Nothing was coming out right. *Why is your hair so thick?* my father would ask. *Why are your arms so hairy? You're a Sasquatch.* Meanwhile, my mother had taken me to those open modeling calls in Chicago, where you walked around in front of Ford Models recruiters, shoved pictures in their faces, and hoped they picked you. I hated it. "You can get scholarship money," she would say. But I knew I would get that anyway. Smarts went farther than pretty, but it was pretty they encouraged. And anyway, I was no Kate Moss. Couldn't they see that? Couldn't they see how anxious it made me? My mother rubbed my teeth with Vaseline, as she had for ballet recitals. "It forces you to smile," she'd say.

"Stop it. You're ruining my concentration," I told Mandi with my eyes closed.

This made her laugh harder.

"Seriously, it's not going to work if you keep laughing. You have to focus." I got to be the boss because I was older by one year.

"The book says it takes a lot of practice."

"I've been practicing. I'm so close, I can feel it."

Mandi sat up and crawled over to me, hands planted on the floor next to my shoulders. She stared at me from where my apple should have been floating. "Eat me, soul. I'm a yellow apple!"

I shoved her and she toppled over. We laughed at ourselves, our legs mixed up together on the shag carpet like pick-up sticks. We were still two girls with a thousand shared limbs, each sensing the other's position, no matter how impossibly construed. We were sisters more than cousins.

She unwound herself from me. "Let's read our horoscopes." She reached for my *Seventeen* magazine. We were dead ringers for our horoscopes. I was a serious Scorpio, contemplating my world word by word, drop by drop, comparing everything, making occasional splashes against the beige walls of circumstance. She was a breezy Aquarius, knocking about in the wide gaps of space that opened for her whenever she decided to stand still. A name only took you so far. A family only provided you with so much. We would have to go into the wilderness of the world armed only with our own sense, our own souls, our own flawed bodies and minds, if we wanted to get anywhere or learn anything.

I lay on the floor and tried again, this time without my cousin. I was supposed to be sleeping, a nine o'clock bedtime for a sixteen-year-old. To make projecting easier, I wore the lightest clothing I owned, a vintage slip that I bought at the Presbyterian resale shop. I had dyed it a soft pink with Rit dye from the drugstore. I looked like a crow-haired Courtney Love, passed out on the floor, and I felt just as spent as she typically appeared, just as tired of waiting for my real life to arrive. I was done with hovering apples. I said *rah rah rah rah rah rah rah* and counted backward from 341 by threes in my mind. It took a lot of work to keep myself from thinking.

When I finally rose above myself, projected one aspect of me above the other—my consciousness outside my body—Mandi appeared in my mind. She took my hand and I ran headfirst with her toward water. Time seemed to fall away as we stripped off our clothing and tossed it over our shoulders. We were quiet and we were loud, we were yin and yang, swirling gray. In my altered state, we were red-and-blue pinwheels, spinning with the breath our mothers blew when they were fifteen and sixteen on the Fourth of July in 1975, sitting on a porch and dreaming of daughters who would go to church and wear matching pink dresses. We were blurry in their bellies. We said hello to each other, silently. A preview of the decades we would spend in and out of touch, but always united, always bonded to one another. In my mind, or outside it if I really had projected, we reached the water's edge and jumped, arms stretched out wide and mouths gaping. When the water hit my face, I was alone again. I was floating in it. It was water, then it was air, then it was time and space together, then it was gone. I looked down and saw myself on the floor in the pink slip. *Wake up,* I whispered.

PART II

FIELDS

BIFURCATION

There was one last game of corn tag the summer that we moved—before everyone made their exits from the river. Corey had recently gotten out of the boys' school for delinquent youth, and he was living it up while he looked for a job. Six of us ran through the field beyond the old riverbed. Even in the dark, we knew when to hop over a hole, when to duck to avoid being decapitated by barbed wire. We knew where the bridges built by the generation of kids before us were still intact and could be used to traverse the creek, a trickle of leftover water from the river that had been rerouted a hundred years earlier. We knew the land as we knew our teenaged bodies. Ripe, firm. Yielding in places. In those days, running was nothing but an extension of self. Like breathing. There was no labor in it, only direction and the feeling of blood rushing in our veins. Above us, a silver moon hung sideways from black sky. Soon, the world would swing sideways with it, unhinged, split wide and dripping.

From somewhere in the corn, Corey tagged my face, blinding me with his flashlight. "Gotcha."

"Where are you?" I squinted against white light. His voice came from all directions, his body near. The absence and presence of him at once disoriented me.

"Guess." I saw him in my mind as an amalgamation—the boy I'd whispered to at night, whose bedroom window faced mine for years, and the man who was so now at nineteen by law, by stature, and by a growing rap sheet. His voice was more familiar to me than his flesh, the nights we talked on our walkie-talkies outnumbering the number of times we had touched in the past year. He'd been gone for a few months, with weekend visits home. Though he was hardly around anymore, he would still come back to me when he could and we would play like kids, even though we weren't. At fifteen, I wanted to tip that balance in favor of flesh. I reached out for him with both arms, ready to grab either version, boy or man, but grasped nothing.

Corn rustled around us. The sound, when you stand inside it, is like water, the dry husks loud as tides. Feet darted from the light in staccato beats. Corey's light went out. "Now can you see me?"

I heard his sneaking smile even in the dark, getting nearer, our bodies like homing pigeons for one another, no matter how long he'd been gone.

"I can't see anything." I stepped forward, but he stopped me with an arm around my waist, restraining me against his body. Wrapped around me from behind, he made me feel small. Crushable. *Why did this feel good? I asked myself later. Should I have been afraid?*

We stood there, conscious of our breathing. This was a feeling like love, I thought, if love was a pull, magnetic and inevitable as gravity. If it was a secret, best kept slow and steady and unspoken. Once, we had swung from the thick vines that grew along the trunks of our backyard trees like strangler figs. He caught me when I flew across the patch of ferns below. He held me half a second longer than necessary to right my footing, the near fall staged for the express purpose of knowing whether he'd catch me. I suppose I had always been attached securely around his trunk, leaching what nourished the center of him. Or feeding it. It was hard to tell the difference, to pinpoint whose pulse triggered and whose pulse chased.

My brother appeared in front of us and we stepped away from each other, caught. "What are you doing?"

"Nothing," I said. "Game on." I lurched toward him, hoping he'd run off.

Corey flicked his light back on and tagged him. "You're out, little bro. It's home base for you. That's what you get for spying."

Marcus was always half a beat behind, a little too young to know what was going on but old enough to want to be a part of whatever it was. Corey had stopped smoking cigarettes in front of him because Marcus was afraid that everyone around him was dying. He'd spend hours sobbing over our dad's black lungs. "Don't you know alcohol kills people, too?" I'd ask, and he'd cry more. Corey couldn't bear the thought of upsetting Marcus, so he only smoked around me because I didn't care.

In a few more months, a combine would plow through the dried stalks and eat up our playground, flattening the field into nothing over the course of a few days. After the combines, winter would come. After that, spring, when the forest along the perimeter of the field would thicken and green and the deer would bed down in it with their young. Another machine would turn the soil over afresh, opening it to receive the next crop's seed. Spring would heal the land's wounds. It would heal us.

Corey's older sister, Rhianna, had died when he was twelve. After that, he entered a period of stunned quietude. I had barely known her. She had gone to college on a basketball scholarship when I was eight, a rare academic exit from our neighborhood, where only half of the kids would finish high school. A few months later, she was gone. I had watched Corey get locked out of his house after she died, the loss of one child too great for his mother to give a damn about another. His father was a trucker and on the road most of the time. For years, his mother worked the night shift at a twenty-four-hour restaurant near the interstate and slept during the day, only waking to holler at us to quiet down from her second-story window. When he wasn't home in time for supper, Corey tried the door and found it wouldn't open. He'd wait a minute, give it one more try, then jump off the stairs—a six-foot leap, landing squarely on his feet. He would wander over to our place to eat and sleep, as if nothing were wrong. He would tell me later that he thought his sister died because she got smart. He thought that if he did well in school, like her, he'd die, too. To stay alive, he rejected school and authority. A child's logic that stuck.

Back then, when my mom asked if he'd like to go to his sister's grave, he'd nod and we'd all get into the car. We'd park on the gravel road near the cemetery, and he'd get out without saying a word. I saw the headstone up close once, a tiny picture of her wearing a pink shirt, framed and mounted in the slab of granite. I couldn't imagine it, losing a sibling, and so I didn't even ask him about it.

When Corey was fourteen and I was eleven, we would sit on top of the swing set my father had built for us and all the other neighborhood kids, long after we were too big and too old to enjoy its primary function. Once a place for hanging by the backs of our knees and looking at the world upside down, it had become a retreat as we grew older. A higher-up place to sit and feel away from the world. Our feet dangling below us, Corey told me he'd been taken to a psychiatrist. "I see things, then I have to do them," he said. "Compulsion. That's what it's called. Or compulsive behavior." He spoke softly, as if saying it out loud confirmed something.

I was never comfortable with serious talks about death or love or what was inside another person's mind. "That must be tough."

We swung our feet, and our ankles collided gently. I thought of my own behaviors—watching him in his window on nights when he slept at home, lit up like a drive-in movie, until I fell asleep; tapping my fingers in patterns on my thigh; repeating something someone had said over and over in my mind until I'd found a rhythm that made my skin stop crawling. *Maybe,* I thought, *I have compulsive behavior too.*

Later, I misremembered what he'd told me. I told my mom he'd gone to the doctor for a heart condition. "Something's wrong with his heart. It's compulsive." It felt true enough. I worried about it. I thought his heart would forget to pump his blood. I would wake up in the middle of the night, look across the grass at his dark window, and wonder if he was still breathing.

Things had started to go really wrong for Corey when he got in trouble for taking a gun to school and stashing it in his locker. He'd taken it to give to someone else, on loan. Guns were allowed in our school's parking lot and plenty of teenagers owned their own guns, so it wasn't outlandish. Before we were ten, my brother and I each had our own .410 shotguns for messing around out back. Target practice. The unspoken rule was that guns could be kept in kids' cars if the kids had been hunting in the hours before school started. The mere mention of a gun was not, at that time, cause for the local news station to arrive. The important thing was that the kids came to school, not that guns didn't. But Corey was the first kid to get caught with one inside the school. Now the school would have to rethink whether guns in kids' cars would still be all right. At the same time, gang violence had reached frightening heights in nearby Chicago, and rural outcasts idolized gang life. Fear was on the rise, and knee-jerk reactions to the potential for violence rapidly became common. Almost overnight, rules and regulations seemed to increase in severity tenfold.

The school made an example of him. Corey was expelled and put on probation. His next infractions—stealing his mother's car, marijuana possession, and running away from home—would earn him time in juvie. When he ran away from there, he'd be sent to a special boys' school, where he would eventually get a GED. His crimes were not entirely out of the ordinary for teenagers with troubled home lives, teenagers in general, even. But it seemed that only the ones from the "wrong side of the tracks" were punished for it. I'd known several kids who regularly carried knives in their socks or kept them in their lockers, and kids who kept brass knuckles in their back pockets and wore swastikas or anarchy symbols on chains that hung beneath their T-shirts. I'd seen both boys and girls beat each other bloody. The pulse of violence was nothing new.

After the expulsion, Corey came over less and less. As I boarded the school bus in the morning, he'd show up looking sleepy and disheveled, smoking a cigarette. We'd look at each other until we were out of sight. Strangers passing. I had no idea where he'd been sleeping, but I missed him. Once in a while he would call from wherever he was, and it would make my day.

The next time we sat on top of the swing set, Corey, then seventeen, told me he'd found out the father he'd known his whole life wasn't his father at all. That he had another family in Arkansas. His brothers had taunted him for years, telling him he wasn't their real brother, forcing him to do things that they themselves would never do—fight his own friends even though he didn't want to, stand still while they pegged him with baseballs. Now he had no choice but to believe it—he really was adopted. He decided he wanted to meet his real father, whom he didn't remember at all. He planned to find his new family, get a job down there, and live with them. I hoped he would, though I hated to see him leave again. I hoped the new family would love him and make him whole and feed him and let him in at night. But he had only been gone two weeks when he returned to the river. He never talked about his father again.

I had watched Corey come and go, missing him, so much in envy of his freedom and wishing he would take me with him, while I stayed, confined to whatever terms my parents set for me. Usually, *home* and *yard,* for my own good. Restraining me nearby, in the vicinity of the place they perceived as safe, was the only way they knew to protect me. It was successful on some fronts—I had never seen a drug more serious than weed, and I had only once been to a party where alcohol was available to me.

After the game of corn tag, I spent three hours choosing the perfect CD from Walgreens for Corey's birthday: Guns n' Roses, *Use Your Illusion I* and *II*. Emboldened by that first kiss, I called him on the phone and asked him to come over. I told him I wanted him to be my first. We would be moving soon and time was running out. He'd do one more stretch of time at the juvenile center and then he'd be moving out and getting a job, and we'd be living three miles down the road in the cornfields. He came over while my parents were out, knocking softly on my window. I was jumpy, and my eyes refused to settle on his face like I wanted them to. We talked for a while, and soon he was tickling me and we laughed ourselves into another kiss, which lasted for the better part of an hour. But when he upped the ante, unbuttoning my pants and touching me lightly between the legs for a second, I stopped him. I didn't want to stop him, but I was scared. My brother was home, and I couldn't risk being caught. Corey said that he had promised my father to stay away from me anyway—I was too young and he was too much trouble. His body betrayed the promise. I felt him hard against the flat plane of skin between my hip bones, but he left anyway. I was angry that two men had negotiated this experience without my input, before I'd even thought of the question. I wanted to be with Corey and I wanted him to wait for the timing to be right, to fight for me, to stand up to my dad, but he wouldn't.

In retaliation, I invited another boy over to do the job instead, with a plan to leak the information to Corey the next time I saw him. If he thought I was too much a girl still, I would force him to be wrong. I kissed this boy, too, but when things seemed to be going too far I said no—I didn't know him like I knew Corey, and it wasn't worth it, even if it would mean getting back at him. This replacement boy wasn't the one I'd intended and no one else would do. I tried to back out, but it was too late. The boy had already decided on an outcome. Throughout the brief ordeal, I looked out my window, into Corey's window and through another window beyond that.

The week we moved, I helped my father cut lilies and hostas at our old house by the river, preparing them for transplanting at our new house. We were moving half our yard from one place to the other—everything but the grass itself. I disliked this idea and thought it in poor taste, bringing the old purposely to live in the new. At fifteen I was quickly gathering regrets, and this was not a clean start. There had been plenty of good times at the river, but there was also enough bad to make this a legitimate concern. I felt similarly dissevered, leaving half of myself rooted by the river while my other half would grow afresh down the road. And where would Corey go next? What would happen to him? He was moving to another nearby town, leaving the river too. It wasn't the future I'd imagined for either of us.

We cleaved the hostas between growth points at the root, dividing them into old and new. "First you cut, like this," said my father. "Right between the notches. Then you loosen the two portions apart, gently. See that?" His voice was thick and slow, purposeful, like Bob Ross's demonstrating on PBS how to paint a waterfall.

It was harder than it looked, to cleave the growth. I watched how he cut the roots before trying it myself, eyeing his precision with the tool and the ease of his pull. I made a single chop into the plant's root bed and wiggled the severed portion away from the old growth, trying to minimize the damage to the root hairs, jumbled up like old phone cords, only far more delicate. I looked up at him. "Like this?"

"Not bad. Little less off the tip, if you can." He showed me again. I liked working with my dad. When he was teaching me something he knew how to do and I was quiet and obedient, things were all right.

I attempted the maneuver again, without much improvement. He didn't seem to notice. When we'd cut all the plants that the yard could spare, we packaged the spliced roots of the new-growth plants in wet dirt. We wrapped them in flimsy plastic bags, loaded them into my father's truck, and drove away. The plants slid up and down the length of the truck bed for three paved miles to our new yard.

When Corey finally got out—done doing time, at last, for his juvenile crimes—I had my license. Our incident of sexual misconnection was a year behind us, and we had never spoken of it again. I picked him up and drove him over to our new house. On my map of home, we were still in the patch of yellow between the pink dots, but the new home was three miles due east and a half mile due south of our river house. Mapwise, we'd barely moved below the blue wavy line, but it felt farther.

We sat across from each other at the table, and I asked Corey what it was like where he'd been—the detention centers, the boys' school. "I've seen a lot of things I shouldn't have seen, and I've learned a lot of things I shouldn't have learned," he said. "Criminal things."

But what I heard was, "Nothing you need to know." The window of time in which he would share things with me had passed. Our easy bond had taken a new form, in which withholding was the only language we would speak.

I didn't ask him anything else, but I knew that what he told me was not good news. We sat at my parents' kitchen table eating store-bought cookies, smiling, happy he was home. I tried not to be distracted by the questions forming in my head about what he had seen and learned, questions about what he felt for me, if anything. I was anxious to be out of my parents' purview, so I took him for a drive in my new car while they waited nervously for me to return, their standard fears—safety, boys, etc.—etched across their foreheads. Corey wore his seat belt and leaned toward me, letting his shoulder rest on mine as he turned up the radio. A void swelled between us, but neither of us would be the first to touch it. He shook his head. "I can't believe you're driving. Little girl, all grown up."

I saw a flash of light in his eyes. I thought it was a promise that he was back, that the future I'd imagined between us might become real despite his silence. That the night we had almost spent together had meant something. Did he even remember it? I wrote headlines about us in my head: *Window Boy Falls in Love with Girl Next Door. Couple Runs from River, Chasing Happiness.* But he confirmed nothing. He offered nothing. We said nothing. We exchanged a quick hug and a casual good-bye. He would probably be bedding someone else by dark, and I hated him for it. Hated myself for my own muteness.

When I dropped him off at his house, I had no idea it would be the last time I saw him. If I could have done it differently, I would have put my hand on his knee and kissed him. I would have cracked a window and let the air out. I would have gone upstairs with him, closed his door behind us, and stayed.

Bifurcation comes to mind when I think of Corey. As in the division of the common carotid artery. As in the shape made by the branching of the Kankakee River and the Illinois River. As in me going one way and Corey going another. As in the way people lose themselves, splitting further and further from their origins. As in the roots of hosta shoots, separated by mutation or by force. As in young flower buds arrested in early development that never bloom. What confluence of time and geography can split roots?

I didn't hear from Corey for a few months after that visit at the new house. He could have called, but didn't, and he had no phone at the new place he was staying. By then he'd been in enough trouble that dating him would have been out of the question—my parents wouldn't have allowed it. When it became clear that nothing would happen with Corey, I dated the first boy I came across. I'd been hanging out with a girl named Kelly, and Trevor was her boyfriend's best friend. It was a convenient match. He was cute and nice, so sure. Fine by me. I would project all that Corey love onto him. He even looked a little like Corey. I still wasn't allowed to really date, but I could hang out with him in groups or when parents were present.

Four months went by. I heard nothing about Corey or from Corey until I heard the news of the murders. Our old neighbors had been stabbed and everyone thought that he might have done it. When I heard this, I felt myself divide further. That part of me that had held fast to my idea of him—so much better than he really was, so out of touch with who he was becoming—split and split again. I was at work, back at the River, so hysterical that my mother had to pick me up and take me home. Then I ran. I had no heart, no head. The horizon tore, directing me away from my home, away from the river, only to be met with mile after mile of land that was indifferent to me. The land was so flat that when I stopped running, standing in a field, I could still make out our house as a blip of color on the horizon. It seemed the world would have its way with me no matter which direction I fled. *Stabbed? Like with a knife? How could that be true?* I'd hopped an irrigation creek and my ankle bled, cut open by barbed wire. I didn't care. I wanted it to bleed out, run the whole river red in protest against what was happening. I wanted to stay in that field until he was home, cleared of all accusations.

I had to bring myself back from the field, eventually, and give in to the truth. I was unable to look my parents in the eye as they hugged my shaking shoulders, because they had known, all along in their heavy hearts they would tell me later, that it was so. He had done it. He had been on a bad path for a while, and now he'd made his own dead end. But by then, Corey was in another cornfield, four towns away, throwing gasoline on the sedan owned by the couple he'd killed in an attempt to erase what he'd done. He had stolen their car afterward and set it on fire in the field, like some bad television crime show. It made no sense to me why he would do this, except as an act of panic, indicating to me that whatever had happened in that house had not been planned. They sent dogs after his scent: spearmint gum, shampoo, cigarettes, and sunshine. Corey was fast, but the dogs were better runners.

People all around me, at work and at school, discussed motives and the possibility of drugs playing a role in Corey's actions. Was it a drug-fueled robbery gone bad? Did he have an unchecked mental illness? Was he involved in a gang? Or was he just a thug, some punk who'd lost all respect for life? Everyone had a theory, the small town shaken by the crime. I had no answers and no guesses. I found myself hiding in bathroom stalls, compressing all the noise into my clenched fists. Today, when kids experience trauma or violence in their towns or schools, adults thrust grief counselors on them. There are vigils and public attempts at closure. But not then. For us, there was crime scene tape, a double funeral, and the front page of the weekly newspaper. Nobody asked if I was all right. My government teacher used Corey's case as a conduit for discussing opposing views on the death penalty. I excused myself and threw up in the bathroom.

The worst I had heard before the murders was that Corey had been huffing gasoline, and that was a far cry from murder. At work, I tried to catch bits of information when the regulars talked about it, but they all hush-hushed when they noticed me listening and smiled at me, shielding me from whatever news they had uncovered. I internalized a new label for myself: girl who had kissed a murderer. Or, worse, girl who had possibly loved a murderer. And what did that make me?

· · ·

The most mundane of all that happened that week stuck with me: The sting of the dry corn leaf fibers that had rubbed against my calves as I ran. The rash that stippled the skin of my shins the morning after they arrested him, right after I'd said, "He'd never do this. Not possible." Not someone I'd kissed with my own mouth. I remembered that itch, how it hung around for days.

I didn't see the slit carotid arteries, the open necks of our two elderly neighbors or the blood that must have poured from their severed viscous tissues. I didn't see how it must have spread, thick and terrible, across their linoleum floor, where I'd stood on half a dozen Halloween nights and held out my pail in hopes of full-sized candy bars. I saw, instead, only two purple lines that had been fashioned across their necks by a mortician in an attempt to blur the evidence of their deaths. To conceal the aftermath of a vicious death, for the deceased and all who mourned them.

I'd been forced to go to the funeral so that I would know it had happened. That my beloved boy was in fact a killer. Capital K, facing the death penalty. My refusal to believe it would have to end. My belief in his inherent goodness would have to end. I could not recreate the violence in my mind or reconcile the facts. *But they had always given out such good candy,* I thought stupidly as I stood at their caskets. *And Corey had always been so gentle.* I looked in shock upon the lifeless faces of our neighbors, even as I mourned the loss of their murderer, who had been some part of the blurry future I saw for myself. How had I lost him, exactly? How had he lost himself? Leaving the riverbed was supposed to be a good thing, but so far, it hadn't proven so. How had I clung to this illusion of him for so long?

Everyone else immediately reduced him to his rap sheet. The list of reasons I had that explained his behavior was longer than the rap sheet. Nothing could justify or explain away that level of violence, but I was certain his life leading up to that point was a factor in the life of crime he had sunk into. Standing there, I tried to feel something pure, find something in my bones that I could believe. But instead, there was only the sense that everyone still living knew I had loved him, that it existed outside me now like an extra appendage, and that I loved him *still* even though he had done what he'd done. Had he known it? I'd never said so. Not even to myself. But there it was. I stood there among the grieving, struck dumb with my own selfish loss.

Generally, the town newspaper was a thing you decidedly wanted your name in or out of, depending on your status. If you were Bridget Trotsma with the brownest eyes and leanest thighs and eagerest stage mother, you wanted to be in. You said, "Look at that. I can't believe I made front page. Again." You smiled to yourself knowing full well you'd be on the front page but not knowing that your life would never be better than it was in that moment. If you were Corey, on the other hand, and you had killed two elderly, innocent persons and torched their car in a cornfield, you wanted to be out. You said nothing, if you were smart. But Corey wasn't that smart. He talked to someone who talked to someone else who talked to the police.

Or, he was smart once, but only had a makeshift upbringing as the fifth of five children, one dead too young, to guide him. This is what I remembered him being told: *get out, shut up, go away, your sister is dead, your father is a lie.* Growing children, like transplanting spliced plants, is a delicate endeavor. "It is easier to build strong children than to repair broken men," Frederick Douglass wrote in the nineteenth century. It is still true. Thugs are made, not born.

I walked the aisles of the grocery story—a mistake, in retrospect. In the bread aisle at the IGA, I heard a man say, "I hope he fries." Firing squad, another said. In the frozen section: "Those people living in the old riverbed ought to be self-incorporated, if you ask me. Those people ain't never been fit for this town. Draw a line between the northern farms and the river and be done with them." Some folks are born evil, someone said. "Ain't nothin' you can do about it." But that wasn't true, was it? Hadn't lots of kids from more well-to-do families smoked weed, stolen, and joyridden in their parents' cars? I was a regular reader of the police blotter, and it almost never contained the name of a Dutch teenager. If Corey hadn't spent four of his formative years in juvenile detention centers for crimes that rich kids had been let off for, would it have gone this far?

His case never went to trial. His attorney, I learned later, advised him to plea-bargain to avoid a jury trial for the death penalty. So Corey confessed and pleaded guilty. He confessed, too, because he was not at heart a person who would do what he had done. He would not sit in front of a judge, the room full of the victims' family members, and disgrace them by pretending he was innocent. I was sure of that, no matter what anyone else hypothesized. It was true that his actions were horrifying. But somehow I held out hope against hope in Corey's civility, in his true self before he shattered, over time, into other broken versions of himself. I knew his soft lips and lean body, those tender hazel eyes, his childlike laugh, his kind heart, his benign presence in my own bedroom on countless occasions. There was light and love at his core, and I had known it as my own. It had corrupted, somehow, dividing and dividing, rooting low, far from the sun.

A prison would take his body, and my parents would take his name. "You'll never say that name again in this house," my father said. It was if he'd never existed at all. As if he hadn't stayed over, eaten meals with us, laughed with us. Loved us. Loved anywhere but his own home. I didn't even talk about it with Marcus, not for years. They could not take everything from me, though. Hidden in my closet I kept:

A white and purple striped hat that Corey's mother had knit
Twenty of Corey's Nintendo games, including a Game Genie
His cassettes and CDs

Corey's paperback copy of Stephen King's *It*
His walkie-talkies
His soccer ball
A stuffed turtle he won for me at the fair
His Rollerblades, men's size 12

I could not reclaim my own innocence, bodily or otherwise, to add to the collection, but in my mind I returned to the night we'd gone to the county fair two summers before the murders. Around and around on the Ferris wheel we went, teenagers a little bit in love, our faces alight under fluorescent bulbs and our bellies aching with laughter. I wanted to stay there with him, looping that moment forever to keep him from all the wreckage that was to come. We had stayed at the fair that night until we puked, sick on too much sugar and grease. We two never knew when to quit.

Corey was sentenced in winter, at the end of February. A leap year. The newspaper showed the judge, a middle-aged white man, grimly doling out his sentence. I couldn't look at his picture in the paper. I already knew the last of the light in him had faded. I convinced myself that whatever I thought I knew about him, whatever closeness we had shared, had been one-sided. Contrived from my loneliness, made of my girlish fantasies. The night at the fair. The almost night in bed. So many moments before those. I smeared the parts of the newsprint where my tears had landed with my thumb, then with two fingers, then my whole palm, until I'd botched up every word they had.

I drove to the field, four towns away, where he'd spent some of the last free moments of his life. The soil was frozen, charred. A petrified crime scene. I said his name over and over, calling him back to ground he'd never set foot on again. I wondered if life would ever grow there again, what corn or wheat could sustain itself in his waste, what mutations would fester as consequence after a plow turned the black dirt brown again.

MAP OF CORN

In 1997, before Monica Lewinsky was the punch line of jokes, before zooming was a thing you could do on a phone with two fingers, before *organic* was a word in my daily vocabulary that referred to my groceries, I was living in the middle of a test field of genetically modified corn. I had no idea what this meant, other than the fact that seed alterations of both a chemical and a physical nature were involved. We had moved three miles down the road from my first home, and flat farmland replaced our view of the Kankakee River. The river was still near—half a mile due north, beyond a row of trees at the end of a field. We were out of the floodplain, but barely.

Life along the riverbanks would not shake off so easily. Corey's life had already been cut short, but mine extended into a horizon that I couldn't see. It was strange leaving a place where I'd lived for fourteen years—where virtually everything I knew about life had happened. We'd moved from the swamp to the fields, which was the equivalent of up, according to my parents. Only poor people lived by the river, and my dad was climbing the economic ladder of the construction industry. This was a symbolic move as much as a practical one. Flood insurance had been pricey. My parents could now actively save for my college education, which would commence, somewhere, in a few years. But it seemed like too much work for such a short distance because not a lot was different at the new house, except for an increased isolation and the view from my window. Corey was gone—from my window and from my life. Falling asleep became more difficult. I had gone to sleep watching his window for ten years. I was like a baby who'd lost her security blanket. That was the worst of it. There was nothing but stars and silos outside my new window. I interpreted the stars and silos as possibility, as an uncertain future.

My father tried to convince us that this rural home, with only one neighbor in sight, was a good thing. I liked the house, but I didn't buy his reasons. The move was a reflection of his personal improvement, his success. *Maybe things will be better.* Maybe a new place would make us into new people, better people. By the initial changes, it seemed to be true. We ditched the Sox and became Cubs fans. The law office my mother worked at provided third-base-line tickets, and we went to games as a family.

Our new road had only numbers for a name—an intersection of directional coordinates that was not like the attractive names of the roads in the subdivisions closer to town, where my would-be friends lived and where I wanted to live. Names like Michelle Drive, Poppy Lane, and Daisy Street suggested a place where life was beautiful and sanguine. Where families were knit close, and mothers and fathers stayed up late laughing and drinking Manhattans and popping maraschino cherries into one another's mouths after their children were tucked into bed. Pies cooling on kitchen tables on Saturday mornings, casseroles for after-school supper, and such. A place where teenagers weren't privately grieving the loss of a friend to a prison sentence. Did moving slightly closer to town bring us closer to that ideal?

I had no real love for the cornfields, no appreciation for the systematic coordinates of their gridded, numbered roads. The fields bore no marks of the land's history, like the riverbed had. A sense of the origins of my surroundings had been constant at the river— where clam shells sprouted from the dirt and arrowheads were readily unearthed with my fingertips. To recreate that reassurance here—place as lifeline—I had to go two miles down the road to

Aukiki, a preserved portion of wetland that lay beyond the shoulder of a state road. Marked with only a brown-and-white state park sign and a narrow gravel road, the land opened up beyond the first bend: water-filled gravel pits for fishing, wildlife preserve, and protected forest. I felt at peace when I visited it, removed from the agricultural fair of progress we had moved into, thrust into an authentic representation of the land where blue herons stood long-legged in the shallow water as they had for eons.

The fields that surrounded my new home were laden with a history that I could not yet unpack. They were neither romantic nor scary. They were nothing but flat strips of earth, dotted with the occasional rise of silo or telephone pole, barn or irrigation machinery. I felt nothing about those fields, or those human-made structures, until later. Our new house did, however, have three stories to it, and that was a palpable difference. The old farmhouse sat on an acre of grass that was plunked down in a gigantic cornfield. It was supposed to be part of the larger surrounding farm, a mother-in-law's residence, I was told, but it wasn't anymore. It had been sold off, piecemeal, like so much else in that town. And now it was ours— tacked onto an operating farm.

The world, of course, was bigger than us and our new little plot of land. In 1997, Bill Clinton was president and times were good, in general. The country was not at war, for one thing. Farmers in the Corn Belt, where I lived, were reaping benefits from the Freedom to Farm Act that granted them windfall subsidies in 1996 and 1997. These monies were given in addition to the regular Farm Bill subsidies that meant, basically, that no matter what happened, the farmers would be guaranteed profits. Fields previously kept idle to meet subsidy requirements were now abundant with soy, corn, or wheat, depending on each field's stage of the soil rotation. Some years, the fields seemed to be filled with mostly corn, which reached high above our heads and enveloped the property. In 1997, whoever owned agriculturally zoned land was raking in dough. Farmers bought expensive new equipment and repainted their barns. They bought condos in Florida for their mothers. The heartland was new and shiny and colorful. A place, much like a family, could reinvent itself, distance itself from the past. So could a government, or a nation.

Most everyone who owned huge tracts of land in our town was Dutch, and by Dutch, I mean many of them had parents or grandparents or other extensions of family still living in the Netherlands. People of Dutch descent owned not only most of the land, but also most of the local businesses. Their collective identity defined the town. They were the teachers and coaches in our school district. Their children constituted most of the varsity sports teams, their last names emblazoned on plaques and pendants above the basketball court. They were the handful of professionals the town boasted, as well as the school board. They took annual family vacations to Disneyland and to see national landmarks like the Grand Canyon and Yosemite National Park. I had never myself seen a national park. I used the Dutch as an association to help me pass my high school history test: they were the rural American bourgeois, rich people who had everything and could decide things; river people, who had nothing and held no power, were the working class proletariat. Bourgeois equaled them, proletariat equaled me. Easy A. I broke down meaning in this way a lot, because history, as it was taught in high school textbooks, made no sense to me. It was a half truth, a culled record of facts.

There was a saying around town: "If you ain't Dutch, you ain't much." Every time I heard it, it reminded me that this town wasn't ever meant to have me in it. Nor them, since the land had been taken from Native Americans in the 1800s. But what did anyone care about that now? Kids who went to school in the towns bordering ours, which may as well have been foreign countries, called us "clickers." It was meant as a derogatory term having to do with wooden shoes—a derivative of a Dutch cultural relic whose meaning and use was several generations removed from us. It grouped us all together. But how, I wondered, could I be a clicker if I was not Dutch? I had always thought that our community was a vestigial culture, the last remaining small part of something that existed before. We lived on land that was stolen. Our social mores were Dutch colonial holdovers. Our laws and penal system were adapted from English common law. Federal subsidies initiated by government officials who were no longer in office benefited the land-rich. The soil was hauled in from elsewhere, filling in the dune sand that had once been covered in wet marsh. I still had the river in me. Still had Corey on my mind. Yes. We were vestigial, at best.

My father's first order of business at the new house was planting a garden. During the first weeks at our new house, my dad began tilling a rectangular section of the soil in our backyard. I helped him. I couldn't wait to stop eating vegetables from cans, though it would take a while for my taste buds to recognize fresh produce as food at all. Our new neighbor, Amos, who owned the big house on the adjacent farm and whose family had leased the surrounding fields for generations, noticed my father working and walked over to us. He put his toes right up against the property line, which extended invisibly from a row of Italian cypresses that marked the eastern edge of our acre. It was probably strange for him, too. It was his mother who had lived in our house before, and he had lived in it as a boy. I knew how unsettling it was to watch other people inhabit a place that had been yours and begin to change it. I had met the new family that moved into our house by the river. Our emotional connections to property were more complex than the legal transactions that transferred it from one person to another.

"Putting a garden in?" Amos was a Deere man, which means a

lot was fancy with him despite his being a third-generation farmer. He had gone to college, then come back to the fields, like many of the town's wealthy farmers. They were educated laborers and small-business men.

My father was a member of a carpenters' union local based near the South Side of Chicago, but on the Indiana side. He had no college education, which meant there was nothing fancy about him except for the things he built with his hands. You learned after a while that there were two kinds of workers in this town: union and nonunion. The union workers commuted to the politically Democratic cities in the more industrial northwestern corner of the state—Gary, Hammond, East Chicago—where union labor jobs were more common, while the nonunion workers were employed locally. It was the union job that had allowed our family to move away from the river. The pay was good, as were the benefits. If I kept my grades up, which was a sure bet, they would even provide a scholarship for my college education.

I stopped what I was doing, stabbed my hand shovel into the dirt next to where I was planting our freshly spliced hostas, transferred from our old yard to our new one along with our aboveground swimming pool. I got a fistful of black soil in my hand and moved it around slowly, sifting it through my fingers as I listened. We had had the dirt hauled in. If you dug down a bit past the topsoil, you'd find that the ground was largely still comprised of sand and clay, remnant of the Lake Michigan dunes to the north and the former marsh. I came across a white grub and sent it flailing across the grass with a flick of my index finger.

"You can't put any corn in it," Amos said, still on his side of the property line that he had once crossed freely.

My dad stopped tilling and stood up straight, squaring his shoulders. "Why's that?"

Amos wiped sweat from his forehead with a faded handkerchief. "It's a genetic test field. Federally funded."

He proceeded to explain the detasseling process, which sounded a lot like sex to me. The female stalks had openings into which the male stalks' seeds would blow and seep to begin the fertilization process. That kind of thing. I turned red and rocked nervously on my feet, which were tucked under me in a way that would leave a wild, itchy pattern of grass marks on my skin once I stood up. But nobody was watching me. They didn't even notice that detasseling was about corn vaginas and corn sperm. More than that, though, I couldn't believe that corn could be manipulated at the gene level. The most I could figure out was that it must have been like making blue eyes brown with the fine tip of a needle.

"If you plant corn in your garden, it'll cross-pollinate with these test rows after detasseling and muck up the whole harvest." Amos didn't like cursing. "We can't have that."

"Which ones are the test rows?" my dad asked, crossing his arms.

Amos moved his hand in a circular fashion above his head.

"All of it? You gotta be shittin' me." My dad loved cursing. He worked a *goddamn son of a bitch* into most sentences, even when the emotional tenor of a conversation didn't necessitate expletives.

"All of it along this stretch of road anyway. Every fifth row's a male. In between are female. Different test strain every nine rows. I lease these fields to a breeder. That's the corn of the future right there." His hand glided through the air, gesturing at the perimeter of our yard as if he were Vanna White. Looking more closely, I saw the wooden posts marked with a numbered code, indicating each strain.

"No wonder they call it Millionaire's Mile," my dad said, and shook his head. "I'll be a son of a bitch." But I didn't understand why this would equate to wealth.

Amos snorted. "You can pick whatever you want to eat once it's grown. It's all sweet corn. Won't nobody miss a few here and there."

My dad nodded by way of agreement and returned to tilling. He didn't like being told what to do, especially on his own property. It was odd the way people ruled their tiny plots of land like kings. Were people who lived in cities the same way? Did people in downtown Chicago or in New York behave like that? It seemed a universally American tendency—to subordinate those who threatened your personal property, especially land and buildings. We were wonderful at fencing ourselves in, moating our little kingdoms. But from what? And to what end? The actual Dutch weren't like that. Many years later, on a trip to Amsterdam, I would be astounded at the vast differences between the "Dutch" I'd known in Indiana and the Dutch in today's Holland. Communal space and neighborly communion seemed to be core values, dictating both building and land design as well as social interactions. Despite the issues of strict dominion over the garden at the new house, we crossed the property line to pick corn from the test rows every night for dinner that summer. We found stringy, shucked hairs in strange places long into the fall.

When we moved, Latino immigrants seemed to have become as populous in town as the non-Dutch. With more land producing crops and more money to spend on production, more workers were needed, and the Latinos provided that labor. Our town now had three kinds of workers: union, nonunion, and migrant. There were plenty of field jobs available in our county, and the only people who worked them were teenagers and migrants. Occasionally a teacher who needed to make extra money over the summer would sign up. But there were no other able-bodied adults in line for these wages. I had heard that some of the migrant workers lived in rows of bunks in outbuildings scattered among the fields and farms. Hidden away.

With their new faces, their dark hair contrasting with so much Dutch blond, came an inexplicable buzz of fear. "If they're gonna live here, they best speak English," my dad said, as if playing a stock character or caricatured bigot. His prejudice was one of the worst kinds, citing patriotism as the reason he held his beliefs and claiming that's the way he grew up. I was to stay away from the goddamn bunkhouses if I ran across one that summer, because there was no telling what could happen. I ought not single him out, though. To be fair, this attitude was representative of the majority of adults with whom I was acquainted. My father's voice was simply one that I heard loudly and often.

I thought his beliefs—this unilateral dismissal—were flawed, and I told him so. I could not understand our differences, where they had come from, or how it was possible to hold on to beliefs that were, to me, so obviously uninformed and unkind at their core. Before I was sent to my room for having an unpopular opinion, my mother piped up. She cited a Hispanic-on-white rape incident she claimed to have seen on the Chicago-based news, which is the only news we got. "But I'm not racist," she added. "I'm only saying you have to watch out." They were always trying to protect me from the wrong threats.

Despite recommendations that would curb immigration, a 1994 report submitted by the commission on immigration policy under the Clinton administration stated that "hostility and discrimination against immigrants [was] antithetical to the traditions and interests of the country." It claimed to disagree with "those who would label efforts to control immigration as being inherently anti-immigrant," calling management of immigration "a right and a responsibility of a democratic society," with the aims of such management to serve national interest. The report refuted its own assumptions about the impact that more-educated versus less-educated immigrants had on the American job market, stating that the commission had "called for favoring immigrants with more education and skills on the grounds that immigrants with relatively low education and skills may compete for jobs and public services with the most vulnerable of Americans, particularly those who are unemployed or underemployed." The claim that immigrants were taking American jobs was refuted when the commission found and reported that, in fact, low-skill jobs performed by immigrant and native-born workers tended "to 'complement' rather than substitute for one another." It showed no correlation between immigration and unemployment among the native-born, a belief I'd heard championed by many adults. The commission recommended measures to remedy their findings, including that any new policy "must give due consideration to shifting economic realities" and consider ensuring lawful entry for those who contribute to our society. But any progress made on that front was halted when former congresswoman Barbara Jordan, the commission chair, passed away before President Clinton had acted in any substantial way, as once promised, on immigration policy reform. The topic rested where it lay for the remainder of Clinton's time in office.

My school couldn't accommodate the new Spanish-speaking kids, or "Mexicans," as they were often referred to, regardless of where they were actually from. There appeared to be no interpreters available, nor any effective way to integrate these new students into the population. Whether that was the unfortunate consequence of a funding deficit or a conscious choice, I do not know.

Within a few years, a Mexican restaurant would open in town. But nobody would complain about that.

For one summer, I worked as a corn detasseler on Amos's farm. A whole crew of us signed up, over seventy in all. Each farm throughout our county and beyond employed hefty numbers of kids and migrants in the summer months, but the two sets of workers were strictly separated, coming into contact with one another only at long views sneaked across different fields. I walked over at six in the morning each day with my brother, Marcus, who was now thirteen, the state's legal minimum age for corn detasseling. We wore gym shorts with warm-up pants overtop and tank tops under flannel shirts. Cubs hats on our heads. The early mornings were wet and cold, but by ten the temperature would reach ninety-five, which made walking in the space between rows of corn feel like being in a sauna. By eleven, breathing was nearly impossible due to the aggressive humidity.

"I hate this job," I said every morning. But a paycheck would mean I wouldn't have to wear the clearance-rack clothes that my mother would buy in the fall, when school started. I planned to buy clothes that were in season and in style, and preferably from the Limited—like the clothes the Dutch girls wore. I wanted new books and blank journals from the bookstore, which was a forty-minute drive away.

"At least it's easy," my brother said, lugging his water cooler in one hand and his lunch cooler in the other. We drank a gallon a day each. Marcus had inherited my father's unflappable work ethic; he rarely complained about physical labor.

"You call this easy? Look at my arms!" A few days after the work had started, I yanked my flannel sleeve up to expose the pink mess of scratches and bumps that was my arm. We'd had corn rash since the first day on the job, and it stung when it was recut fresh each morning. But you had to keep going. The rows felt endless, a rural hell that, until you had worked a field, was unassuming and picturesque from a distance. I felt something about corn now. The fields had looked inviting from our front porch, gently rippling for flat miles in the wind and catching the sun's last shine at the end of the day. But up close, *this* close, the corn was violent with leaves as thick and sharp as thorns that cut right through the skin—*ts ts ts.*

We would visit Dr. Vanderveen, one of a handful of Dutch doctors in town. He would prescribe salve; we would hand over our union health insurance cards and be made well again.

As my relationship to the farmland's layers grew more intimate and palpable, as I learned which scrubs and fowl were native and had been there longer than the Dutch, my understanding of anthropological shifts in society over time also expanded. In school we studied the hunters and gatherers; the agrarian societies; the industrial, technology, and postindustrial eras. The commingling of societal-era strongholds present in the region in which I lived perplexed me. We lived sixty miles from the dead center of downtown Chicago, and from here to there, one could encounter successful agricultural, industrial, technological, and postindustrial ventures—to all of which corn or soy was an integral commodity in some way. Farmers were producing it in mass quantities for almost innumerable purposes— among them, as feed for livestock, as fuel, as building materials, and as an additive to foods and everyday products. I could not help but feel that, considered in the context of federal subsidies, I was living in a country that was governed, to some extent, by corn. The belief in corn's usefulness was reinforced on the consumer end, too. The food pyramid, for example, whose standards were issued by the federal government and mandated in schools, was comprised of a large daily helping of American-grown grains as well as a quantity of dairy products derived from cows that consumed the grains. My curiosity about and knowledge of the way that this crop was bound up in our country's wealth and history, as well as its future, were rudimentary. Yet I sensed an orchestration whose scope and scale were larger than I could imagine. Corn, as a multifaceted industry, seemed a gorilla against whose chest one might futilely beat one's tiny fists and not begin to wound it.

The first time we saw the crop duster, there was no warning—it simply arrived as noise, drowning out the clucks of distant hens and the intermittent lurching calls of the scant blue heron population. We watched the plane buzz the field, spray a fine yellow mist from below its wings, and lift its nose right before it reached our house. And then we went outside to weed the garden, mow the grass, and breathe in the country air. Until that day, I had never thought about what might be on our food, what was unseen. Would it impair our health, sticking around in our bodies for an untold amount of time? We had been eating that corn all summer. We had certainly breathed in the chemical as well. What was the life span of fertilizer-laced corn products inside us? In this way, a place or an experience could potentially stay with you forever, corporeally.

As I learned about the agricultural industry in the United States, and about the country's economic system, I became fascinated by the life of a dollar. Where it had come from, through whose hands or accounts it had passed before it reached me, where it would go afterward, and how its value would be reduced as portions of it were given back to the government. I wasn't interested in comprehending vast economic systems that reached across countries and oceans, but rather in the individual level of my own experience and how it fit into the larger picture. My thoughts scrambled when I thought of how many times each dollar from my detasseling paycheck had been taxed or transformed in its value before it reached me. My mind stretched sideways when I considered that I could, in theory, bear children, hold a job, go to jail, and pay taxes, but I could not vote for how my money was spent by the government.

I could construct a similarly complex life cycle for corn. The seeds that were planted each spring behind our house had been manipulated at the gene level and sealed into a chemical fertilizer coating before they ever touched the farmer's machinery. Their future was set before shipping. Once sown, they were watered with irrigation drawn from surrounding lands, water that was abundant due to the land's original status as wetland marsh, fed to soil rich in minerals due to being drenched with that water for centuries. As the corn sprouted, it was lacquered with another chemical fertilizer to ensure an optimal yield for its producers and investors. I came into direct contact with it each morning when I worked those fields for one laborious summer. In the fall, the corn was harvested and stored in the silos I gazed at as I fell asleep at night; their massive drying fans hummed in my dreams through the morning. When the corn was siphoned out of the silo, it was piled into a truck and driven to market. And that was only the beginning. After passing through an unknowable number of hands, machines, and facilities, it came back to me in the form of fuel and oil, in my breakfast cereal, in the milk produced by the cows who fed on it, and in my lip gloss. I could neither see nor name all the things it had influenced or into which it had been inserted.

My brother was right. The field work itself wasn't that hard. You got used to the corn rash, and the heat was harder than the work. We got a lot of breaks, and I often rode piggyback on my friend Josh to work the rows I was too short to reach on my own. Josh would kiss me behind the bus sometimes, which left me rapt with anticipation and excitement. We were making a hell of a lot of money, too—thirteen dollars an hour if it was your first year in the field, and more for returning workers, which nearly tripled the federal minimum wage. After work, a few of us would skinny-dip in our pool before our parents got home. Sometimes we'd see the Latino workers lined up in a field, waiting for a farmer to pay them. I hoped they were getting paid what we were, or more, given that they worked harder, but I had a bad feeling they were not. If they were, they'd probably have looked happier about payday.

One morning I told the foreman, who was only seventeen, that I was too tired to keep working. "It's almost lunch," he said. That would be at half past ten. Our work would be done before noon so that none of us got heat exhaustion.

"But I'm getting a sunburn." It never occurred to any of us to wear sunscreen.

"Fine. Take a break."

I nodded for Josh to follow me. We headed for the bus that had brought us out a short distance into the rapidly growing corn. Traditionally, you knew whether the crop was on track for a good harvest when it was knee high by the Fourth of July. In recent years, though, the corn was well over our heads by that time—the seed and fertilization further refined toward perfection each year. If it weren't for the years of flood and drought that affected the yield, they'd have attained that perfection. From the field, I could still see the roof of our house, but I couldn't see so far as the road. The top of our back-yard pool came barely into view when I stood on the steps of the field bus, and I wondered if I could sneak away for a dip. Cool off, then come back to work. But I wasn't nearly that brave. I sat down on the steps of the bus next to Josh, so that I was out of the sun. It was too hot to go all the way inside. Despite the heat, it felt nice to lean against him. He was six-five, easy.

"Want to go to the beach later?" Josh asked.

"I don't know. I think I'm getting heat exhaustion. I feel sick. Let's go to the beach tomorrow."

Because my mother worked with Josh's mother and she was a CPA, he was the one boy I was allowed to be alone with, no questions asked. Perhaps they thought he was a promising match for a boyfriend. I spent most of that summer with him. We would drive up to Lake Michigan and wade out to the sandbar. Or we'd drive around in his truck and listen to Janis Joplin or Jimi Hendrix. Some days we'd smoke doobies in his garage. The term was outdated, but we didn't care. We were sure we were living in the wrong decade. Sometimes we took the South Shore train to Chicago and shopped at the resale stores on Clark and Halstead, where we took turns trying on the same vintage T-shirts and fedoras, unable to decide who wore them better.

Josh and I huddled together on the bus steps, gazing at the field across the dirt road, accessible only to the farm staff and secluded entirely from any real roads. We watched a group of about twenty men sweating synchronously, moving in perfect rhythm. Reach, yank, toss. Reach, yank, toss. Their muscles flexed along with their motions. Their skin was deeply tanned and their eyes were dark and shaded. They were loads faster than our work crew, and it was obvious that they took their work more seriously. I couldn't understand the few utterances that broke their silence. There was no bus around for them. No shade, no breaks. I wondered whether we were working for the same farmers, or if the land they worked was owned by someone else. I wondered where they had come from and whether they were happy. Mostly, I wondered why we were kept separate.

"I can't believe we get paid to mess up this stupid corn and make out." Josh laughed, then quieted, looking at the men. "Jesus, this is fucked up."

We looked away from the men embarrassed by our privilege and our own futility.

By the end of the summer, I no longer wanted new clothes or new technologies paid for with my detasseling money. I put it all in my savings account, and my brother used his to buy a PlayStation, Cubs jerseys and tickets for the bleacher seats, and new Jordans. I was transfixed with the old—bell bottoms, hot pants, terrycloth jumpers, record players—while Marcus wanted every new thing available. Josh and I had discarded our CDs and listened, instead, to dusty albums that we found in our parents' garages. *Saturday Night Fever,* the Moody Blues, Lovin' Spoonful, Ella Fitzgerald. We spent our time running our fingers through the air as we sped along the country roads, stopping to scour yard sales and dip our feet into creeks. We never talked about the strange work we'd done, or how terrible we had felt watching real men do real work while we made a mockery of it in the next field over and collected paychecks that we hadn't really needed. Instead we drove until we hit water, until we'd put all that troubling land behind us.

By summer's end, my father's garden had produced more vegetation than our family could hope to consume. He was proud of having cultivated his own garden, having successfully improved our immediate surroundings by getting us away from the river, but that ownership was relative. The land was not ours. Not really. We were there, living on it, but we did not know the implications of its past, nor those of its future. We would not possess it forever. It was connected to everything else around it, not separate, despite the lines of the paper deed that cut it away from the fields. Borders are only real because we say they are real.

One morning, my father burst through the kitchen door lugging a basket of vegetables. "You won't believe how big the zucchinis are this year. Picked these goddamn sons of bitches first thing this morning." He pulled one of the zucchinis out of the basket and put it on the countertop next to a butcher's knife, for scale. "That sucker must be sixteen inches long and six inches thick."

"They're supposed to be about seven inches long and barely two inches wide. They taste better that way, too." It was something I'd recently learned on a cooking show—that zucchinis were meant to be harvested long before my father had picked ours. The plump, overgrown ones held too much water, making them soggy and flavorless when cooked. Yet he insisted they were perfect. It was one of those discoveries made after childhood that, although a seemingly minuscule and unintended deception, made me question what else I'd mislearned from my parents.

"The bigger the better," he said. My father also used a fully out-fitted tractor to mow our one-acre lawn, and he had furnished our new home with plasma televisions in nearly every room; before we moved my mother had obsessively gone on home tours, enviously eyeing homes we still could not afford. I never grasped my parents' desire for excess. It was one more difference between us. But my brother seemed to have inherited the gene: he lined the shelves of his new closet with a dozen pairs of Jordans, more shoes than any boy could ever need.

I kept arguing with my father, though it was useless. He was going to deep-fry the zucchini and douse it with hot sauce either way, ruining it completely. And besides that, you couldn't argue with my dad.

"It's all-natural," he went on.

"That's impossible."

"It sure as shit is. Didn't put a damn thing on it."

I reminded him of the planes that had fertilized the fields twice that summer. "Don't you think that might have something to do with it?"

"This is why they call it Millionaire's Mile, baby. Richest soil in the Corn Belt right here."

I counted to ten in my head to calm myself down. Maybe the chemical bath was not only on our food but also in our water, and had spread to our brains. I feared the corn we had eaten all summer, sampled from a dozen genetically experimental strains that bordered our little chunk of land, was a kind of poison that was silently wrecking our DNA. The hostas we'd replanted from our old yard, our old lives, were thriving in their new environment. I had thought they were hardy plants, able to root anywhere and survive. But it was only the fertilizer, the rich soil, the relocation, that had enabled their growth.

THE REGULARS

When I was seven, a babysitter walked me and my brother to the River to buy cigarettes. She stole the money from the old water jug my parents saved change in for vacation. She left us at the water's edge while she made her purchase. "Don't tell anyone," she said. But I did. Not because she had taken the money for cigarettes, but because I didn't like being left outside by all that water with nothing stopping it, or me.

The summer I was twelve, my brother and I would walk to the River from our house and order steak fries and Pepsis while our parents were at work. We would watch the men sitting at the bar, smoking and drinking, most of whom lived nearby and knew our father. We would use half a glass bottle of Heinz ketchup for our fries, licking salt from our fingertips. When the bartender brought the bill, I'd slide it back to her with sticky fingers and tell her to put it on my dad's tab, that he'd be in later, I was sure of it. And she would, and he would.

I got a job at the River as soon as I was old enough to obtain a work permit. I could have worked anywhere in town, but I wanted to work there. I liked being near my old house, near Corey's house. It was a rite of passage. Corey had worked there and planted the plants around the restaurant, and I would weed them. He had washed the dishes that I would clear from tables. I liked this continuity. I liked seeing people from my old neighborhood. It was a familiar and comforting place. My father usually sat at the bar when I was working, both to keep an eye on me and to socialize or entertain people from work. At home he seemed to barely speak to me, and when he wasn't working in the yard, playing golf, or watching television, he swung unpredictably between being a shadow of himself, exhausted from work, and being a battle-ready brute with the vengeance of a wrecking ball. He was unpredictable, throwing hammers and expletives in equal measure. He had left his own dismal past on the banks of another body of water—the Conococheague Creek, a tributary of the Potomac River in Maryland, but I could not name his ghosts. I only sensed their presence in his anger, in his detachment. His father had been a brick tanner, and the tannery had let their family rent an empty home on its property for one dollar per month. Though the home was a large, sprawling plantation, it still had no indoor plumbing in the 1970s, when my father lived there with his family. He had joined the army at eighteen, and he never went back except to visit. At the bar, he was a different person than he was at home. Jovial, pink-cheeked, spirited, and conversant. Generous in his affection toward me. I preferred him half-drunk to sober, in the bar to at home.

At the River, my father celebrated his promotion to general foreman, then later to superintendent of a union construction company. He bought rounds of drinks for everyone, and he called me *baby girl* when I walked in with a tray full of dirty glasses. Some nights, he ordered prime rib for the two of us, then danced with all of the women in the bar, spinning them silly and singing into their ears. He was still a stranger to me. But he could afford to buy me painting lessons now, and in the bar he squeezed me close and told everyone about my good grades and that I'd received an honorable mention in a painting contest for the national duck stamp, which had something to do with duck hunting. We had the watercolor picture framed and hung in our hallway at home. In it, a sleek male wood duck floated in a pond, water rings spreading out from its richly colored plumage. It was easy enough to do. I copied it from a picture in a book, visually dismantling the duck into its core shapes and allowing myself to see that brown is actually made up of grays, greens, yellows, blacks, blues, purples, and whites. Later, this painting would earn me an academic scholarship to a nearby college—the only one I'd ever consider in my listless search. *You're so smart,* everyone insisted. I had the grades to prove it, but I told them I wanted to be average.

At work, I kept waitresses from crying or fighting, inhaled secondhand smoke, and smelled like meat juice. During my first week at my new job, a woman named Toni was canned for giving blow jobs in the men's bathroom. A woman named Lonnie told me while we were rolling silverware that her new thing was screwing her boyfriend while he was driving, straddling his lap and watching the road get smaller and faster behind the truck. "You have to try it. It's a rush," she told me as she slipped a buck from someone else's tip into her apron.

From the age of sixteen on, my Saturday mornings began as most people's grandparents' do: I drove my four-door sedan with the sparkling champagne paint job to the bank to deposit my paycheck, then I bought a cappuccino. My father had brought the car home as a kind of gift. He had put a down payment on it, but I was responsible for making the monthly payments until the $12,000 loan was repaid. I had a checking account with pink and blue pastel checks for a baby, and each month I mailed a few hundred dollars to Ford Motor Credit. My evenings were as strange as my Saturday mornings. I didn't spend Friday nights at the Pizza Hut in town with kids who wore letter jackets, and I rarely went to parties. I spent my weekend nights with the regulars, listening to jokes told in poor taste and wrapping myself in the raucous bellowing of men's voices and women's laughter. I caught glimpses of myself in the mirrors that lined the bar's dark paneled walls—my face puzzled out beneath the Budweiser and Miller and Leinenkugel decals, shadows splitting my cheek crosswise. The curve of my own smile, a mystery. The layers of smoke and grease carried home with me each night like party favors. The way I knew they would never fully wash away.

I bused tables, carried empty glasses to the dishwasher in the bar, lugged trash to the Dumpster, churned the film on the salad dressings, answered the phone in a voice that sounded like my mother's, and managed the waiting list for the restaurant. I married the ketchup bottles in silence, connecting the bottle necks with a steady hand. I watched the Kankakee River freeze over into big white plates of ice and snow while I washed the restaurant's windows. I felt they were my windows, the Kankakee my private sanctuary. I enjoyed the peace that came with physical work.

I took baskets of bread to the family of the boy who had broken up with me. They barely spoke to me. Only to say *Water, please. More napkins.* Trevor, my first real boyfriend, did not once even look at me. I still did not know what I had done wrong. There was no explanation. The brusqueness of that ending was an affront I could not digest, an affection I could not relinquish. I could have hidden in the break room, asked my coworker Shannon to take them bread. Instead I sought the masochism of it—the horror at the lack of conversation when I faced them each Saturday night, the way I could nearly cry each time as an assurance of my own body, alive and feeling. I stared at Trevor until his face turned red. I wanted him to know with certainty that he was a coward and that I was not invisible, hard as he tried to make it so. If he felt anything at all, he was a better actor than me. No one in his family seemed to remember, there in the restaurant, that I had spent the previous Christmas with them or that they had given me an expensive porcelain doll with angel wings, which was still propped up on a metal stand next to my bed. She had blond hair as fake as mine and my same blue eyes. *A doll.* I still looked at her, with her tailored golden dress, quietly mocking me. I believed this gift was chosen for me as something to aspire to. This was how a girl should be: demure, mute, polished. Should I want to continue dating their son, I ought to discard the resale bell bottoms and men's polyester pants, the 1950s housedresses and the flowing gypsy skirts I'd sewn myself, and become more like her. But I couldn't settle on a style. I lacked sophistication. As I had with religions, I cycled through a dozen looks, and nothing seemed to fit, so I would make what I wanted to wear. In the employee bathroom, I retied my apron, wrapping its long black strings around my slim waist. I washed my hands, washed my hands, washed my hands.

I worked harder and faster than most everyone else because it felt good to use my body and to make everything new and clean, to put everything in its proper place. To complete the tasks set before me. For the first time, I began to understand my father's relationship to work. Physical work offered tangible accomplishment, and it eased a busy mind, almost like a sedative. Working at this pace, lifting and moving, my quads and hamstrings hardened over time. Work left me no time to think about anything other than the dirty dish or phone call at hand. It kept at bay my instinct to question and lament all that seemed wrong in my world. When even the work was not enough, I tried to make a game of it by bettering my wait-time estimates and by doing so much of the work myself that I made the other busers look lazy. And most of them were. Many of them had bigger problems than mine: abortions, anorexia, absent fathers. One night in the dry-storage room, which was really a narrow hallway lined with unstable metal shelves and boxes, a dishwasher named Josh caught me alone. I'd been jumping vertically to grab and pull down reams of white napkins from the top shelf. He put his hand up my shirt and kissed me, without any warning, without even speaking to me. It took me longer than it should have to push him away with both hands. Still, I never said no, although I was not attracted, even remotely, to him and I did not want him to touch me. Later, he followed me to my car after my shift and tried to get me to go to a party with him. For once, I was glad my parents were too strict for that to be a possibility. "My dad's in the bar," I said. "He said I have to go straight home." Away from the river, back to the fields. I didn't belong there anymore, but I kept holding on anyway.

At sixteen, I was the youngest person on the floor staff, so people were inclined to teach me things. Betty was the head waitress, with fluffy white hair and tiny feet and red lipstick. She told me about her sweet old husband and her sweet old Cadillac. She called me honey and promoted me to head buser, a title for which there was no pay increase, only more work. She taught me to put on lipstick the right way, which meant outside the lines of my already plump lips, in order to attract a man. It was not unlike the showy green and purple feathers of the male wood duck's crested head. We were not far from our animal instincts.

One night while we were watching the nightly news, a spot ran about the AIDS epidemic. We were loading empties into the glass washer, and Betty said to me, as much as to the television, that AIDS existed because black women couldn't keep their knees together. Horrified, I told her she was ignorant and a bigot, and she was never kind to me again. She tried to have me fired, and nobody said I was right. I went home in tears and in shock, and I was too embarrassed to speak of it to anyone.

At the River, a waitress who was forty and pregnant asked me to babysit her eight-year-old son. When she came home hours later than the time she promised, she was gone in the eyes and barely on her feet. She never mentioned the little boy's name, not before she left and not after she returned, but she had told me on her way out the door that there was mac and cheese if I wanted it. The boy was already in bed; his face twitched with sleep in the moonlight. I wanted to hold him, name him, make him meatloaf with green beans and chocolate chip cookies for dessert. But all I did was dab my cheeks with his mother's CoverGirl powder in the bathroom and wait, playing house in their home. The baby was born with Down syndrome, and everyone at the River loved him and squeezed his chubby hands when she brought him in. I never stopped thinking about how the older boy didn't know I was there, even as I layered him with extra blankets and thought about how I could save him.

At the River, my friend's dad came in drunk and ordered prime rib *au jus*, two inches thick. He ate the monstrous cut of meat with his bare hands, slopping it into the juice like a puppy mauling a rawhide. I watched him from the buser station. He slapped the steak onto the table and tried to speak to me through his wide grin, but I couldn't understand what he was saying. His face was red and his eyes were red and he dumped the juice all over the table, then he rested his face in the mess of food and fell asleep in it. After he was carried out by his friends, I cleaned the mess alone while everyone else smoked. I watched the Kankakee rush by while I mopped, wondering where all that murky water ended up. I called my mom and told her what happened, crying into the pay phone as if it could comfort me, because it seemed like the only thing to do. The more the men at the River surprised me, the more the women seemed to glaze over. They quieted, as if in silent prayer. Their calmness frightened me. My mother called the man's wife, a friend of hers, to tell her where she could find her husband, and I tried and failed to imagine her surprise. Would I, too, become immune to such spectacles? That day I learned that there were different ways to be a drunk and that a bar was another kind of church.

One day, a man called Muddy who had known me since I was ten fell backward off his bar stool. When I rushed to help him up, he stormed out in horror, the bells on the door jingling after it slammed behind him. He never, ever returned. Sometimes I wondered if he was dead on a couch somewhere, with a bottle of

whiskey between his thumb and index finger, sitting in front of a
static television, or if he found another place to pray.

I stayed late after my shifts ended because it was better than
going home. After a while, people no longer invited me to go to the
Pizza Hut. I didn't want to go because I felt as though I was between
worlds when I was around them. The kids in town didn't hang out
in bars. They didn't feel more comfortable around men nearly their
father's age than boys their own age. They lived in subdivisions and
had golden retrievers and mopeds and crushes on one another,
while I was being hit on by men in my father's work crews when he
wasn't looking.

One night, I played "Strawberry Wine" on the jukebox and
sipped a virgin daiquiri at the employee table in the corner. The
song reminded me of Corey, of how I had tasted him and, with a
few different decisions, he could have been mine. It was homage to
our lost chances, what with him in prison. A sort of tribute to my
longing for him. As I listened to my song, a man named Tim sat
down across from me. He bought me french fries and smelled like
mouthwash. His voice was high-pitched, although he was twenty-
seven. When I was younger, I had watched him fly by my house on
a crotch rocket, his curly blond hair blown back by the speed. I was
eighteen now. Fair game. "You want to go for a drive when you're
done with that?" he asked. He came in a few times a week. That
night he told me that he was separated, getting a divorce, that I was
pretty, that we could go to his house. Maybe for a drive, I said, but
we never made it out of the parking lot. His truck was brand-new,
the spoils of his job as a carpenter. The bench seat was covered in a
red-and-black plaid blanket made of wool, and it scratched against
my bare skin.

At the River, a man named Dave, who had known my mother
for more than twenty years, stayed at the bar from early afternoon
into early evening when it wasn't harvest time. He talked to me

about planting and irrigation, about books, about nature, about the presidential election, which I could now vote in, about taxes, about the Farm Bill, and about the college I would go to the following year on a partial scholarship, where he used to party when he was my age. An avid reader of the *Farmer's Almanac* and in possession of an MBA plus his father's farm, he knew much about nearly everything. One day while we were talking about waterfowl that make their habitats along the old Kankakee marsh—blue herons, wood ducks—he told me that only some wood ducks migrate south along the Atlantic Flyway, while some stay put through winter. "You can't tell which are which, not by looking at them, or by where they live." He meant that it was determined genetically. "They're programmed as one or the other—to stay or leave," he said. The ducks had the get-up-and-go gene or they didn't. Dave was very tan, year round, from having worked outside all his life. He was always alone, always at the bar, elbows up and smiling wider as liquor took hold of him. A happy drunk. Once, I had gone to his house with my family for the Fourth of July and swum in his pool. I could feel him looking at me from time to time, and later we were alone, briefly, in his big empty house. He told me it would sure be nice if I were ten years older. And I felt like I already was, standing there in a bikini and dripping pool water all over his floor. I went back to the pool and dove down to the bottom, where I lay on my back holding my breath and looked straight up to the sun, wondering what was programmed in my own genetic code.

At the River, I read on my work breaks, and everyone got mad because I took the full fifteen minutes. It was only fair—I didn't smoke and everyone else took a smoke break every hour. That logic was lost on them, so I ignored them. I read books about witchcraft, the Louisiana bayou, Henry VIII, Elizabeth I, and apartheid. I read books by V. C. Andrews and Stephen King and Thomas Hardy and Mary Higgins Clark and anything by the Brontë sisters and anything Oprah said to read. One day while I was reading, a boy with long hair whom I'd never met sat down with me. He bought my meal at my discounted employee rate. He told me he had read *Jude the Obscure* already. He said that I was beautiful and that he would like to sit there all day until I was done working. "And then what?" I asked. He said then he'd take me to a real dinner. I thought he might be crazy, but I also loved his candor. It was not every day that someone had read the books I was reading or said I was pretty—men I knew only implied it by assuming I was available to them, that I was appreciative of their advances—so I was an easy sell. He asked me to meet him in the parking lot after my shift. I found him sitting on the hood of a blue car with a guitar, waiting for me. He patted the hood, inviting me to join him. Then he got up, stood five feet from me, and sang to me in broad daylight, putting my name into the refrain and looking me straight in the eyes. He didn't tell me his name, didn't try to kiss me or touch me. Just a smile and a good-bye. I never saw him again. He was proof of something, but I wasn't sure what.

At the River, I took dollar bills from men who wore guns in black holsters beneath their overshirts but over their undershirts. I picked the music, and they smiled. We listened to all the Hanks, the Stones, Stevie Nicks, the Judds, Merle Haggard, Joni Mitchell, Aerosmith, Genesis, Bon Jovi, and the Eagles. I danced and sang while I worked—with Kimmy and Dave and Lonnie and Tim and Harvey, and by myself. I called home to lie: they asked me to stay till close. I put on more makeup in the bathroom and stayed late at the employee table because I was still too young to sit at the bar. The regulars, who were friends with my dad, friends with me, took turns sitting with me, and everyone tried to get the bartender to give me a drink, a real drink, but she wouldn't and I didn't want one anyway. I wouldn't learn until college how much I liked to drink. Then, the company was enough.

The men told stories about dogs and ex-wives and fishing and teenagers and motorcycles. The women talked about men who were farmers and steelworkers and carpenters and bricklayers and alcoholics and wife beaters and no good and a little bit good. One night, when the talk went a bit sideways and the pours of liquor went a bit heavy, two of the men argued and tumbled onto the patio, where they drew their guns. But the women were swift to cull their brutes, reducing them back to size, and with a few soft moves no shots were fired.

At the River, I was five and nine and fifteen and eighteen and twenty and sixteen and seventeen. I talked to Kimmy, who had begun dating Dave, and she told me how he made her ache with love. I wanted to ache as she did, but none of the men in the bar produced in me even a flicker of that exquisite pain. I studied the two of them, the way they smoothed one another's forearms and shoulders in a kind of primal dance, one wood duck spinning gently in the water of its mate's wake. An undertow that, when seen in miniature, looks almost like love. They were different sorts of people, Dave and Kimmy—as different in appearance as the male and female wood duck. He was mostly quiet and smart, while she was at the edge of unraveling, teetering between precipices of elation and melancholy. Dave talked to me less frequently, and Kimmy never remembered what we talked about, relaying the same anecdotes of her life present and past, again and again. She got lost in her own bubbling laughter, in the perfect harmony of a song only she could hear. And I hoped that I'd grow up to be a little more fun like her, a little less serious, a little more disarming and open-armed and fragile, but I never would.

Kimmy came to my high school graduation party, all the regulars did, and they hugged me and gave me money and said *Good goin', girl. We're proud of you.* They were the sum of me, divided into different kinds of pain, different kinds of happiness. Or perhaps I was the sum of them, our common denominator the River and a hard-earned history. Kimmy gripped my cheeks with her long fingers and told me that she loved me. It was her lasting memory, a compilation of many smaller, specific ones that had been lost inside a bottle, a feeling that was true. Still, she knew we had shared something important, if not the details of it. She said, "I could be your aunt. I could be your *sister*." She told me to stay blond, blond, blond and to marry a man with money and to not get pregnant in college.

That summer a group of men and women painted my portrait at a watercolor workshop. We stayed in a barn on a sunflower farm for a week where there were flower heads big as pies for acres—I had never seen such beauty. In those days before I knew what the need for morning coffee was, I'd get lost in the flower fields before breakfast and show up for class with yellow cheeks. I was there on a work-study scholarship—my parents had paid half the fee. In exchange for the second half of the fee, I washed the artists' dishes, helped cook the meals, and sat for portraiture. The participants gathered around me like children at the storyteller's knee. They could hear me breathing, and I could hear their brushstrokes, the soft spray of their water spritzers, the scrub of their sponges against my paper temples. I heard them whisper, as if I were not there, "The mouth. Can't get the mouth right." I was a plate of shapes. Apple cheeks, hay hair. No longer a hostess, no longer a student, no longer a daughter. I wore a sundress and cowboy boots that never made it to the page. At the end of the week, I saw my face in seven interpretations, each more surprising than the last. Did I look the way they saw me? Were these the eyes I'd been seeing with all these years? I couldn't tell. I felt foreign in my skin, wrong bodied. I have wondered whose closets I haunt. Where those seven alien selves have traveled. Whether anyone knows my name, or gave me one: *Plain Girl above Our Fireplace* or *Nothing Special in the Hallway* or

Woman Who Could Literally Be from Anywhere. But at the time I only wondered, *Where is that woman going?*

By summer's end, I had paid off my car in full and purchased a computer with leftover graduation money. I'd received three annual scholarships: one from my father's construction company for keeping a high grade point average, one from the arts council for my painting, and an academic scholarship from the school itself. One for each of the three things that had paved the way for whatever the future held. I packed the duck painting in a flat cardboard box and took it with me to the one college I'd applied to—one town over from home—and later to several apartments, evidence of my having crossed over from once place to another. But I never hung it up and I never painted again. I was embarrassed by it, having copied it from a picture. Only an idiot would recreate exactly what was already there and call it art.

DISPATCHES FROM ANYWHERE BUT HERE

M y need to flee began long before I called it that. It started as a series of adventures, and then it became more pressing, more intentional. Sometimes I thought my aimlessness might have been friction resulting from Corey's absence. I was still troubled by losing him, though I never spoke of it to anyone. The fact that I still thought of him in this way worried me. Why couldn't I incriminate him like everyone else and bury it? In addition to English literature, I had decided to study criminal justice in college, and that choice was in large part motivated by the idea that if I could somehow intellectually understand how he had ended up imprisoned for life at nineteen—understand the reasons people commit violent crimes—then with enough education, I could also save him from the fate he'd earned. I could beat the system for him. Or at least make it better for others, on both sides of crime.

I'd selected a college based on proximity to Greg, my hometown boyfriend. Greg worked as an excavator, rearranging the terrain. I liked his job as a metaphor. On the weekends, we would obsessively scour the newspaper for vacant land that we could buy for a future home, but as soon as I started school, I realized we were worlds apart. I was interested in books, in sociology and criminology. He was interested in fishing and heavy machinery and wrestling.

Living one town over from home was barely leaving. Tumbleweeds on the plains traveled farther than I did. I'd wanted so badly to leave, but when the time came, I recreated what I'd already known because I couldn't think of anything different. Greg was a safety net. If I had a boyfriend I was committed to, around whom I could plan my life, I wouldn't have to figure out my actual life. I hadn't seen or experienced much else, hadn't known many educated women, so everything that wasn't home was foreign and thus frightening. The first sweatshirt I bought from the college bookstore had the school's year of establishment printed on it: 1889. It had been operating for over one hundred years. The first in my family to go from high school to a four-year college, I was shocked to learn that people my grandmother's age had gone to college. I'd considered higher education a "new" thing because it seemed as though my family was just now learning of it.

I still went home on weekends to do my laundry. If I was hungry, I ordered the same kind of fast food I had eaten at home. I stored frozen quarts of my dad's homemade chili, filled with vegetables from his garden, in my dorm room freezer. If someone had said, "Here is a blank piece of paper, draw a living room—anything you want," I would have sketched my mother's sofa and pine furniture. My dad visited me at school once a month when he was passing through for work. He would take me to lunch and we made small talk for thirty minutes, and he offered life wisdom: "Don't sweat the small things," he reminded me. Before we parted ways, he'd hand me a fifty or a hundred-dollar bill and I would want to not take it, but then I would pocket it reluctantly and kiss his cheek in thanks.

Soon, though, even that was too much. I needed more independence. I broke up with Greg and got a campus job tutoring basketball and football players to earn spending money. I imagined myself a satellite gathering information about the unknown world, extending sensors in hopes that an alarm would go off when I'd found a place that "fit." As if it were easy to know what was what, where one belonged, what one should do. In "Some Dreamers of the Golden Dream," Joan Didion cites California as one such destination— where people seek destiny, or, at least, a refuge from "somewhere else." She writes, "Here is the last stop for all those who come from somewhere else, for all those who drifted away from the cold and the past and the old ways." West as a Hail Mary. But I didn't have the West. I had wherever my car and a few hundred dollars in the bank would take me. It wasn't California.

My cousin Mandi's golden dream consisted of getting a smattering of tattoos, changing majors half a dozen times, massaging hundreds of aching bodies before finally settling on acupuncture school, living in half a dozen states. Eventually, she bought a dog named Bodhi and moved into a small house in Evanston, Illinois. Greg moved to Las Vegas and lived with his friend James in an RV as a remedy to our breakup. He left a fifteen-page letter on my windshield, like a time capsule that recorded our brief history together, before making this journey. I didn't think he'd really do it, but, to my shock, he never came back. Had he left an address, I would have written him and asked him to return home. Not because I wanted to be with him, but because I couldn't fathom making a one-way trip to a distant state. People didn't *move to Vegas* and stay there.

My own launch and exploration was more timid and piecemeal, oriented toward a fascination with selvage, run-down places and meaningful interactions with strangers. Sometimes I would visit a place and stand in its center, inviting it to transform me. In truth, I never had a plan for anything. Whatever came my way, I accepted, as if I had no choice in my own tomorrow. But after excavating the river and fields of my home, I turned that curiosity outward and slowly became an eclectic tourist of America's towns and neighborhoods, an interlocutor in silent commune with other scarred lands and depressed buildings. I set out to my destination, sometimes accidentally and sometimes on purpose, applying my new knowledge to each new landscape. I analyzed the metallic remains of postindustrial wastelands. I mouthed my secrets into the hallowed valleys that marked the paths of ancient glaciers. I sketched the scenery, recorded my conversations as journal entries or poems, then reported back home to Indiana.

Broken Windows Theory

After Corey disappeared from his bedroom window forever, I was fascinated by abandoned structures. Places that once held people, businesses, animals, cargo, but were empty now. Barns, silos, houses, warehouses, Cabrini Green. Places where the past was scooped out and the shell remained. I liked to imagine the stories that happened inside—the chain of events that culminated in each place's specific emptiness, the people involved, and where they were now. How it had changed them. I still remembered watching the news when residents of Cabrini Green, a Chicago housing project, were evicted, then watching its demolition on television. They had to drag the last few people out by force. *Where on Earth would they go?* I wondered. *What would happen to them all?* There was no way to know whether emptying out and dispersing the violence-plagued community would scatter the people, the problems, or both.

The Sandman Motel was a different kind of empty, a rural empty. It had been vacant since I was a kid, having closed down for good in the late 1970s. I wanted to stay there for a night. I thought if I could sleep there, spend some time there alone, I'd learn its stories. I remembered my mother's face when I asked her if we could rent a room there. She looked at my father as if to say, "See what I mean about this one?"

She called one day when I was away at school to tell me the motel was on the news. "They're calling him 'the chicken fucker.'"

I wanted to see it for myself. My preoccupation with dissecting crimes now extended beyond Corey's. At night I watched *Unsolved Mysteries* with my roommate, and by day I read the local police blotter. In my criminal justice classes, I had learned a number of criminal theories. Policing theories, behavioral theories, psychological theories, economic theories, theories of socialization. There were endless theories to learn, and I wrote them all down on three-by-five note cards. I had also learned the names for the various crimes one could commit: larceny, burglary, murder one, murder two, manslaughter, trespassing, criminal trespassing, rape one, rape two, and so on. I memorized them and regurgitated them for exams, wrote papers about a growing, untenable American prison population that teemed with broken men and women, an untenable lower class, an untenable middle class, white-collar crime, the escalation of violence, the effects of the misguided war on drugs, earning perfect scores in all my classes. It was easy to understand the world from the top down. It was easy to comprehend a massive, layered problem when it was flattened out, two-dimensional as a flowchart, or as a series of smaller problems and solutions into whose connective tissues you could interject theories on little note cards like heroic antidotes and create a kind of sense. A way out of the mess. But in practice, it falls apart. Theories are not useful as cultural medicine.

The broken windows theory stood out as being particularly troublesome. The theory, developed by criminologists George Kelling and James Q. Wilson in the early 1980s, was based on the idea that the appearance of neglect in a given neighborhood lends itself to actual crime. In other words, in a neighborhood whose residents didn't maintain its upkeep and safety, criminals were emboldened to commit crimes. A "no one else cares, so why should I?" mentality. Though likely only coincidence, the theory emerged as gang-related crimes at Cabrini Green escalated. In interviews, Chicago police officers years after the housing project was shut down for good termed the neglected area the "perfect place to commit a crime." The buildings in the project had suffered from severe disrepair, and law enforcement and community boards either wouldn't or couldn't do anything about the situation. And when they did try, they faced difficulties in gaining access to the buildings, as they had been overrun by criminal operations.

I never saw Cabrini Green up close, or the redevelopment that followed its demolition. But I could go to the rural motel and see for myself. I remembered the Sandman Motel as a categorically seedy place built as a long line of square rooms with thin walls, each with a separate entrance and a single cheap window framed in faded barn-red trim. Its rooms had held decaying beds, rotting nightstands. Old Bibles. The police had found feathers, and a blood-stained mattress. I saw on the news that the man had stolen chickens from a local farm, and he plucked out their feathers before committing bestiality.

Like a womb, the motel had held that crime inside it. The soft underbelly of our rural area, which was supposed to be a haven from "city" crime, was scaly, flecked with brown and green rot. It, too, had its dark and empty places where people lugged their worst secrets and tried to conceal them. But looking at that motel from outside, I couldn't have guessed.

The problem with the broken windows theory is that it fixes property, not people. Certainly not systemic poverty or oppression. Moreover, the theory assumes that a place can have psychological influence over people's actions or state of mind. And it would seem that that's true: for example, we long to visit beaches and climb mountains because we desire the physical and mental experience of those places. In 1981, Jane Byrne, the first and so far only female mayor of Chicago, lived in a Cabrini Green flat for three weeks to get firsthand experience of life in public housing. During that time, various upgrades were made to the buildings and surrounding land and no one was killed. The violence subsided to a simmer. But when she left, it started right back up again. The baseball diamonds that were built during her brief efforts were soon overrun with weeds. The windows were broken again.

I once heard that New Yorkers are anxious because they can no longer hear silence or the chirping of birds, which seemed a logical correlation to me. Unbroken windows are an illusion, like small towns, meant to tell us that "nothing bad happens here." But it's not true. The problems of humans manifest wherever humans are, razing each landscape raw as freshly tattooed skin.

Routine Activities Theory

At the time of my first trip to New York, Corey had been in prison for two years. The trip was organized by the private Catholic college I attended in rural Indiana. I paid for the trip with money I had saved from working at the River—I'd continued working there even after I left for school, commuting for shifts once or twice a week. A group of twenty students and faculty members would fly into LaGuardia, take a train to a youth hostel in lower Manhattan, and meet once a day for group activities. The rest of the time would be ours, to do with whatever we wished. I didn't know any of the people who had signed up, and that, too, was encouraging. Unsure of what lay waiting for me in New York, I packed my sketchbook, three pairs of leather pants, tank tops, a trench coat, and one comfortable walking-about outfit. We had only three nights in the city, and I planned to see as much as I could and sleep as little as possible. A classmate from New York had given me a list of things to see, taught me how to read my pocket-sized laminated subway map, wrote down which trains to take where, and wished me luck.

I did all of the regular things—Statue of Liberty, Ellis Island, MoMA, the Met. I had to buy new pants, having mistakenly imagined New York as some gigantic nightclub. Wearing new cotton pants purchased from a gated parking-lot bazaar in Greenwich Village, I looked out over the city from the top of the World Trade Center, which would fall nine months later. I went to an Internet café, a novelty for its time, where you could pay to use a computer while you drank coffee or beer. I ordered beer, and no one asked for an ID. I drank it and checked my e-mail. I had never before experienced the two activities in public, or at the same time.

My nineteenth birthday fell in the middle of the trip, and I debated mentioning it to someone. It was my first birthday spent away from home, and I kept it a secret until I didn't. It was too lonely, I decided. I didn't call or e-mail home—no one carried cell phones, though a few people had one, and my parents didn't yet use e-mail. I had written Corey a letter for the first time since he'd gone to prison, and perhaps as a gift to myself I had timed that letter so that his reply, if he wrote right away, would arrive around my birthday. It was in the back of my mind the whole trip, this letter to a man in prison, while I attempted to befriend regular young people who came from nice Catholic families. Some of the students had heard there were "triple X" bakeries in New York, and the boys on the trip were determined to find me a penis-shaped birthday cake. They settled for a flaky, chocolate-filled penis-shaped pastry, which I ate, laughing, as they sang "Happy Birthday" to me on a street corner. For dinner, my new friend David took me to a restaurant in Little Italy, where we pretended to be married and cosmopolitan, in hopes of being served wine, which we were. In one of my classes, I had learned about the major U.S. gangs and the criminal activities in which they engaged, so when I spotted the Hells Angels bar in the East Village, I wanted to get closer. I jaywalked and presented my ID at the door but was denied entry, as expected. Still, I'd gotten a glimpse inside: smoky, dark, loud. I didn't want the day to end, and so, when everyone else turned in for the night, I selected a train line by its color and took it to anywhere, which turned out to be Queens.

I walked from two to four in the morning, utterly lost. I had read about the routine activities theory in my criminal theory class, and I was growing paranoid, watching for crimes everywhere. The theory's geometric representation was triangular: it converged a person's daily routines and regular haunts, a motivation to commit a crime, and a clear opportunity to do so. The space enclosed by the three "sides" was the criminal activity. In broad daylight, glimpsing crime had sounded interesting. But nighttime was different. I passed dark alleys in which I could make out people's shadows, and I passed vacant buildings with broken and barred windows. I wanted to stare at everything, despite my quickening pulse, but couldn't: the urban fears I'd acquired in my rural upbringing had come to the fore. I had changed into the leather pants. Would I be mistaken for a prostitute? Was I *asking for it?* When I passed men on the sidewalk, I told myself, *act like you live here and don't make eye contact.* How does one blend into a foreign place? By mirroring the behavior of the locals—size them up and quickly assimilate. And then, the darker thoughts: *say you have AIDS; say you have children; pretend that you like it to undercut the desire.* Every woman had a rape plan, didn't she? Mine involved verbal manipulation. But no solicitations for sex arose, nothing bad happened, and no motivated individual saw in me an opportunity to commit a crime. I eventually found the train that took me back to the hostel.

Three Chinese men sat outside the hostel in the early dawn. They offered me a joint. I hesitated, thinking it a trick for a moment—*Are they cops? Will it be these men who hurt me? Is the joint laced with PCP?*—but then accepted. We sat on a bench together, our four sets of hips colliding, and blew long, straight trails of smoke into the air. I showed them my sketchbook—the spade-shaped bridge in Central Park, the gazillion windows of the city skyline—and they asked me to draw them. I drew each man, one by one, as they taught me words from their language. I didn't know what we were saying, but I took it to mean, "We are all here together now and everything is all right." Sometimes the differences in where we are from and where we are sitting are irrelevant.

Biological Theory of Deviance

As we were nearing the top of Grandfather Mountain on a hiking trip in North Carolina over my summer break from college, my aunt Eileen told me she sometimes felt a compulsion to throw herself from heights. Most any were problematic for her, she said—bridges, balconies, the top of the Sears Tower. "Do you ever want to jump?" she asked, and stepped nearer to the edge of the mile-high overlook bridge.

"Too conspicuous." I checked for signs that she was kidding. "Dramatic. If we're talking about ways we could kill ourselves, I'd rather find a cave to crawl into. Starve. Rot away quietly. Eat poison berries. Avoid the free fall and the newspaper article afterward."

As we trekked upward toward the highest point, I watched her. Though it was rarely if ever spoken about openly, a clear pattern of depression ran through my mother's side of the family. There were also incidences of schizophrenia, and I suspected that there were other undiagnosed mental health issues as well. Deviance was once believed to be phenotypically linked, but today's biological theories of deviance associate certain brain functions with deviant behavior. Maybe we were on the biological fringe of deviance. But maybe we were just human.

My aunt and I silently convinced one another not to play out those potential ends—knowing glances, pretend lurches toward the edge in an attempt to laugh away the seriousness of the implication—but I saw the way she eyed the spray-painted arrows pointing toward paths that led to the edges of cliffs.

I understood her compulsion. But for me, the lure was the locked cellar, abandoned and untouched by light or humans for decades.

Empty structures of any kind with the suggestion of a ceiling would do—the warehouses that lined Chicago's South Side with rows of broken windows screaming skyward and graffiti mural walls. I didn't want this cursed attraction; I wanted to be a person who embraced mountain overlooks—who found those sorts of places life affirming and rejuvenating. Mind quieting. I was hell-bent on trying, anyway. Is it possible to best a psychological ill though willpower? Whenever I'd had a cold, my father would look at me scornfully and tell me to stop coughing. When I had chicken pox: just stop itching. "Mind over matter," he'd say.

On the last upward thrust of the hike, perched on a ladder climb that had us scaling a mile-high cliff, I panicked. A familiar paralysis took over me, and I couldn't breathe. Aunt Eileen, three rungs below me on the ladder, coached me upward. She was a paramedic, level-headed and at her best when she was faced with trauma. If there was anyone you wanted around in a medical crisis, it was her. It took several minutes for me to make it up the last few rungs with her verbal assistance, and when I reached the top, I collapsed and curled into a ball. I sobbed and she lay over me and held me. "You're all right," she said. "You're having an anxiety attack." She held my hands and face, soothing me until I could inch my body away from the edge, still pressed fully flat against the rocky ledge.

I didn't know if I could make it back down the other side of the mountain after that. "We'll take our time," she said. "Don't stand up until you're ready."

I realized then that what I experienced on the cliff was the same "heart attack" I'd had as a kid. Only now did I realize it was connected to fear. On the descent, I tried not to wonder about what in my childhood had been bad enough to give me anxiety attacks. I looked to the trees for solace. I constructed poems in my head. Anything to keep me from thinking backward—to keep me rooted in the present moment and in the flat land that awaited us at the bottom of the mountain.

On the way down, we saw a dried gourd hanging from a barbed-wire fence line. How I wanted to steal it and take it with me. I wanted to weave a blanket of thatch in there, curl into it, and fold my wings. A tiny bird prison that left no room to expand into the air around me.

Differential Association Theory

My great-grandmother lived near Seven Mile Road in Detroit until she died when I was in college. She was Hungarian and tough, with a real mouth on her as I recall. She had been married to an Irish man who drank and gambled and left her. She had several children, each of whom was struck with one of the classic, stereotypical Irish ailments: drinker, gambler, physical abuser. I'm told that my grandfather had an inclination toward two of the three, and though I never met him, I know that my mother and her siblings suffered.

In contrast to biological theories of deviance, the differential association theory said that behavior was learned, communicated primarily through the nuclear family. Even if people who witnessed deviant behaviors didn't become deviant themselves, they may learn the rationales anyway. That made sense to me. My mother and her siblings were raised in an abusive home, a consequence of my grandfather's alcoholism. It accounted for my mother's willingness to let things happen that ought not to happen, to explain them away. I worried I was repeating the same behaviors—letting things happen in my life as though I had no choice. I wondered what marks, what effects of witnessing my grandfather's deviance, had carried over, inadvertently passed down to me.

Seven Mile Road and the surrounding blocks are notoriously known as Detroit's deadliest neighborhood. The city's Mile Road system, made famous by Eminem's biopic, *8 Mile,* is fraught with disproportionate crime and blight within a city that is known for its crime, abandonment, and blight. When you google Seven Mile, page after page populates with links to violent crime reports, news articles about the atrocities that have occurred on Seven Mile, and statistics about murders. The numbers are staggering. It was recently dubbed Carjack City by local police, who cite carjacking as a serious issue in the area, with incidents annually numbering in the hundreds in recent years. We were told as children that her neighborhood was too dangerous for us to visit. My mother had told us stories of visiting there herself as a child, when they'd more than once had to drop to the floor during a drive-by shooting, and it had gotten worse since then. That my father wouldn't allow us to visit I found most disappointing. I felt they were hiding the real America from me, and I loved peering into those unfamiliar cultures, which to my young eyes were like dystopian snow globes. There was the shake and wonder as we sped by in our car, my mother white-knuckled at the wheel, having taken a wrong turn; the litter like a futuristic urban snow; and the wide black streets a plastic bottom that held up an insular world that might shatter if it was dropped. My great-grandma's funeral was held in a Catholic church near her home—it was the only visit I ever made to the city. My mother made us duck and run from our car into the church, but again, nothing happened. I had seen worse things in our own neighborhood.

In the film *8 Mile,* the place where Eminem grew up is both a physical and a symbolic barrier to his achieving success as a hip-hop artist and, more generally, as a productive member of society who is not simply rendered irrelevant and unsavable by his own past—his lack of privilege and his familial instability. Eminem has a dichotomous relationship with the neighborhood where he was born and raised: it's both the source of his art and the limiting factor in his personal wellness. The film itself depicts pure transition, a big reach for a golden dream, retelling in a way that is contemporary and culturally relevant the classic American story of pulling oneself up by one's bootstraps. It reflects an ongoing struggle to shed the past, shed place, shed experience derived from place. Pack the memories and move somewhere better. Differentiate his association. Never mind the bootstraps, which haven't been worn for decades. But I bet even Eminem goes back home. I bet even Eminem lets slip a few learned behaviors in the presence of his daughter. I felt a kinship with him—both limited and empowered by my river home, like a strange new species trying to jump out of a koi pond of overgrown goldfish even though it was the only place I'd ever known or would know as home. Cursing it even though it was part of me.

Defensible Space Theory

Near Indianapolis's downtown, a now-defunct Eli Lilly laboratory facility stands three stories tall beyond the enclosure of a chain-link fence. I first visited this building with a young man named Dustyn. I'd met him at my second job, where I was working evenings at a café after putting in nine-hour days as an intern at a nearby government association. Dustyn wore a mustache before mustaches were cool again. He looked like a disheveled Salvador Dalí, with his slick black hair and the detached air of an artist. He rode a stunt bike to and from work at the café, even in the winter. On a cold night in October, I'd insisted on giving him a ride home, which was more for my peace of mind than for his convenience—he had no problem with the temperature that I had noticed.

We set the café's leftover food on the bistro table in front of the restaurant, where each night a handful of the city's homeless would pick it up to distribute among one another. Dustyn and I wedged his small bike into the backseat of my car and set off for the city's near south side. We turned onto Orange Street, a name that had inexplicably been assigned to the cheerless gravel alleyway that ran parallel to a string of businesses whose operations weren't apparent upon first glance.

The defensible space theory, similar to the broken windows theory, was also about discouraging criminal behavior through property management and a place's projection of a certain type of image. The theory asserted that building design and layout that created naturally defensible spaces, a layout that allowed people within to watch what was going on outside, for example, would deter criminals. The building on Orange Street featured none of the theory's cornerstones. Its first floor had virtually no windows. The parking lot had no streetlights to speak of.

I was suddenly unsure of my decision to drive Dustyn home. Once at home in an environment that bespoke neglect, I had somehow grown afraid of it. Experience and age and the American media had ingrained in me a kind of fear of the nonsuburban, of being alone with a strange man in the middle of the night. Dustyn was, actually, more or less a stranger to me. He asked me if I'd like to come up and take a look. Though I was skeptical, recalling those moments in which the first fatal violence occurs in your average horror flick, I could not resist the opportunity to enter the building. I wanted to see what was inside.

The building's foundation slid at a diagonal into the ground, crumbling on one side. Several of the windows—small rectangular inlays that composed a larger plan of windows on the second and third floors—were broken. Dustyn opened the heavy metal door and led me inside. One lightbulb swayed slowly in the center of the entryway, a dull yellow orb. He told me that the building had once been part of the pharmaceutical company's sprawling campus. Now it was pieced out and sublet to so many folks—four artists to a room in some cases—that none seemed compelled to bear responsibility for its common areas. The place smelled of mildew and finger paint.

"This way," Dustyn said over his shoulder as he walked toward the freight elevator. "Lights don't really work." He had devastating brown eyes, a perfect pink mouth. But he himself was a kind of defended space—designed to keep people out. It was obvious that he made an effort to avoid embracing his natural good looks, what with his unkempt beard and haphazard appearance, his greasy hair, though I couldn't understand why. He would not blend into any setting no matter how he tried.

Once we were both inside the small elevator, he grabbed hold of a dirty rope and pulled. A wooden door crashed down, whacking the floor with a thud. I jumped. "You get used to it," he said. We were forced to stand close together, which seemed to make him uncomfortable. He smelled like basil, not unpleasant, but earthy. I decided I could get used to his aroma, though I wasn't particularly drawn to it.

On the third floor of the building, I followed Dustyn down a dark hallway. He pointed to a few vacant rooms, whose walls were the color of verdigris. "This is where they used to test syphilis drugs. This one over here was for Prozac." I wanted to stop to look longer, but he kept walking. He led me into a room at the end of the hallway. It had high ceilings and big windows. The blinds were drawn up, revealing row after row of single-paned windows, arranged like wall-sized checkerboards that overlooked the industrial south end of Indianapolis. The night skyline was the best view of the city that I'd ever seen. When he turned on the lights, I saw the rest of the room. Every surface was covered with poster-sized works of graffiti art. Easels and worktables and empty spray paint cans and stacks of art in various stages of completion littered the floor area. On the walls, brilliant sprays of color formed finished portraits of men and women, their images layered over detailed graphic designs. It was some of the most striking work I'd ever seen. It was electric, and it made a strange logic against Dustyn's blasé nature. I wanted to dip my fingers into whatever swirled inside his mind.

"I'll show you something else," he said. "A little field trip. Follow me." He grabbed a flashlight and we walked out the building's back door, down an apparently unused set of train tracks, and beneath a bridge. He turned on the flashlight, directing the light against the cement underside of a bridge. He was not only an artist, but also a vandal.

"It's stunning," I said as I stared at what was his best work. A gigantic mural of a woman, her face familiar.

"Next stop," he said. I followed him back inside. Instead of going into his studio, we walked up two more flights of stairs and then he began to climb a ladder and flung open a trapdoor at the top.

I'd been leery of ladders since the Grandfather Mountain incident. I could barely look at it without freezing up again. In my mind, I was right back there. I've heard that smell is the strongest link to memory, but I'm not sure that's how it works for me. For me, memory flashes resurfaced when my body was oriented in a remembered way in a remembered place: up a ladder to a cliff.

"Where does that go?"

"To the roof," he said.

I couldn't tell if the tour was turning into a romantic experience or if he really did want to show me things. After a few seconds of deliberation, I followed him. The rooftop was skirted by a two-foot-high brick wall and large enough to sit at a comfortable distance from the ledge. I followed him to a spot in the middle of the rooftop and we sat down and looked out over the city skyline. He didn't say anything and I didn't say anything. Would he kiss me now? Or were we really just looking? I was game, either way, and happy to enjoy the view now that I was safely sitting down. When nothing more happened, I told him I was ready to go home. We stopped by his studio again so I could get my keys. I looked around again at the artworks covering the room—this place that I never would have guessed belonged to the dark-haired boy on the stunt bike, much less was hidden in a building in an old alleyway. I was in awe of him, and he seemed entirely disinterested in me. And what could I say for myself? That I had painted once and rolled it all up and stuck it in a closet? I wasn't even trying. I was a half-assed writer, a sometime doodler, roaming around looking for something I couldn't even name. I complimented Dustyn's work, asking him questions about his process and spray paint methods and whether I could buy something to take home with me. He uttered a noncommittal response and would not look at me. I couldn't determine what code I'd violated, but I sensed that he regretted bringing me there, and so after a few minutes, I left him there with his hidden art and his darkness and his too-handsome face and his secret, empty building.

Self-Fulfilling Prophecy

The shoe barn sat in a thick patch of pine trees between the old funeral parlor and a crumbling row of apartment homes in my hometown. I'd go there even after I left. The appearance of the surrounding buildings reflected the way this part of town was built: on dreams half-launched between bankruptcies, destined for swift abandonment, eventual and total disrepair. After removing the faded *No Trespassing* sign that hung askew from the rusted, unlocked chain, I'd crack the sliding hinge door open wide to reveal the heaps of boxes. The boxes of shoes stored in the barn that once formed well-organized towers—someone's bounty of hope—were now dashed across the floor, as if toppled by a child's whim. The dream of a family's business abandoned. Or so I believed. All I knew for sure was that the family was gone and the shoes remained, decades out of fashion and rotting. Slim pairs of weathered go-go boots made of crushed velvet and black-and-white saddle shoes with platform heels covered the barn floor. A range of mismatched sizes and varieties formed piles at the base of the heaps like skeletons ejected from their coffins.

When applied to criminal theory, the self-fulfilling prophecy, a concept developed by sociologist Robert K. Merton, asserted that deviants became such after being told that's what they were: bad. It was the manifestation of belief or prediction that involved labeling a young person a criminal, or a future criminal.

I began stealing shoes from the barn in high school. Sometimes I would take friends there and invite them to help themselves, as if the place were mine to give away. In college, when I learned the nuances between the various crimes involving theft, I was able to retroactively categorize my actions as burglary, defined as petty larceny *plus* breaking and entering. Trespass with the intent to steal. But did I consider myself a criminal, either then or now? No. Again, I thought of Corey, who, before the serious crime he committed, had committed crimes similar to mine but, unlike me, had been told he was a criminal and treated as such. He'd been labeled *bad* from the first incident of deviance, which had not hurt anyone and had not been intended to hurt anyone. Somehow, I was still *good*.

Condemnation

For several years, beginning in college, I was an active member of a Habitat for Humanity chapter. In addition to doing work on new homes being constructed locally, the group made trips each year to other states that needed work crews and to places that needed repair after disaster relief programs had ceased to be helpful in restoring residences. Illinois, Mississippi, Missouri, Louisiana. One year, we went to North Carolina to provide reconstruction relief in homes that had been severely damaged during Hurricane Floyd—which had swept through that area of the coast in 1999—and remained severely distressed in 2002. Though some of these properties had been condemned, deemed unfit to inhabit, some of the homes could be salvaged.

My efforts seemed futile even at the end of a full day's work—there was so much work to do. I took inventory of what remained. A few families had begun to move back into their homes, but the restoration was slow. Five in six houses were still empty. I walked into these vacant homes, their doors not even closed, let alone locked. They held little worth protecting from intrusion, completely undefended spaces. Once the water swept through, I imagine the families felt a simultaneous fear and relief at the knowledge that no mere person could violate their property the way that nature could. I imagine people became less frightening after that, and weather more so.

I walked through the front door of a small blue box of a home and toured its empty rooms. In the kitchen, a baby's bottle sat on a shelf in a cupboard whose door hung from a single hinge. It was the only possession that remained. In another home, this one an aged white color that looked more like gray, I sat on a small wooden chair and gazed out the window at a desecrated backyard. The walls of the condemned homes had sustained water damage that rose several feet up the drywall.

Condemnation is also a process by which a government can exercise eminent domain to obtain privately owned property for some kind of future public use or redevelopment. With respect to criminal law, it has another meaning: a person deemed guilty and sentenced to a punishment.

I stood inside a third small house stripped bare of all evidence that humans had recently lived there except for a 2Pac poster on the living room wall. It was the only thing completely unaffected by the flooding, pinned up in the middle of all that destruction.

By then, it had been three years since 2Pac's death. Rumors that he was alive were still circulating—my friends and I among the hopeful believers. We had attached ourselves to hip-hop and rap music in the 1990s, even though most of us were not part of the culture it represented. I watched his image eerily watching me from where it hung on the wall, amid the destruction and the wasted space. He was the Mona Lisa of rap, looking down at me. He'd been bought up with bail money and transformed by a Compton gang leader into a symbol, which ultimately led to his death. Despite that, his music had helped to bring to light a segment of America's population that had previously been shadowed. He told stories that needed to be told. I wondered what he had thought of himself in that position. Whether it felt authentic or performative. Whether his death by drive-by shooting was simply another incidence of self-fulfilling prophecy. Hardened street life, hardened street lyrics, hardened street death. Because 2Pac wasn't from Compton, as some of his music would lead you to believe. He was from the East Coast and made his acting debut in *A Raisin in the Sun*. Born Lesane Parish Crooks, he became Tupac Amaru Shakur, then 2Pac, then Makaveli. He had gone west, inventing, reinventing. The current took him.

I wondered whether the family who'd lived in that empty house would ever return. Whether the kids who had put 2Pac's poster up would come back to claim it and how they would be changed by the flood. Whether the poster meant something important to someone who had lived there. I wondered where the family had gone. Why they had left only the poster behind. What would happen if I stole it. What would happen in the empty home's next life. What remained after condemnation. What was "west" for me. I wondered how to bulldoze the past, or at least excavate the topsoil. How to fix the windows so that it looked all right from the outside. Or let come what may if I shined the light on the trouble inside.

THE BADDEST MEN ON THE PLANET

I first visited a prison when I was only twelve. My uncle Pat had been sentenced to twenty years for attempted murder. He had shot his boss in the stomach after being assaulted by him and his wife in a deserted parking lot. Uncle Pat had been asked to meet them there to discuss their disagreement about the legitimacy of the license plates on the rig my uncle was driving for the couple's trucking company. The story goes that the three of them had come to blows before my uncle, outnumbered and recovering from a recent heart surgery, retrieved an unregistered handgun from his truck's cab. Uncle Pat said he believed they'd meant to kill him. It was their word against his, with only telephone poles as witnesses.

My mother prompted us to write letters to Uncle Pat while he was incarcerated, keeping him apprised of our grades and art projects and goings-on, and eventually took us to the Plainfield Correctional Facility to visit him because, she said, he needed us. He was still a Good Person, she said, despite a conviction that would, in the case of anyone else, indicate otherwise. Our visit would be beneficial for him and help him survive, she said. He was depressed again, afflicted with one of the episodes of blanket-like darkness that came and went, I understood, like an emphysemic cough that could never quite be shaken off.

I was excited about the visit and fond of Uncle Pat. I'd spent that summer doing little but reading and staring into the sun, which gouged black holes that burned in my periphery well into the night. When I slept, I'd slip through one of them, to the other side of life's motion-picture screen, into whatever romantic landscape I'd been reading about that day. To the moors of *Wuthering Heights*. To the plains of *Little House on the Prairie* or the colonial coast in *The Witch of Blackbird Pond*. To another place and time. Gone. The feeling that came over me as we approached the prison's treacherously razored and fenced perimeter was multidimensional. It was a story world become real, raw experience at my fingertips rather than seen through a dream hole or the pages of a book. It was an invigorating and controlled brush with danger. It was also a harrowing revelation: freedom, once I saw it constricted up close, seemed even more necessary.

Alison Lurie, author of *The Language of Houses*, told me in an interview about her visit to a prison. She was studying the messages buildings send. Her husband was teaching in an education program for prisoners administered by Cornell University, and she'd gone to see him at the prison. "I was really scared the whole time because the whole atmosphere is of being shut in and closed and dark," she said. "There's a gloom over the whole place." In *The Language of Houses*, Lurie examines the architectural intention underlying a prison's design. "Once you are an inmate of such a building," she writes, "the physical signs of incarceration soon become apparent." She compares it to other spaces of confinement, reaching as far back in time as a baby's playpen. "When we were children there were times when our own homes, however comfortable, felt like prisons."

Before we went into the visiting room, we put our belongings into a small steel locker. A prison within a prison. Escape from the heavily guarded facility would be miraculous. A female guard patted me down, and I stepped through a metal detector. We waited in our assigned sitting area for Uncle Pat to be called down for the visit. Every prisoner who emerged from the door near the guard's desk adjusted his belt and scanned the room in search of some remains of his dignity. Perhaps he momentarily willed himself to believe that he was not altogether human and thus he could not be dehumanized. This could not be his actual life, he might be thinking, his body disrobed and inspected for contraband a few feet away from where his family waited to see him. He had surely been someone else before this. *How long until they begin to forget what came before?* I wondered. *How quickly does the erosion of self-identity begin in a place like this? What does a place like this do to a person? And how does one ever recover?* In prison, I imagine time must expand and contract in the minds and bodies of inmates, even as it is measured and counted, every second the same as the last.

Revealing objects concealed in the rectum—that is the purpose of the squat and cough, an examination required of the inmates upon entering and exiting the visiting room. I watched the men try to relax into brief hugs shared with their families and friends after having just been strip-searched on the other side of the cement brick wall that divides the visiting room from the hallway leading to the yard and cell houses. Beyond that wall, the prisoners were housed like caged mice, and violence swept through like a riptide: destructive, random shakedowns, aggressive outbursts between inmates, and occasional attacks on staff occurred without warning or logic. I found myself trying to see through that wall to what lay beyond it. Even as their visiting periods commenced, the men remained hyperalert, stiff in the jaws and shoulders, their eyes darting erratically over their shoulders, their bodies jolting slightly at any sudden commotion. In this kind of man's life, trouble interjects itself like a misplaced comma, rendering a reading of his life's transcript choppy and piecemeal. Everything was fine, and then—,—.

When Uncle Pat came in, he walked slowly and heavy-footed, as he, too, readjusted his belt. He looked familiar but altered: long, unkempt hair, a loss of focus in his eyes, a bit jumpy. He tried a joke. We'd heard him tell it before, and although the beat before the punch line lasted several seconds too long as he paused to watch a fly perched on the arm of a chair clean itself, we laughed anyway.

There is a picture of me as a child in which I'm sitting in the grass in our front yard, next to a patch of overgrown lilies. The flowers have already bloomed for the year, their fibrous green leaves spilling out from the cement blocks that encircle the flower bed. In the background, a fence encloses me within our yard—that boundary that would later seem to mark the limits of my own existence. I'm wearing a sundress that dips low across my nipple line, revealing scrawny ribs and tan lines. The dress is handmade, constructed from a patchwork of fabric scraps. In the picture, four sickly calico kittens, whom I named Jo, Bo, Mo, and Flo, are brandished across my chest, presented for the camera like living trophies. *I was present at your birth,* I might be thinking. *Don't you remember when I bent down over the cardboard box and named you?* My arms strap the kittens' fragile necks tightly against me. Their newly opened eyes seep with disease, and their soft pink tongues flail as they kick and wail, desperate to be released from my hug. I'm smiling for whoever is behind the camera. I can still smell the lily of the valley, its thin tendrils occupying a corner of the picture's foreground. I'd mistaken the kittens' fearful mews for the sound of tiny white bells tinkling in the breeze.

Shortly after that picture was taken, I dreamed my father placed the unsalvageable kittens—"They'll die soon anyway"—into an old pillowcase, one by one. He cinched the top into a loose knot as they shrieked and tumbled against one another. He dunked them into the four feet of standing water in our backyard and waited and smoked his Salems, one by one, until there was nothing left to smoke. It may not have been a dream. I can no longer remember. Someone drowned those cats. Was it my father? Or our neighbor, Wild Bill?

After the kittens' demise, my eager brand of love landed on an abandoned baby bird. I found it in a nest that had fallen from our sycamore tree. The nestling survived under my care for one blissful day of chopped worm meals and soft strokes to its downy head with the tip of my index finger. After it died, I watered the sun-scorched grass, but it would not perk with color as it should have. I aligned a series of shells on our front steps, inviting any passing crustacean friends to adopt them as homes. I sang loudly at my window, but not even a mockingbird replied.

Though many functional aspects of the prefrontal cortex are not understood by the scientific and medical communities, it's well established that this particular area of gray matter regulates high-order decision making, the expression of individual personality, social responses, and emotions—including both romantic love and violence. In individuals who experience outbursts of aggression, prefrontal cortex functioning is often lower than normal. The prefrontal cortex's functioning level is also related to obsessional jealousy, obsessive-compulsive behaviors, emotional overwhelm, dark mood swings, and poor self-esteem. The brain as landscape, barely mapped, seems a most isolated frontier. I would like an English word for "fear of sitting alone with one's own unknowable frontal lobe." Or "being loved and still lacking meaningful human connection." Or "the feeling that the self has unhinged from the body."

There are countless case studies that demonstrate the range of psychological and physical effects that solitary confinement, imprisonment, and deprivation of affection produce in humans. But perhaps the clearest anecdote is that of the infant monkeys on which psychologist Harry Harlow conducted his famous experiments on the nature of affection. His studies showed that monkeys, when confined without love and care from birth, will nuzzle a wire doll representation of another being. And, barring even that illusion of physical contact, will simply freeze up, rock, cry, or curl up. It would be unethical to conduct such a study on humans, but certainly we have all seen a variation of this case before.

Whenever a boxing match was on cable television—a novelty at the river in the early 1990s—my family would gather in the living room to eat Red Baron Supreme Pizzas and cheer as we watched two men pound each other. I'm not sure how it happened that one of the few happy traditions that we collectively enjoyed was a celebration of organized violence, of refereed concussive strikes to the head, but I grew to love these rare, sacred evenings. Together, we rooted for the favorites: Julio César Chávez, Mike Tyson, Evander Holyfield, and Oscar De La Hoya. What I liked most about boxing was not the hit landed squarely on the contender's brow bone, which in fact made me shudder, but his getaway, the near miss. Just out of reach, like a secret. My enthusiasm expanded into the space created by the unexpected sashay that drew the boxer out from under a punch that would have wrecked him. What I loved next best was another negative space: the sweat-drenched theater that occurred in the corner between rounds, where the cutman's hands tidied ravaged blood vessels with salve and the cornerman leaned over the ropes, shouting and waving his fingers in front of the boxer's face. I loved the boxer shaking with adrenaline as he leveled his eyes in preparation for the next round. I loved the boxer on his back, briefly unconscious. I loved the idea of the TKO's afterburn that bleated in his brain like a black curtain closing and opening behind his eyes.

We awaited the much-anticipated Tyson-Holyfield match set for 1991, but it didn't happen. Tyson, the reigning champion, seemed to me as ruthless and powerful outside the ring as in it, behaving as though his boxing titles had granted him superior status in the rest of his life. Above law, above consequence, above rational decision making. Had he always been that way? Or had too much time in the ring changed him? Tyson pulled out of the fight after breaking a rib and shortly thereafter was convicted on one rape count and two criminal deviant conduct counts, crimes committed against women in Indiana, a jurisdiction that had landed him in my home state for trial. He did not win his case, and was sentenced to two ten-year sentences, to be served simultaneously in a state prison.

I watched my father fight another man once. He prepared us for it before it happened, telling us to stay in the house when the man, whom he worked with, came over.

"Why do you have to fight him?" I asked my father. "We like him." He was a friend of our family we had known for years. Once, during a barbecue at our place, he told me he'd marry me when I was old enough.

"He called me a liar," my dad said. As if that were the worst a person could do.

"So what?" I said. "Talk it out." I looked at my mother in hopes that she would support me. She offered nothing but a shrug.

"He'll be here soon," he said to me and my brother. "You go to your rooms and stay in the house."

I refused. "If you're going to do it, you'll have to do it in front of me." But even that wasn't enough to change his mind.

I watched them from the kitchen window, my mother trying to pull me away the whole time. The men's bodies, bathed in porch light, moved irrationally before me. They lacked the control and grace of professional boxers. There was no dance, no sport, to an unorganized fight between men who had been drinking. When it was over, I wiped away my tears and lay my disgust at the doormat. My mother nursed my father's damaged knuckles. "He shouldn't have said that to your dad," she said. My parents were a lot of things, but liars they were not.

·   ·   ·

During my first prison visit with Uncle Pat, he nodded to his right and told us quietly that Mike Tyson was sitting nearby, visiting with professional basketball player Chris Webber. My brother and I were ecstatic, starstruck, and we gawked at them for a few minutes. I fumbled with my quarters, eager to beeline to the vending machine because the path would put me within five feet of Iron Mike. Tyson noticed us, my brother and I, unable to contain our excitement, and told us to come over, he'd have Webber buy us some chips and pop. We ran across the room, and I stood in front of Tyson, smiling, as Webber handed us our treats. Tyson was everything you saw on television, only slightly smaller in real life. He seemed dulled, less shiny. I'd only ever seen him sweating and waxed with salve. As he spoke, you could time the pauses between one sentence and the next, as if he might be trying to see through permanently starred vision or still counting down a knockout in his mind. How many times to ten? How many times straight to black? He told us a Bugs Bunny joke, slowly, as if he'd nearly forgotten the punch line, and though I'd heard it before, I laughed anyway and admired the gap in his smile.

When we left the visit with Uncle Pat, I imagined the men returning to their cells, or "cages," as they are crassly referred to on the inside by both guards and inmates. Slightly renewed, momentarily cheered. As we drove away I gazed up at the tiny rectangular windows that lined the exterior walls of the prison's housing units. One window for each cell. I wanted to know what they were doing behind the bars. Uncle Pat said many of them read. They slipped through the pages of books as if they were the back panels of magic wardrobes and came out the other side in Narnia. But all the bad things you heard were true, too—guards abusing their positions, racial divisions, gang violence, sexual exploitation, dehumanization. He had seen it all. I wondered what the men saw from their cell windows. Small bits of sky, clouds, a sliver of moon, sometimes the wings of a bird? What effects did those views have on the men? What did they think of when they looked at the sky? Of what came before? Or of what would come after? Of anything at all but the present? I wondered whether seeing the sky had a positive effect, translating in some way as hope, or if it made their confinement all the more difficult, the sun like a bully waving a long stick and stars like a thousand knives. I waved at the windows as we drove away. I don't know whether anyone on the other side was looking.

When I was eighteen, studying criminal justice as a freshman in college, my uncle Dave, Mandi's dad, was the lieutenant of a nearby county police precinct. He offered to take me along on a patrol ride. I didn't know what I wanted to be—I thought I might go to law school and become a public defender or start a nonprofit that provided education and counseling to incarcerated youth. I had built up empathy for them over the years—first through Uncle Pat and Mike Tyson, then Corey. I didn't think Corey's attorney had represented him as well as he could have, and I thought that becoming one myself would be a karmic deposit, a righted wrong. I didn't want to be a cop, but I wasn't afraid of criminals. To me, inmates were regular people who had been caught doing something society deemed impermissible and who had likely had some misfortunes along the way. I was optimistic about the prospect of rehabilitation.

We toured the jail first, and I peered up at the familiar barred windows, which I had eyed with intense curiosity from the street since I was a girl. I was fascinated by incarceration as place: they couldn't get out and I couldn't get in. Uncle Dave paraded me around inside the joint, introduced me to everyone, and gave me a fried chicken leg from the break room. He showed me where they processed people and let me get fingerprinted for fun. I signed a waiver and he strapped me into a bulletproof vest. My fingers itched with adrenaline. I somehow felt I could move faster under the weight of the vest. The illusion of police invincibility was real. We got into his car, cranked up the dispatch, and drove around until a call came across the airwaves.

The call was for a domestic violence report. We flipped on the sirens and raced over to the address with intoxicating speed. The house was a modest ranch, completely average. "Do you want to go in with me?" my uncle asked as he got out of the car.

"Hell yes," I said.

"Okay, stay behind me and don't say anything. Let's hope he hasn't chopped her up yet." He started laughing. It was police humor, sick humor, he explained. The same kind prisoners resort to, warding off hopelessness by forcing the least appropriate joke. People try to make light of facing the worst there is in humans, or in themselves. Striving for civility and sometimes failing. Pressing onward anyway. It is one reason some police officers have resisted cameras that run continuously. Aside from any argument about what they might see, the public would find the audio unpalatable.

I followed him to the door. We were ushered into a sparsely furnished living room. Lots of shades of brown—sofa, carpeting. Paneled walls. He began questioning the couple and pulled the truth out of them like a pro by getting them to talk. "You have kids here?" he asked.

"The baby," the woman said.

My uncle nodded to me. "Go find the baby and stay with him until I tell you."

"10–4," I said, and he gave me a look like *don't be cute.*

I walked down the hall and poked my head into the rooms. It was strange being in someone else's home like this, intruding into their lives. Being in a position of authority among someone else's belongings was private and vulgar. I thought of Corey, who had broken into the home where he committed crimes that would land him in prison for the rest of his life. It was one thing to cross property lines, to trespass onto land or into vacant buildings as I had done many times, but it was quite another to enter someone's private residence without permission. Surely he had felt this sensation of utter violation of a personal space. I was still slipping from my mind into his, as if there was something there that I needed to extract.

A curling iron sat on the back of a toilet. Clothes were strewn around the couple's bedroom. Drawers hung open. The baby was in the room at the end of the hall. I could hear him whimper. The light was on. I bent over his crib and placed my hand on his fat tummy. He smiled at me, then looked scared, so I picked him up.

I cradled the child against my chest and the bulletproof vest. I sang to him softly, then louder. I didn't want him to hear anything being said in the living room. I was afraid it would taint his childhood. Some foreshadowed future hung in the balance and I wanted to clear it away for him. But it was probably too late for all that. I looked around his room—the walls were still white. I had thought one of the primary things you did when preparing for a baby was to paint the nursery, prepare the space, creating the feeling of love and safety. The expression of emotion via decoration was a function of place I found fascinating. I had transformed my cinder-blocked dorm room with blues and greens, with posters and a new rug. These parents had done nothing. This oversight of care, however insignificant, spoke to lack—a metaphor of irresponsibility and a shotgun start.

When my uncle walked into the bedroom, he gave the baby's toes a soft pinch. "Hey, kiddo. You're going to be all right."

"Do we go now?" I said.

"We go now."

I carried the baby into the living room and shifted him from my arms into his mother's. Back in the squad car, I asked my uncle what he said to the couple.

"Not much. They needed someone to listen."

I looked out the window and tried not to cry over the fact that I had soothed a stranger's baby. It confirmed what I already knew—I wasn't cut out for my uncle's job. I was too emotional and prone to overthinking. The reality of the world was too much a shock for me. The child's tiny fingers curled around my finger, his white walls that wanted for pale yellow or blue—that was too close. I thought I would be better off looking at it all from a slightly greater distance.

"Now let's do the fun part," Uncle Dave said.

"What's that?"

"Get free doughnuts, of course."

Uncle Pat and Mike Tyson were freed the same year, both having served less than four years of their original sentences. It was decided in an appeal that Uncle Pat's acts had been justifiably committed in self-defense, a claim previously disallowed as a defense in his trial, and thus the sentence was overturned. Tyson, by all appearances, got out on good time and good attorneys.

After Tyson's release, he racked up insurmountable debts, his wealth evaporating in a cloud of smoke shaped like Vegas, and eventually wrote an autobiography called *Undisputed Truth*. As if anything could be considered absolutely true, much less undisputed. The Associated Press reported that Tyson said that while he was incarcerated, "I was having so much sex [with female prison visitors and a prison drug counselor during his three-year prison stint in the '90s] that I was too tired to even go to the gym and work out." The AP reported, too, that since his release, Tyson "constantly warns that he's not far from slipping off the edge, or slipping back into a strip club to party with drugs and women. 'Sometimes I just fantasize about blowing somebody's brains out so I can go to prison for the rest of my life,' he writes. 'Working on this book makes me think that my whole life has been a joke.'" Kid Dynamite was about to implode. The Baddest Man on the Planet, they called him. Another self-fulfilling prophecy?

I remember the day Uncle Pat was released from prison. Though they had overturned the ruling, they could not give back the time, nor erase it from his record. I was there with my mom to pick him up. He emerged from the razor-wired gates carrying a wrinkled paper bag. His clothes sagged from his body; his long beard, graying and frayed, grazed his chest. The sun on his face illuminated a man unconvinced of reality. Maybe a place is a turnstile that you pass through on the way to somewhere else. A small token for each ride is dropped into a narrow slot. Over a lifetime, a fortune piles up in the meter. The price of a prison sentence, exorbitant, no matter how long.

Postincarceration, Uncle Pat's depressive states worsened, and he isolated himself from people by staying in his apartment most of the time. My brother and I would walk over from the Boys and Girls Club, where, as teenagers, we sometimes spent our summer days while my mother worked, to visit him, but we would quickly feel trapped in the tiny studio and wouldn't stay long.

During my first year of college, Uncle Pat met a woman online. She lived in Texas, and he asked me to write her an e-mail that would vouch for him in anticipation of their first face-to-face visit—to ensure he wasn't an ax murderer, I assume, but I suppose that was relative. If the bullet he'd hit his boss with had lodged a few inches to the north or south, everything would have been different. He would have been categorized as a murderer, like Corey. This difference, while having vastly different consequences for the victims, struck me as also a rather small difference with respect to the violent act itself. Was there much difference, then, in the *person* who had almost killed someone versus the one whose act had resulted in death? Measuring out the wrongness, the *badness,* of a person, was therefore complicated. Nonetheless, Uncle Pat was happier than I'd seen him in years, which left me little choice but to agree to help. Regardless of the gravity of his near-murderous act, be it self-defense or not, I believed he was still good enough to deserve love. Within the space of two paragraphs, I talked him up as kind, loving, good-hearted, funny, and well-intentioned. I wrote nothing that was not true, then sent it off to her using the e-mail address he'd given me. When he set off to marry her, a road trip with a wedding waiting at the end, it was with fanfare elicited by his enthusiasm. We crossed our fingers and waved him off, sharing his hope. But a week later he came back alone, and we never spoke of it again.

A few times, I went over to clean his first-floor apartment. It was sparsely furnished with an alcove that held a daybed that doubled as his sofa. The space was small enough to discourage inviting visitors over. I did my best not to show a physical reaction to the stench that had built up inside, tried to make it a bit homier for him by hanging a few pictures on the wall and ordering his canisters by size on the short length of kitchen countertop. I coated his counters with 409 and scrubbed them clean. I removed the yellowed light fixtures, dumping dozens of bugs into the trash, and wiped them clean with Windex and paper towels. After another surgery, I came to change the dressings on his scars and examine his stitches for infection, even as my stomach threatened to empty itself onto his kitchen floor. Not long after, my aunt found Uncle Pat face down in his apartment, unconscious and nearly dead. He had gone and done it, finally, we thought. At the hospital, his stomach was pumped, the liquid mass of dissolved pills extracted from his body through a thin tube. Death, redacted.

In college, when I still couldn't shake my feelings for Corey, I had written him a letter. I was sure that some part of me had been locked up with him. I heard his voice in his reply. At first, his words were a deep comfort and a reminder of the boy who had always taken care of me, tending to me as if I were a fickle houseplant. But as the months of school passed, he became guarded. He lectured me about the actual ins and outs of prison gangs as I learned about them, theoretically, in my criminal justice classes. I drew the symbols of a dozen prison gangs on my midterm exam and wondered whether Corey had any of them tattooed onto his skin. In addition to the prison education he was getting, he was taking college classes in anthropology and sociology. At times he was more open, relaying to me what was required of a person in prison and how survival sacrifices humanity and reason. How there was so little light, so little sustenance. Almost no growth save for what he could create for himself. He told me he was fighting, building muscle, boxing, making a name for himself. What did that mean? A reputation that people would fear? He had no choice, he said; he was preparing for the long haul of a lifetime in prison. Nineteen to ninety, if he lived that long. Part of me hoped he would, and part of me hoped he wouldn't. I couldn't imagine him at seventy with the onset of Alzheimer's, which ran in his family, still sitting in a prison cell five decades after the bad in him had run dry. "That's justice," he'd say. "That's what I deserve." At some point, the reputation he made for himself would have to be stronger than his physical body. It would have to protect him.

Corey asked me about how I found an address to which to send that first tentative letter. In turn, I told him about my search on the Internet and the e-mail I had sent to the correctional facility staff late one night from my college dorm room, in hopes of obtaining a mailing address for him. I told him that he had been my first love, a confession made on paper out of desperation—if I could admit to that, I thought, I could let it go. Be happy with a real boy in the real world. Or just be me, something that rarely occurred to me as

a pursuit worthy in and of itself. He did not acknowledge my confession in his reply. Eventually, I became a little bit scared of who
he had become and stopped writing, only to start again and again,
year after year, with the same unsent letter: *Dear Corey, I've been
thinking of you. I've never stopped. Do you think of me?* It was the
only thing left to say, some catch of water in my throat that I could
not clear.

That same year that I wrote Corey for months, I paid a man to
tattoo my back. I paid another man to pierce my belly button as
I lay on the floor of my dorm room. On a date with a guy named
Tony, we had the cartilage of our ears pierced. There was some
comfort in this control. Some relief in knowing exactly how and
where pain was inflicted on my body. *Here,* I might have said.
*Right here, this is where it hurts. This is why. In three days, I'll feel
nothing.*

After prison, Mike Tyson got a tattoo on his face while he was party-
ing in Vegas. The tattoo, scrawling wisps that lap at the edges of his
left eye like black flames, is a symbol of the Māori tribe. When he
was asked what he thought immediately after getting it, he said it
made him look "sexy." He acknowledged that he had no knowledge
of its meaning at the time.

After prison, Mike Tyson returned to organized violence and finally did fight Evander Holyfield. In the first fight, Holyfield
achieved a technical knockout after seven rounds. In the second
fight, Holyfield head-butted Tyson, who was disqualified when he
bit off a chunk of Holyfield's ear in retaliation. The media outcry
after that offense was louder than the one after his rape conviction.
Some types of violence can still shock us. After prison, after biting
Holyfield's ear, Tyson lost and regained his boxing license. He made
a movie and apologized to Holyfield on *Oprah.* If only we all had the

world's ear for the making of our amends. "It is nearly impossible to hate anyone whose story you know," writes Andrew Solomon in a *New Yorker* article. Mike Tyson had done bad things. So had Corey, so had Uncle Pat. I didn't hate any of them.

Violence happens in a negative plane, like a dug hole. First you're digging, aware of the shovel in your hands, aware of the pressure as the dirt flies behind you, and then you're simply standing over a hole, black and gaping like a foul mouth. Regret is fill dirt, settling and settling, always leaving a dimpled impression—one that never quite smoothens—in the topsoil. Domestic abusers will apologize, swear up and down to never do it again, swear they didn't know what they were thinking. Inmates who have had long enough to think will walk themselves through their crime, again and again, not only to understand it but to pinpoint the moment that brought them to prison, to imagine the inertia of the decision that would wreck lives landing instead a fraction to the left or right, avoiding the knockout punch with a sidestep. But instead, this happened, then this happened. Then suddenly, everything went awry. Cut straight to the bruised and bloodied aftermath.

I had to give up on Corey. Though he was always in the back of my mind, I had to live my life. I moved on without fully letting him go. There were many boyfriends over the years, and I wasn't picky about who they were. Men were distractions for me, placeholders. A way to keep me from being alone with my thoughts, a way to keep the darkness of my mind at bay.

Just after college, I was living back home, sharing a little apartment with Jo, my closest high school girlfriend, while I was working on a political campaign. I fell blindly in love with the idea of a man named Steve. Politics is a training in optimism; you learn to inflate positive qualities to make up for negative ones. The relationship lasted four months. And during that time, I was enamored of Steve's vision of his future self, which he described to me in detail, as if it were part of a stump speech, over screwdrivers that he'd sweet-talked the bartender into giving him for free. Steve was starting a construction business. He was making a website. He was an *entrepreneur.* He complimented me generously, and in return I was going to help him connect his current self with his future self. He could get to his construction jobs if only he had a car, so I loaned him money to buy one. He could call me more often and line up more construction work if only he had a cell phone, so I added him to my cell phone plan for a mere $9.99 a month, which he would repay to me in cash on the fifteenth of each month. I liked to help where I could, I told myself. A few weeks later, he lost the car he had purchased with the money I'd loaned him; he put the car up as collateral for a title loan, the sum of which he squandered in less than two hours at an Indiana casino. As an apology, he took me on a date to a Vietnamese restaurant in Chicago. I drove. When we left without paying, a wave of shocking regret jolted through me as we hauled away in my Mustang like Bonnie and Clyde. I did not recognize my own eyes in the rearview mirror. Shaking, I dropped him off at his mother's house. I changed my phone number and locked my bedroom door, donned sunglasses and poured a bottomless gin martini. *Thank goodness I never slept with him,* I thought, as if that mattered. *Thank goodness I had only needed his feigned affection.* Like Harlow's monkeys, I would have curled up with a wire doll if I thought it would love me back.

The guilt was unbearable. The next day, I mailed cash to the restaurant, along with an anonymous note that explained in rough terms that I had forgotten to pay. Steve came to my apartment the following Saturday and pounded on the door for a full twenty minutes. I sat inside with the lights off and the blinds drawn tight, holding a flashlight over my phone bill. He had racked up a debt of $863 in four weeks. A very deep hole.

After prison, Uncle Pat's freedom was relative. He had difficulty obtaining a job due to his felony conviction and mental health state. Whatever issues he'd had before prison had been exacerbated by his four-year stint. After the attempted suicide, Uncle Pat entered a period of reentry and recovery, respectively, names for the new shape of his life. He determined that a move to Michigan, away from people, would suit him well. He planned to breed rottweilers and write a screenplay. He planned to watch the snow pile up around him, whitewash for a new future. He would buy a tractor to mow a big lawn to stretch out the summers. But even a new life is a kind of prison after prison. In Michigan, he began composing lengthy e-mails to members of our family, berating me and my cousins and aunts for not making the six-hour trip to visit him frequently enough. It was unfair to his nieces and nephews—we were starting our own lives and could not, in our early twenties, save his too. He called me once and told me that he had been used by the government for information that only he had about the 9/11 terrorist attacks. When I raised concerns to my mother, she conferred with her sisters. But ultimately, nothing happened. No one could force him to get help. I wasn't even sure they recognized it as mental illness. They resisted such labels, tending to sweep undesirable facts of life under the rug. Meanwhile, Uncle Pat entered long, intermittent periods of no contact, going silent and electronically dark for months on end. Sometimes, my mother and aunts persuaded neighbors or friends who lived within driving distance to check on him. They held their breath through the long winters, awaiting the reports. Alive? Well? Alive, at least?

One Christmas, Uncle Pat returned to Indiana with three dogs in tow. "Meet my kids," he said, flinging the bed of his truck open wide, looking and sounding well. He introduced the enormous beasts one by one—a German shepherd, a rottweiler, and a Lab mix of some kind. He explained their personalities and their lineage, and shared heartwarming anecdotes from their life together. I had never understood dog love, but I tried to mirror his enthusiasm.

I pointed at the rottweiler. "What's that one wearing? A diaper?"

"That's Ginny," he said. "She's in heat." Ginny shook her hips, trying to free herself from the plastic chastity belt. The German shepherd wouldn't leave her alone.

It was determined that the dogs would stay in the garage, against my father's wishes. Uncle Pat would check on them periodically to ensure that nothing had been destroyed, and that Ginny was penned away from the two males. At dinner, as my father began to carve the Butterball ham, we heard a desperate yelp from one of the dogs. Uncle Pat stood up, on parental alert, and rushed to the garage. "God damn it, the kids got out."

No one made a move to help. But the garage could not have opened itself.

Uncle Pat flew out the front door, took two quick steps, and then thought better of it. He hollered for them by name, then collectively. "Kids!" he called. "You kids come back here."

The rest of us sat at the table, smirking as the German shepherd caught the rottweiler and tried to mount her in the front yard. We watched her break free, run a little way, and then get caught again. My father continued slicing the ham. Had he let them out of the garage? On purpose?

"Shit," Uncle Pat said. "Ginny's gonna get nailed."

At twenty-three, I moved to Indianapolis. Life in the city was quite different from life in rural Indiana. In the city, my new friend Rachel introduced me to good food. I ate sushi and curry for the first time. I drank wine and dirty martinis and we went to art exhibit openings. I got credit cards and bought expensive shoes and pants at Nordstrom. I took taxis and brunched with new girlfriends. I joined a book club, where I met Jen. She was smart and empowered and beautiful. We went to museums, festivals, and political rallies together. We shared bottles of wine and our impressions of novels we had read. Meeting these two women was a saving grace. I hadn't had close girlfriends, other than my cousin Mandi, who were sharp and worldly. Who read the news and formed educated opinions. The world was opening up more widely for me, and they were a part of that growth.

My discernment with respect to both wine and men became more advanced. I dated a fairly successful musician, a surgeon, a former NFL player, then a couple of attorneys. Men my father would approve of. When I fell in love with an actual man, rather than the idea of one, I was relieved. He too had a real job, a career even, as an airline pilot. Mike was sweet and generous and steady. But I began to rub off on him: I was a party girl. He slept less, drank more. He stopped training for cycling races. He burned through his savings account as we toured Indianapolis's best restaurants and went on vacations to Colorado and England and Canada and Washington, D.C.

Mike and I could never determine when it was time to go home, when to turn off the lights, and so we sometimes had to call off work. Together, we made friends who were similarly reckless, who also had a hard time differentiating between fun and self-destruction. Our friend Martin came over one night to swap records—My Bloody Valentine for the new GusGus album. After the trade we went out, as usual. We'd been a dynamic threesome of friends for a time, our nights unfolding across the city's haunts. We had no destinations, only arrivals. We walked to one bar, then took a cab to another. The west side, the east side. The near north, downtown. One night, we ripped a paper towel dispenser from a bathroom wall. We left wads of cash to compensate for the damage and went dancing at a gay bar. Later that night, I was in love with both of my companions. At one point, I crossed over into another plane of consciousness. I became suspicious of my own face in the mirror and then of Mike. A plane ticket stub fell out of his pocket, and I couldn't remember his telling me he had been in the city listed on the stub for any reason. I'd lost track of the sprawl—mine, his, ours. It was bound to happen with how much he traveled. Still, I was enraged.

In response, Mike handed me a twenty and told me to take a cab home. He left me with Martin, and we kept dancing. When the bar closed, we began to walk toward home. After a few minutes Mike pulled up in my car, too drunk to drive it, and I screamed at him. I overlooked the gesture, that he had come back for me even though I had been unreasonable, and focused on the danger of the situation. I refused to get into the car and demanded that he leave it there, that he walk home the rest of the way with us. When the men tried to quiet me, confining my flailing arms and rendering me immobile so that they could place me in the car, I reacted by pushing and kicking them. In the morning, I remembered very little. I vomited all day, and by evening I still couldn't stop. First it ran clear, then there was blood. Mike took me to the hospital, where they sedated and rehydrated me. I made him stay in the waiting room so he wouldn't hear me tell the doctors I'd only had a few drinks. So he wouldn't hear me say no when they asked me if I drank often. *What are we before we become something else?* I thought as I lay in the emergency room bed. Before I was a woman, I was a girl. Before I was a woman who lived too recklessly, I was a girl who loved too reactively. But can I pinpoint the change? The point at which love and fun and danger and self-destruction had melded into one continuous event? Everything was fine, and then—,—.

One of Uncle Pat's unique attributes is his ability to recall details that others typically forget. With startling clarity, he has recounted for me, many times, each time he took me to Dairy Queen for hot fudge sundaes between 1985 and 1989; whipped cream, no nuts. He has recounted the dates on which he played video games with me for hours past my bedtime the year he lived with us. He has reminded me that he has, to date, purchased nine books for me, the names of which he can still recite, in order of date of purchase. *The Boxcar Children #1*, 1989; *Nancy Drew and the Secret of Red Gate Farm*, 1990; and so on. I understood that documentation of this nature was proof of his love for me; the only thing he could give me was an accurate recounting of a chain of events that, taken together, undoctored by memory and perception, had a larger meaning. But they were currency in a bank account that I didn't realize I borrowed against when his phone calls went unreturned, or when I failed to send him a birthday card each November. He kept a close eye on the balance.

The night after the dog incident, we ordered pizza. I rode with Uncle Pat to pick it up. The dogs lay in the bed of the truck. We parked in front of Papa John's. We were early. "You know," Uncle Pat said, "you only like pizza because of me. I gave you your first slice of pizza when you were two."

He turned to me then and delivered a lengthy monologue about how little I appreciated everything he did for me—the account balance apparently well into the red. As he talked, I eased my hand onto the door handle, not out of fear but to ready myself for an escape, should I need to make one. Part of me knew that he had wanted badly to have his own children and, in lieu of that experience coming to fruition, had displaced that desire onto his nieces and nephews. But it was more responsibility than any of us could bear. He did not make it easy to love him. Or, he did, until he didn't. "You should go visit him in Michigan," my aunts and mother would say. "That would make him happy." But I was getting tired of making men feel secure in their broken selves. My mother had said the same sorts of things about my father. When I brought a black boyfriend home to meet my parents, without mentioning his skin color beforehand because I didn't think it was relevant, my father didn't speak to me for six months. "You need to talk to him," my mother had said. But I didn't. I was done talking. And I was done shifting myself—my own beliefs and behaviors—to fit the preferences of a man, no matter who he was. My mother's advice was ever mask, bury, deny, submit.

"You know what?" Uncle Pat added, leaning slightly toward me. "I was going to shoot every last one of you when I came down here to visit. Your dad, your mom, everyone. But I didn't." He paused, his eyes wide and plucked completely free of lashes, which he claimed was a medical condition. *All of this is a medical condition,* I thought. *Why won't anyone call it like it is?*

I shifted my gaze subtly, as one would if one were confronted with a bear on a hike in the mountains—enough to note that the doors on the car were locked and that there were no nearby weapons. The words *unregistered gun* flashed through my mind. Had he decided not to kill us before driving down from Michigan? Or had he decided just now? Had he brought a gun with him? I imagined for a moment my brains splattered across the dashboard. "Thank you," I said, disbelieving my own words. *Now I'm thanking a man for not killing me,* I thought. *It has come to this.*

When he exited the truck to retrieve the pizza, I pictured him sitting on his bed in the dark, mindlessly pulling eyelashes out, his blue-green eyes farther away than Neptune.

The truth is that Mike and I probably would have broken up if he hadn't pitied me. We had both moved into the apartment building, where we met, for different reasons. I had hardly any money despite working two jobs, one low-level government job and one as a barista, but had wanted to live in downtown Indianapolis anyway.

He had no money because he was still paying rent on another apartment he had lived in with his ex-girlfriend—he was that generous. He had never wanted to live in Indiana, and only moved there to take his job. He wanted to leave the state as soon as possible. The building, historic and with decent views of the city, had a mixed tenancy. There were students, a few young couples, middle-aged and elderly men and women who lived alone. The neighborhood was rough, though not unlivable, but I chalked that up to life in the city.

Two years after I moved in, though, I learned about Indiana's online sex offender registry, which was state-of-the-art for its time—replete with details of people's criminal backgrounds, their photos, their addresses and places of employment. I immediately searched my neighborhood, and no less than sixty hits popped up within a one-block radius of my address. When I widened my search to a half-mile radius, there were over one hundred. My building, as it turned out, neighbored a halfway house for sex offenders who had recently been released from prison, and several others lived in my building. Worse, I had moved from the fourth floor to the garden floor because it was even cheaper.

I had never been afraid of the city. My car had been broken into three times in three years, and I was resilient. I would call the cops, who would write it up because they had to but would inevitably tell me, "Don't expect to get any of your stuff back." I would shrug and call the glass company. A standard $140 repair. When I'd lived on the fourth floor, I often curled up in my balcony window with my cat and a notebook, comfortably watching drug deals on the sidewalk below as I penned bad poetry about city life: the catcalling men, the public debauchery, the homeless, the unexpected kindnesses, the insane beauty of it all. But the long list of ex-rapists, some of them with multiple offenses, paralyzed me. I began to fear coming home at dark and being alone, which only made me stay out longer to avoid returning to the building, spend more money, have one more drink, and, before Mike, stay over with men when I didn't even want to, pushing further into my own danger zones.

I memorized the faces of the men on the registry, memorized their crimes, their scars, their tattoos—all of which were documented in their individual registries. There were three main categories: Sexually Violent Predator, Sex Offender, and Offender against Children. I focused my memorization efforts on the first. Face, Name, Race, Convicted of. Scar on L eyebrow, Tattoo on Upper L Arm ("HONESTY"), Piercing on Face (EYEBROW), Piercing on Tongue (ONE PIERCING), Tattoo on L Hand (4 ACES), Tattoo on R Breast (SKULL), Tattoo on R Breast (BOXING GLOVES), Tattoo on Neck ("SALINA").

Shortly after I began noticing the people I was crossing paths with regularly, bracing myself when I saw one of the men from the list, a man began harassing me. First he'd say hello to me in the parking lot. Then he'd say hello in the mail room, shuffling in with me, always a bit too near me. When he knocked on my door one afternoon, I opened it a crack. Before I could say anything, his dog, a boxer puppy, nosed its way in and disappeared into my apartment. The man threw my door open, pushed me aside, and ran after his dog. "Sorry," he said over his shoulder as he stepped into my bedroom. I stood in the doorway, holding the door wide open as I inched into the hallway. There was no one around. "You need to leave," I called into my apartment. "You need to get your dog out of here." I wanted to say that if he didn't I would call the cops, but I didn't want to provoke him. He did leave, though, carrying his unleashed dog with him. He never mentioned why he had knocked on my door in the first place.

When Uncle Pat had a stroke, my mother went to Michigan to visit him and clean his house while he recovered in a care facility and attempted rehabilitation. It was late winter, and feet of snow buried northern Michigan. When she opened the bed of his truck in search of Uncle Pat's snow shovel, she found the rottweiler, Ginny, lying dead. Frozen stiff.

We had hoped the dog was in the truck's bed because the ground was too frozen to dig. Because Uncle Pat's health was too poor to shovel. We had hoped the burial had been interrupted by his stroke. But we were wrong.

"I was waiting to bury her when she thawed out," Uncle Pat said, "so her brother and sister could say good-bye."

"When did she die?" my mother asked him.

"Two months ago," he said.

When I talked to my mother on the phone, I asked her what she was going to do.

"Bury the body," she said flatly. "What else can be done?"

"He could get on some medication. That's what," I said. "You do realize he intentionally froze the dog and planned to thaw her out for the 'siblings'? And you do realize that storing a dead animal in a car is not a mentally healthy behavior?"

She couldn't disagree.

In Indianapolis, I started exercising at the gym instead of jogging outside, and whenever I walked from the parking lot to the building, I popped Mace in one hand and my keys in the other, positioned between my knuckles like a knife. Jo, who had moved to Indianapolis too and also lived in the building, told me a man had put his hand on her bottom in the elevator. When I asked what she did, she replied, "Nothing. I just ignored it and walked off when it got to my floor." I was surprised because she had had self-defense training. She had worked for years as a police dispatcher and had even attended the police academy for a while. My plan was to stab a man in the eyes or neck, depending on his height, if he attacked me or put his hands on me in the elevator, and in my mind, I watched myself do it over and over so that when it happened, I could simply react without hesitating, without the anxiety attack I knew would come over me if I wasn't prepared.

One morning I was studying for my first law school exam—I'd been accepted after a bumbling, unstudied stab at the LSAT—when someone knocked on the window of my apartment that faced the small garden courtyard. I yanked the blinds up to find the man whose dog had run into my apartment standing at the window with his pants down. I dropped the blinds and ran to the door to check the lock, pulled the chain to make sure it was set. I hid in my room, and by the time he started knocking, I was on the phone with a 911 operator. "There's a man harassing me. He had his pants down at my window. He's at my door and won't leave," I whispered into the phone. They told me to sit tight, that an officer would be over shortly.

For the first minute that I waited, the man laughed as he knocked at my door, randomly calling out, "Woo! Woo!" By the time the cop arrived, he was long gone. The cop wrote it up, but since I didn't know the man's name—his wasn't one of the faces I'd memorized from the registry—there wasn't much he could do. "I'll drive around your block for a few minutes. He won't come back," the cop said. But I wasn't sure, because he couldn't know that. The man lived either in the building or in one of the buildings next door. Our paths would inevitably continue to intersect. In a sense, I was relieved he hadn't been caught. They wouldn't hold someone in an overpopulated city jail for long, and if he knew I'd called the cops on him, what further harassment would that bring?

I slowly put the incident out of my mind, but I remained on edge. I put two kitchen knives in my bedroom, one on each side of my bed, and kept a second can of Mace in my nightstand. I didn't know what else to do. I had learned a few self-defense moves years earlier, but when I was faced with an actual threatening situation, the memory of them disappeared somewhere unreachable, leaving me incapable of any defense no matter how mentally prepared I felt.

I stayed with Mike when he was in town, returning to my apartment for any length of time only when he was out of town for work—usually a few nights a week. One of those nights, I was awakened by a noise outside my window. I saw a shadow pass by and knew I had to react to whatever was about to happen. I grabbed the knife nearest to where I lay and waited, unable to move. When I heard the living room window open—*my god, had I actually left it unlocked?*—I swallowed hard and forced myself to run screaming up the flight of stairs that connected the two floors of the apartment. I screamed and dialed 911, waiting for the man to come up the stairs after me. I could have run outside, but it was one in the morning and the streets where we lived weren't a great place to be at that time either. This time I stayed on the phone with the operator until the cop arrived. I waited upstairs on the sofa as he swept the lower floor. He turned up nothing but a half-opened window.

"You probably scared him off when you screamed," he said. He consoled me for a few minutes, wrote up the incident, and said he would patrol the neighborhood.

"That's it? Aren't you going to, like, check for fingerprints or something?"

He politely told me there was nothing more he could do. I roped him into a few more rounds of useless questions, but none of them would make him stay much longer.

"But I can't stay here," I whined to the officer as he started walking away.

He looked at me sympathetically, but ultimately I was on my own. "Can you call a friend to come pick you up?"

After the cop left, I walked back downstairs and locked the window. With my cell phone, I took a picture of it that I would later stare at obsessively: two big handprints on the glass that glowed almost white against the darkness outside. I dragged my pillows and comforter into the bathroom—the only room without a window— locked the door, and curled up in the bathtub. I knew I wouldn't be able to sleep, so at four I called my friend Ameet to come get me. He lived a few minutes away. "Call when you're here," I said. I stared at the phone until it rang again.

"I'm right outside your building in my car."

I started crying.

"Ang, you're fine. You're not staying the night there. Stand up, run out the door, and get into the car."

"I don't think I can."

"What do you mean?"

"I can't move," I sobbed into the phone.

He coached me for ten minutes, and still I couldn't move. "I'll come in and get you." But when he knocked, I still couldn't get out of the bathtub. He called me again on my cell phone.

"You're a really good friend," I told him. "The best. But I can't move."

"You're giving me no choice here."

"Can you stay on the phone with me?" I asked.

And he did. Until the sun came up.

When I finally walked out of my apartment that morning, to take my Property I exam, I knew everything was going to end. I would fail the test. I would never become an attorney, and if I was honest, I didn't really want to anyway. That was my mother's dream, not mine. I also knew it was the last time I would go inside my apartment at night.

Mike returned from work later that day. We sat at his kitchen table in his apartment on the sixth floor, and I told him I needed to move. I would find the money somehow, though I had already taken out the maximum loan amount to cover my current expenses and the costs of law school. He sat nearby when I called the property manager's office to see if I could transfer my deposit and get a different apartment in one of their other buildings, but nothing was available. Mike watched me for a few minutes. "I guess you can live with me."

He asked me to marry him a few months later. We went to London thanks to his free flight benefits, and he proposed in front of Buckingham Palace with a well-planned speech and a huge ring. It was extravagant and, like a fairy tale, almost beyond belief. I tried not to think about whether it would have happened if he hadn't taken me in and saved me, or if he weren't so kind. A few days after we returned, we watched the movie *Blood Diamond,* and determined that it was too late now. He couldn't sell the ring back. I would wear the (likely) dirty jewel.

A year later, he married me even after he learned that I had loved recklessly and widely. Even after he learned that I had an uncle who had served time and indirectly threatened my life and with whom I would later ask him to share his holidays. Even after I confessed, as I always did, that I still hadn't gotten over some boy from my childhood who had never even loved me back. And that that boy was a man in a prison and at some point, I would need to go there and see him. Mike loved me even though I was practically consumed by fear and incapable of trusting men and unwilling even to consider why. He loved me even though I had grown up in an old riverbed and had a bloodline that ran brown like its water. But where was the source? When was the water clear? When had the trouble begun? If I was going to survive my own history, I would have to find a way to drain a vein without a wound.

PART III

MOUNTAINS

ITERATION

I

A few years ago, Mike and I discovered more proof of our aging. We were in bed, feeling weary. Time had sped up. Two babies in eighteen months was no easy feat. The world around us had shrunk, as it does with new parents. Neither of us had been able to bring ourselves to wash the Crock-Pot for over two days, and the whole house was starting to smell. It had only been two years since the first baby; the second was six months old. It hadn't been long at all since this part of our life had taken its own form, filling the shape of two tiny people, yet it had also been an eternity. Mike asked me to feel a hard lump near his elbow, and I directed his long fingers to one on my hip bone. He shrugged. "Probably nothing."

I wasn't so sure. I always dimmed the lights now—to shade the evidence of my abdomen in retreat of usability, my uterus like a deflating hot air balloon. A manifested past tense. He moved his hand to the top of my pelvic bone, where I had once been glued shut. "Can barely see it now," he said.

With the second baby I'd had an emergency C-section. Hours after the operation, I woke up in a room, trying and failing to remember the newborn's tiny face. I registered Mike, asleep somewhere near me. The smell of blood, singed skin, sweat, and must filled my nose. I should have been smelling my son's head. I had read that the top of a baby's head gives off pheromones that drive the instincts for motherly love. But no one was smelling my baby's head—its scent was evaporating into nothing, and my maternal instinct seemed to be going with it. When they finally rolled him in, I tried to nurse him, but his mouth was lazy. Already, his innate sense to search blindly for his mother with his mouth had waned, nature's reflexes having been disrupted by the surgery and the hospital staff. Already, I failed him. What he managed to eat, he threw up. Again and again. I was assured by two doctors that this was normal, but I knew it was not and asked for a third. I could tell by their eyes that I was a nuisance, that they'd rather be sleeping, but what else could I do? There was nothing to pray to; there was no matriarch to whom I could defer; there were no ceremonies to perform. My grandmother had just passed away. My mother did not remember this part. The nurses were already busy with the next mother and child down the hall. My body had made it clear that it would not accept motherhood without a fight. There was only me and him, the whisper of instinct, and a stack of books that would guide me.

Mike and I were planning a move to Vermont in order to live better, to find our best selves. Mike's parents had barely spoken to him in fifteen years, while mine were overinvolved. We wanted space; we needed distance to find out what kind of family we would be together. We were drawn to Vermont's promise of green and the height of the land; we would stand on top of it all and feel like we were home. It was everything we thought we were missing: topography above sea level, an outdoor lifestyle that spanned all four seasons, a progressive community that was more aligned with our values and our hopes for our children. In short, it was our ideal—geographically, philosophically, politically.

In the house we'd bought in Indianapolis, we weren't living in fear of any direct physical threat. Though crime was a common occurrence and a worry, our city was not run by a drug cartel. We did not live in a communist state or in a perpetual war zone. Our dissatisfaction was relative. We knew that. The choice to leave was a privilege afforded to us by our flexible employment. As a pilot, Mike could live anywhere. And I did my editing and writing work from home. We were motivated by our fear of becoming our parents and of being a midwestern *suburban family*—the idea like a heavy cape that once donned would never be shed. We feared our children growing up slightly "backward," as we had, and yet we missed the countryside. In Burlington, there were all the cultural and social benefits of a small city with all the beloved features of a rural life. It was positioned between a lake and mountains. We believed that a new location, the ideal place, could change us. Or, at least, allow us to be ourselves in a way that we could not achieve where we were.

I had been increasingly reluctant to set foot in my hometown, to make the two-hour drive alone with a baby and a one-year-old in tow. Mike was gone for days at a time, and I wasn't cut out for solo parenting. I was desperate for help, but there were a hundred reasons I struggled with going home—nothing ever changed, there was nothing to do, and I slipped right back into the subordinate role that I detested, required to play the part of the accepting daughter who kept her mouth shut when she didn't like something she saw or heard. I couldn't stand not feeling like an adult around my own children. I was in charge now, and being home threatened my control. I didn't like who I was in that town, and there were too many ghosts there for me. And now I had my kids to think of. A racist comment, a homophobic suggestion impressed upon my children by my father or anyone else, a suppression of their natural talents or interests, and I would snap.

But the tipping point was a surprise, even to me. My mother's suggested remedy for exhaustion was that I go with her to a wine and canvas night held at an Olive Garden. She described this event as a girls' night out, attended by pairs of mothers and daughters who had never left our small town. "You used to love painting," she said. True, I had. I had spent a few years studying with a well-known watercolorist, an experience my parents afforded me and one for which I was grateful. But it wasn't that my mother suggested I spend what little free time I had in a chain restaurant creating the exact same picture as everyone else and calling it art. It was worse than that: in all my twenty-nine years spent living with or near her, she still did not know me at all, and I could no longer expect that she ever would. I avoided chain restaurants as a matter of principle, and I had a much different conception of what constituted a good time. Sitting around gossiping with the locals, or even pretending to enjoy the aimless and uninspired conversation, didn't qualify. I knew she was trying to be kind and helpful, but it still bothered me.

My father said I'd gotten snobby. But when I asked them to rise to my level by, say, watching the news or reading a book or visiting a vacation destination that didn't involve a resort designed to make them feel "at home," they scoffed. Probably I overreacted, but I was tired of trying to explain myself when my mother said things like "Smile. Just be happy." And "buy this dress from Banana Republic" and "fix your hair" and "get a pedicure." As if the change I craved were as simple as changing my clothes, or unkinking my naturally wild hair. She wanted to make me into the girly girl she had always wanted, and I could not unbend her understanding of me with a straight iron. What she wanted, I think, was to be friends. But it was an instructive friendship, where I had to bring my world to her. I didn't want that role; in my mind, it was too late for her to take an interest in who I was.

I'm not sure it had ever occurred to my parents to consider what it was like to have felt an impasse between myself and my own community—my own family—all my life. I had begun living defensively around them, the gap between us growing wider with each passing year even as they tried their best to remain close to me. I worried my children would come to know me as a woman in hiding. A woman who had let the best of herself settle somewhere below the surface, or worse, had never identified it at all. I didn't want to smile when I wasn't happy. I didn't want to shop at Banana Republic. I didn't want to brush my hair.

When Mike and I visited Burlington, we'd stolen away to Montreal for the day. A world-class city, an hour-and-a-half drive from our could-be home. We went to the Musée d'art contemporain de Montréal, where an entire room was dedicated to the exhibit *Sometimes I Am Content*, created by Grier Edmundson. Spanning an entire wall was that bold title statement—"Sometimes I am content"—in typewriter font. Black on white. Yes, I thought. I get that. I wanted to find the *somewhere* I was content to go with it.

Richard Yates's novel *Revolutionary Road* begins on the opening night of the Laurel Players' community theater production. April Wheeler—a suburban wife, a mother of two, and a hopeful actress—makes her stage debut to an audience that is at best underwhelmed by the group's performance. After the curtains close, April retreats to her dressing room, eyes swelling with tears as she wipes the lipstick from her lips and casts accusing glances at her reflection in the mirror. On the way home, April and her husband, Frank, argue as the tension of April's disappointment in the play's opening saturates their conversation. Frank pulls the car over and the couple's argument escalates into near violence at the side of the road. "It's not my fault you didn't turn out to be an actress," Frank yells. April screams back at him, and Frank stops short of punching her in the face. His fist, and by extension their shared disillusionment with their life in the suburbs, lands on the roof of their sedan instead. But the effect on the audience, on the reader, is an emotional bruise on April's pretty cheekbone and the innate, pressing knowledge that something must change.

Not moving to Vermont would have been our *Revolutionary*

Road. "The cornfields will kill us," Mike said. "Let's do this before one of us gives ourselves an abortion," he laughed, referring to the dramatic ending of the book.

I laughed, but it wasn't funny. We had begun wondering aloud which of us would be the first to die and had taken out extensive insurance policies on our lives, mine with remarkably less monetary value than his. "I still remember the smell when the doctors cauterized the incision," I said to Mike.

"I still remember seeing your guts," he said. He scrunched up his nose with the memory. "And the sucking sound that came out of your belly when they took him out." We'd agreed, holding our second son in the recovery room, that there was no going back once you'd seen a person's insides. You couldn't unsee it. It colored our love differently, blood-red and ripe with mortality. That memory— the cut and pull, the stretched infant limbs—greeted us as we poured our coffees in the morning and again when we poured our cocktails at night.

Another six months later, we justified all the costs of the move as we unloaded the U-Haul in front of our new garage in Vermont. With a "now or never" mentality, we'd left friends, jobs, and everything that was familiar to us. We left my extended family to their midwestern ways. I was so ready to leave the past behind, leave sameness and smallness and suburban expectations behind, that I didn't even think about stopping by my hometown for one last look. We'd decided to absorb the sheer financial burden of moving across the country to New England, where the cost of living was twice as high as in the Midwest, unflinchingly, and said, over and over, that it was worth it. We never talked about whether we'd be new, too, or whether we'd be the same—our regular, relocated selves, only surrounded by green now, our mouths gaping *O*s of wonder, finally in the place that would content us.

· · ·

Instead of collapsing under her belief that she had failed as an actress, April Wheeler ignites a plan to move to Paris, which Frank enthusiastically supports. *We're not like them,* they say, referring to their suburban neighbors. *We're not meant to be here among them,* they say. April offers to work as a secretary in Paris so that Frank can read and write and discover what it is he wants to do, who it is *he* is. To April's horror, her plan evaporates when she learns she is pregnant again and Frank insists they can't raise a baby in Paris.

Vermont was everything it was advertised to be: plenty of green, enough mountain views to last a lifetime, and a disproportionate share of fresh air. The tightening in my chest that had come and gone for years began to ease. A thought occurred to me a few weeks after we'd settled into our new home. We still had not unpacked the half dozen blue plastic bins that had been through four prior moves—a yearlong stay in Denver, Colorado, two apartments and one house in Indianapolis—never to be opened in any of our homes, but instead relegated to storage. We'd dragged the containers from apartment to apartment across Indianapolis, then to Denver for a temporary work move, then back to Indiana, and then finally to Vermont. Storing them and storing them again, forgetting why. Forgetting what. "I feel like an idiot," I said, and sat upright in the dark.

"Why?"

I told him about the bins.

"Now?" he asked.

I couldn't be stopped. I had to know what was in the bins, and neither of us could remember. We couldn't think of a single thing that was missing, nor could we think of anything we'd be holding on to for later. But I knew the bins held an answer to a question I hadn't yet asked. I knew that even in this new postcard-picture-worthy land, there was still something I lacked. Mike helped me pull them down from the small alcove in the new garage, their fifth home. He was helpful like that—always finessing my environment, providing whatever would make me happy. And my satisfaction was fleeting, unpredictable. Perhaps even impossible. But sometimes, I was content.

When he went back to bed, I opened the bins, perplexed. I'd kept all the wrong things: a brief lifetime of boring. Irrelevant papers and attempts at short stories, old candleholders, small glass dishes that served no obvious purpose, the odd chipped mug, a small ugly lamp, wooden frames for paintings I never painted, a Norton anthology of literary criticism, a textbook on the theory of punishment, an outdated introduction to criminal justice, some VHS tapes. I laid it all out by the curb in the dark, wondering who I'd be by morning.

II

A woman I met through a mutual acquaintance years ago had recently quit her job as vice president of a Midwest-based software company to make herself completely available to be herself. Jory had worked as a jet-setting executive for fifteen years, often detailing her negative airline experiences in Facebook posts—delays and more delays; yoga sessions she barely squeezed in between power lunches and late-afternoon meetings; incredulous faux pas of her professional wardrobe. The Internet, as an extension of place, was a dumping ground for the hassles of everyday life. Though Jory was only arriving at the cusp of her fourth decade of life, and by many Americans' standards had achieved quantifiable success, she decided to enter what she called her "retirement." I received the announcement of Jory's impending job change in my Facebook feed.

Facebook gathers together people from the past, many faces from many different places. It also opens another realm of existence, where we can be slightly better, slightly more presentable versions of our messy selves. It gives us space to love our mothers the way we wish to love them, to forget, at least within the confines of Internet filament, that they are flawed; it lets us forget our own flaws. The Internet, in many ways, is a happy, pretend place. It is a version of reality. It is real life, rivered by the banks of our choosing.

Jory announced that she was through with the rat race, and she had decided to take a new job, effective immediately. She appointed herself "chief innovator" at "[Her] Life," formalizing her transition on both her Facebook and LinkedIn profiles. This period of retirement, she proclaimed on these platforms, would serve the sole purpose of self-discovery. She would endeavor, through systematic soul searching, adventure, and intentional quietude, to find out who she really was, the demands of her corporate job stripped away. "The plan is to take a year or so off to focus on myself," she writes. "To experience life on my terms untethered from the shackles of a job. To make each day what I want and need it to be to move myself closer to my true spirit." When I read that last sentence, the following diagram came to mind:

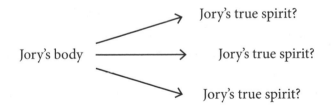

Where could her true spirit possibly reside if not within herself? Afraid of being typecast, I think, as an exec who had worked so hard that she'd forgotten how to live and who had somehow lost something crucial to her personal identity, perhaps even to her humanness, she set out upon a 365-day blogging practice to document the first year of her retirement. As promised, Jory blogged daily about her experience, updating the world at large on her progress. At the time of this case study, she was 174 days into her retirement. Since she began, she had taken a cross-country trip by car with a friend. She had paddle-boarded at sunrise. She had jogged across a variety of terrains. She had sought the expertise of her shaman, inviting her physical and emotional energies to be manipulated, coaxed, and released by his incantations. She had tried to find new love via Tinder (to no avail). She had entered a new romantic relationship (not via Tinder) and moved in with her new partner. She had done a lot of yoga. She had occasionally passed judgment on other people. She had whined. She had set intentions for herself, reminded herself to be present in her own life, meditated, and contemplated her divine purpose. She moved significantly across lands and bodies of water, traversing terrain, moving through space and time in her search, the world wide and her need great. This part, I understood. The need to look at other landscapes for clues about what already lies within us is real. It is a variation on distance, that thing you need to put between yourself and a problem in order to see it clearly.

I read most of Jory's posts, not necessarily because I was interested in or envious of her unfettered pursuit of what I would call leisure activities, but because I was fascinated by the end goal: a core knowledge about herself that undoubtedly awaited her at day 365 like a wrapped gift. Santa presenting Jory with her true self by firelight. I was fascinated by the very concept of her journey toward that true spirit, as if it were something that could simply be revealed or discovered or unearthed, if only one knew its whereabouts and proximity to the body. "I know that everything I write is a documented intention to manifest a result somewhere in my life . . . either now or down the road," she writes. "There are no wrong paths," she writes, attributing the sentiment to Oprah. *But aren't there?* I wondered.

I read Jory's posts and wondered how she would measure her success. On one hand, I wished I possessed her certainty that each day's experience, and by extension its write-up on her blog, was leading to a positive, conclusive, tangible end. That there was somehow sense to be made from experience, or the accumulation of choices and circumstances. But what I noticed most often about Jory's posts was that they were iterations of the same thematic point: she was on a quest for missing pieces; she was clearing the fog; she was staring into a mirror waiting for her own image to speak or blink or sing; she was opening the hatch and letting all the world in for as long as there were pieces of herself left to gather. There was no mistaking that she did not perceive herself as *whole*. And the missing pieces—well, they could have been anywhere. Pieces of this whole self could even be other selves. They could be Earl Grey tea or headstands or sleeping until noon. They could be scattered along the Appalachian Trail, or they could be sitting on her nightstand all this time in the form of the one book that had gone unread all these years, or they could be in the bottle of pills that she saved for emergencies only.

Jory seemed to know for sure that a person ought to be whole. A person ought to be somehow circular and transparent and known, and the individual, as the maintainer of the person's whole self, is simply tasked with finding what is missing. She's charged with putting the sphere back together and keeping all the curved glass parts clear of debris. When this is achieved, the moment when all the dust is wiped clean before new dust can settle on any of the round, puzzled-together pieces, then and only then is the self made whole. Somewhere a bell rings and someone snaps a picture—#selfie #me, finally #whole.

By the conclusion of her yearlong journey, if she were to leave a trail of bread crumbs that marked her daily path, I would expect Jory's search for self in all directions to have taken on a likeness to a Jackson Pollock painting—all lines and motion, but little sense. What would Jory see in a Pollockesque visual representation of her year? Would a pattern or answer emerge? Would she see chaos?

Would she feel like a different person? Failing at a palpable take-away, would she accept instead something beautiful created in the wake of her disciplined pursuit?

Rachel Kushner poses a similar notion in her novel *The Flamethrowers*. Reno, the book's protagonist, endeavors to achieve artistic success by photographing the patterns created by tracks she makes racing her motorbike. This allows her to combine two things she loves—velocity and motorbikes. By taking a good look at these markings from the top-down view of a camera's lens, she assumes they will somehow make an unintended sense. They will transform Reno's physical experience of racing across the desert into art, thus memorializing and intellectualizing the individual tracks themselves. She will take the sum of the tracks' parts and project meaning onto the experience as a whole. Like Reno's photographs, Jory's blogging journey—a daily foray into the physical and digital worlds in search of parts of herself, the shedding of the job, the act of looking for the "self" regardless of what is actually found, of pinning down the day's most important themes through the titles of her blog posts—will become a collective personal truth that stands apart from the intention and the individual "tracks" that sweep across the desert sand of that year of life. A new idea, the year's summary, a result of the exploration of the self, will be retro-actively applied to Jory's experience. She will likely intuit and inter-nalize wisdom—making sense of the things that happened during the course of that year after they've occurred.

In her posts, Jory refers to her blog as a trial run for more se-rious writing—not an uncommon goal for bloggers and diarists. What if Jory writes a book about her experience that then pushes outward into a readership, creating its own ripple effect that is then entirely separate from the writer? To write the book, Jory will have to further assess and consider her experience. New thoughts will mix with old, while time passes on the clock that measures the distance between the experience itself and the ever-changing memory of the experience. Decorative language will be added to make the account of the experience richer and more interesting and more meaningful. Lines will be drawn in the sand. Pictures will be taken from above. Look, here is what happened. Here's who I am. Sort of.

III

I suppose I could have said that I was between jobs, or that I was changing careers. That I'd been distracted by the curious landscape of southern Quebec—the odd roadside businesses barely hanging on, situated between sad-looking homes whose architecture couldn't be associated with any decade's style that I knew. That something was about to happen, though I couldn't say what. I could have said that I was temporarily unemployed, unsure of what I'd hoped to find waiting for me in Vermont. Unsure, too, of whether I was the same as I was before I'd moved, or changed. Whether a new place could actually open the door to a new me. I wanted to be changed. I wanted to be whole. I wanted to think that a simple change of place had that power, or that the work I'd begun to put into writing, having found myself friendless in my new state and inspired by the topography and the very idea of the opportunity to reinvent myself, was leading me to my true self. (*Are you a vegetarian?* people asked me in Vermont. *Are you a locavore or a vegan or a pescatarian?* they asked. *Perhaps,* I thought in reply. Perhaps I would be one of those things here. I could, after all, be anything here. Say it and it became true. A new place certainly presented that opportunity. It's the classic reason for moving to New York: to be someone. And sometimes, to be someone *else,* place equated to anonymity.) In Vermont I had tried many things besides writing (not shaving my armpits for three months, foraging for mushrooms and ramps, yoga on a paddleboard, indoor surfing class, acting as if I liked other people's dogs, sewing, cross-country skiing, a planter garden on my balcony, relearning French, life drawing and drinking classes—at the same time), and only the writing had stuck. I had told Mike that we needed to get away, though we had only recently arrived in our new state, and now I was coming back from Montreal empty-handed.

I could have said that a melon color had been wrenched loose in my life by writer Maggie Nelson's fascination with blue. That I had to have it, the way Nelson had to have blue pieces of glass, which somehow made sense in her life where she could not. Melon-colored Eames chairs, melon-tinted lipstick, a ream of melon and cream damask fabric that never got used for anything, salmon nigiri. That melon did not often occur in nature, at least not in the lush green of Vermont's Champlain Valley, where I now lived, was a fact I lamented. I found myself quickly disappointed. Barely charmed by tiger lilies. Appalled at cantaloupe's watered-down orangey color. I could have said that in Montreal, a man stood next to me at the corner of Rue Saint Laurent and Saint Paul, smoking, his cigarette clinging at an angle such as I had never seen before to lips such as I had never seen before. And that it changed me, and that his mouth was the embodiment of melon. They were the same. That it was my job to explain how this could be so. Pam Houston, another writer, calls these "glimmers." I don't like the word, because it sounds too sweet in my foul mouth, but I know what she is saying. She's talking about those moments and images that strike you midsternum. All of life's messiness and mystery somehow looking back at you in them, with answers toward which language only groped. It was the part of life—experience—that prompted us to do our darnedest with words. The things worth writing about. I had seen these all my life, but I hadn't made sense of them until I came to Vermont. In Vermont, I wrote. I looked. I listened. I questioned.

I formulated tentative answers. I settled into words, and like an old favorite chair's, their comfort was familiar.

I rode in the passenger seat of our rented car as we neared customs. As our turn for readmittance into the United States approached, Mike muttered, "You can't wear sunglasses through customs. What are you thinking?"

He is a pro at travel, packs his suitcase expertly in the dark to catch 5:00 a.m. flights for work, breezes through airport security without a snag. He has systems of efficiency, not unlike *The Accidental Tourist*'s Macon Leary. And Mike has no patience for those less practiced, those who can't keep up, can't fold a pair of pants into a pocket-sized, wrinkle-free contraption, can't pass through customs unmolested.

I, on the other hand, was never quite apace with nuances such as these. I generally couldn't find my passport, never made it through security without being pulled aside for extra screening processes. I have a permanently guilty-looking face. As we were green-lighted for the customs station, I quickly removed the sunglasses.

The customs officer, layered in bulletproof and polyester garments, leaned in, squared her jaw, and set about questioning us. What were we doing in Canada? What did we do for work?

My husband is an airline pilot, so his response was simple and straightforward. Plus, he did this all the time. Being the less-traveled of the two of us, I faltered in the face of such inquisition.

"And you? What do you do for work?" the customs officer asked, looking at me.

I squinted, barely able to make her out as anything more than an outline of black against the summer sun.

I could have said that once, during a Get Out the Vote campaign, I'd sat on a man's couch, a terribly dirty couch in a nameless trailer park, and helped him spell his own name as he registered to vote for the first time. I was rattled, realizing then that people who could not read existed down the road from where I'd grown up. That when he insisted he write his own name with my help, rather than signing X, which would have been perfectly legal, his five-year-old daughter who was still in a diaper and could barely talk came to sit on my lap, and I thought for the first time that I might one day like to be a mother. And that later, it worried me that it was not my own mother's love that prompted this thought. And worse, that I recognized, for the first time and far too late, my penchant for falling in love with strangers would be a problem. Had been a problem. That somehow I felt safer and happier and more alive with them than with people who were familiar to me. And what was that about?

I could have said that once I'd watched a half gallon of milk go bad as proof that time is change, that one thing can become another. As proof that cheese is a sublime marriage of art and nature.

I leveled my smile, hardened my eyes. I matched my face to the customs agent's, something I'd learned that humans do to indicate trust. The long answer, the storied answer, compressed and collapsed in a blink, and I uttered rather unconfidently, "I'm a writer." It came out sounding like a question rather than a statement. *I'm a writer.* The reply echoed in my mind. Was that what I did for a living? Well. It was a living in that I was living it. Not that I was paid, per se, not yet, but that I supposed that it was time I called myself a writer. Publicly.

The officer looked almost amused. Almost. She definitely did not believe me. Worse, I did not believe myself.

No grandmas, no vaginas, no mirrors, no accounts of postgrad summers spent traipsing through Europe, no writing about writers. These are the lessons I've picked up from other writers about what not to do as a writer. Among the not-to-dos, or the cautiously-to-dos, is the timing of proclaiming that necessary statement, "I am a writer." I was struggling to own it, what with most of my friends having ignored the release of my little publications, small as they were, and my efforts at starting the first draft of a novel. Jen and Rachel, my best friends from Indianapolis, were my cheerleaders, along with Mike. But defining terms of the "writer" label was a gray area. Profession, hobby, love affair, compulsion, calling. Whatever "it" is was in question for a lot of people—namely, those without book credits and degrees behind their names, and that included me. But writers are writers before they publish books. Beginnings are locatable. They must exist somewhere.

My own beginning as a writer was in books I read and in journal pages I penned, in terrible poems and desperate letters. It was in the unrest I felt about Corey, whom I kept coming back to, writing and rewriting. It was in the river back home, in the fields. In all that had happened there, which had followed me to Vermont and flowed out of my fingers onto a computer screen. Moving to Vermont was turning out to be more of a link to the past than an escape from it. This melon syndrome, my wild crush on the mundane and the emptied out, the thrill of vaguely intimate encounters with strangers and vaguely intimate encounters with abandoned structures. I had to admit these into my persona, give them a name. Give them room to breathe. Nurture them. Write it all out in a way that meant something and held weight in the world. In a way that became more than a collection of images, more than a cross section of place and time and people.

All the answers I could have given the customs officer meant the same thing. And I hadn't realized it until now. Writing had become more than a hobby, more than a desire. Writing, as a creative practice and an earnest attempt at art, had become greater than the fear of failing at it.

When she pressed for details, for evidence that would amount to my reply and publications that she could google on her government-issued laptop to confirm my claim, I listed for her the few publications I'd acquired over the past six months, feeling puny and ridiculous at the joy I had felt over them. They seemed insignificant under her scrutiny.

She typed away on the computer. "What do you write?" She seemed confident, sure of tripping me up with this question. "Look at me when you say it."

I was glad she said that. To look at her, I mean. Disallowing anything but facts. Demanding an unflinching reply. She didn't mean for it to help me. I know that. She only meant to determine whether I was lying. Whether I was a threat. But it was what I needed to be asked. She might as well have asked me, simply, "Who are you?"

"Oh, short stories, some essays. I'm writing a novel." Spat out in a single sentence, nearly a year of work sounded in a minor key. Hundreds of pages shriveled in the hazy summer air between us. "I'm just starting out, really." *I'm writing letters to a man I haven't seen in fifteen years and putting them in a drawer instead of mailing them.*

The customs officer looked at me, then at my passport, then back at me.

I'd cut off all my hair and looked nothing like my picture. I smile when I'm nervous.

"Don't smile," she said. "Where is your work published?" She fixed her gaze on her computer.

I still hadn't convinced her. Did she expect my name to pop up in a search? It wouldn't. I started thinking about this woman as she worked, about who she was beneath the pepper spray and the nightstick. Beneath the black polyester. She was very short, but not slight. She wore a hard look on her face, but smile lines caught in the sunlight around her mouth and eyes. I named her Amanda.

"On the Internet, mostly. Some journals." I shrugged, feeling smaller each time I spoke.

"*Where* on the Internet?"

At that point, I was pretty sure she wanted to humiliate me, the silly woman trying to wear sunglasses through customs who thought she was a writer and clearly had a self-confidence problem.

I rattled off the short list, my voice flat now, unemotional. I hoped she inferred my meaning: let's stop the charade, *Amanda*. Amanda, who is a real person beneath the polyester who smiles and wears capri pants and flip-flops and takes selfies and likes baseball and probably snorts when she laughs.

"Mm hm. Mm hm," she said, and cleared us for entrance to the United States with a stamp and a nod.

When we crossed back into the United States, I was still thinking of what else I could have said at the customs gate, vaguely unsettled by the ordeal.

My husband put on my sunglasses and pretended to toss his hair. "Uh, I'm a writer? Um . . ." He laughed at himself and gave my sunglasses back, rubbing my knee. "I'm kidding. But you'll have to get better at saying that."

We drove another ten miles without talking, the green intensifying the deeper we drove into the Vermont countryside. "What do you do for work?" he asked.

I looked at him. "Very funny."

"No, really. You should practice."

He convinced me to say it out loud as we rode down I-89 back to Burlington. "I'm a writer," I said, only half-serious.

"Nope, not good enough."

"I feel like I'm in therapy."

"Just do it. When you fly a plane, half the challenge is confidence in your authority. If you don't know you can do it, you can't do it. If I was checking a pilot and asked him what altitude he should be at to turn off the seat belt sign and he said, 'Um, 30,000 feet?' what would that look like?"

He had a point. I repeated the statement until we felt it was believable, and we laughed about it. When we got home, it was night. Carrying my overnight bag up the stairs to our condo, I worried about my new writer self, still a dribbling baby gazing out the window in wonder, falling in love with melon for no apparent reason, my sentences circling back to the very place I had abandoned. I wondered about what remained in me of home. How new I could really be here.

In the morning I wrote home—an e-mail to my closest friends— to update them on life in the Northeast and told them I was writing and starting to publish some work. That I was writing a novel. That I felt I'd found my place in the world for perhaps the first time in my entire life. That sometimes, I was content. Of the six friends I contacted, two replied. Jen and Rachel, as expected. I was devastated because this was a huge transition for me. Didn't they know this was a proclamation? Writing was hard, emotional. It was work, body and soul. It was fragile and I was only a writer-baby. Often, it undid me in ways both freeing and crippling. I remembered something I'd heard Julia Alvarez say at a reading: "When you've seen a thing, what, then, is the obligation?" That has stayed with me, helped me make sense of my writer eyes. Of my moving forward. Of my need to look back at what happened with Corey and figure it out—for me. It helped me stop waiting for the approval of friends or an understanding pat on the back from my parents for all my trying. It propelled me beyond the visioning—this lifelong collecting of images and moments—and enabled me to move more eloquently into that higher-ordered act, the writing itself. And beyond that: owning whoever I was, whatever whole looked like, wet and muddied roots and all.

Could I better understand the significance of the angle of a man's bottom lip, of an illiterate man registering to vote, of rotten milk, because I am compelled to notice? I can, because the people are alive, because it is never too late to empower yourself, because milk becomes cheese. Time is change, more than a beginning and an end, but an ongoing expansion. One thing can become another—gradually, and then suddenly, as Ernest Hemingway once said. And cheese is part art and part nature. I have seen that and more. Writing is seeing. There is an obligation to complete the half-written letters, assemble the tales, stitch together the truths. Of that, I am certain.

ON ROBERT FROST'S LAWN

We are lying on Robert Frost's lawn. We cup our hands around clumps of grass to hold on to what's left of the afternoon. We listen to the hermit thrushes and strain to hear the stream over their song. To do this, we must not speak. And anyway, we can't, because then everyone would know what they are not supposed to know and what we ourselves do not even know for sure. They would hear it in the pauses, too luxurious for mere friends.

This is a school for adults who have too much to say. A grown-up's *rumspringa*. We left our families at home and are here for two weeks. We have divorced technology and shunned reality. We are thinking backward in iambic pentameter by threes. "Do not call home if at all possible," we were told at orientation. "No one will understand." And it's true. My best self has grown here in Vermont. Only it is a wild self, one that knows it was never meant to root down into any ground. One that values freedom above all else. This revelation is an unexpected discovery, but Mike rolls with it and with me. He rearranges his work schedule, taking time off from his own travel so that I can attend writing conferences and get swept away by my intellectual connections with other men and women. I go, he stays. He goes, I stay. We are barely together, but it works out. He never bats an eye. He is an expert falconer, and I am his golden eagle. I fly and return to the nest.

John Elder, the resident Frost scholar and naturalist, stands in front of us. He begins a lecture on Frost's Vermont, Frost's trees, which surround us on all sides. It's an incantation for the dead at this close range. The writers' conference was started in 1926 by the poet, and Elder speaks of Frost as if he were an old friend. Like many of Frost's poems, Elder's lecture draws us into the landscape but doesn't tell us what to make of it. Beyond Elder is a small cabin, one of two of Frost's former Vermont homes. The lecture is part of the program—propping up our minds with speeches, dangling Frost's house in front of us like candy. We're not sure what's edible and what isn't. We stuff gray pebbles into our fleshy cheeks like gobstoppers, tip sunshiny daffodils to our mouths, pinkies up. We are gifted. We are here on exhibit. We are competing. We befriend one another but reserve a teaspoon each of jealousy as an antidote to failure.

The lecturer invites us further, quoting a Frost poem about a thrush wood bird and a tree as we listen and look: the very bird, the very tree. It is too much, too sacred, and on an acid trip of words, we draw nearer one another on the lawn in shrinking orbits, pairing off or grouping together in threes. Our real lives shift beneath us. The atmosphere is so enchanted that we willingly shift along with it. I almost believe I am one of them, the learned and graduate-programmed people on the lawn. I was not accepted the way they were—green-lighted by committee. I was wait-listed and sit on this lawn only because someone dropped out at the last minute. Everyone knows it, especially me. It is possible that in this world, people have mothers who read them Baudelaire at bedtime as children and fathers who quoted Keats during family meals made from scratch. It is possible for me to pretend I belong here or share their history. There is one thing we have in common: we are tired of explaining ourselves with words.

Elder limits his talk to our immediate surroundings. He says nothing of the state's curated legacy beyond these trees, nothing of poetry beyond the context of Vermont. Intoxicating beauty is everywhere in Vermont. You hate to leave it behind, to cross the state line back into New York or Massachusetts. To board a plane at the Burlington airport. It is designed to have that effect on visitors—Vermont will send you into a rapturous stupor like the overoxygenated casinos of Las Vegas that make you forget what sleep is. You'll come back and back again. You'll remember it as a place where the locals have it all figured out. Vermont's small towns aren't failing; they are actually quite lovely. Vermont's politics, if you're even moderately liberal, are exemplary compared with those of many other states. But Vermont is more complex than this lawn, these trees. In the late 1800s, a collapsed agricultural economy resulted in a talent exodus. In the 1920s, the state countered this problem with two remedies. First, Vermont's beauty would be systematically preserved in hopes of promoting a wealthy tourist culture that would create an influx of prosperity. Second, "voluntary" eugenics policies, aimed at curbing the reproductive capacity of the state's so-called "degenerates," would arrest growth of the wrong kind of public. This knowledge makes it hard to isolate my thoughts locally, to bind them within the tree line. At this diversely populated conference, Vermont's overwhelmingly white population is suddenly very apparent.

On this lawn, I am ancient and newborn at once. The whole world pulses in my wrist. I watch my new friend's face grow more familiar by the hour. Soon, I have loved him for five years, at least. I know the structure of his sentences (he favors semicolons, em dashes, and parenthetical asides). I know how he likes his coffee and when (black, mornings, and into the afternoon). I know that when he looks for me across the lawn, scanning the faces of poets, his bottom lip will collapse a little when he doesn't see me amid the crowd. I won't be there. I won't be waiting for him. I'll be far from the peloton, scraping the bark of an oak with my fingernail.

His face is a map of the fields he ran through as a child, gently creased from too much thinking. A picture to go with the story he tells me about the kite that flew too high and never came back down to the boy who cried and cried. Or maybe he is worried about this growing thing between us that won't stay in my pocket no matter how I fold it up to size. Let us say it is the fields. I, too, ran in those fields. I see them still when I sleep. We'll never really escape the landscapes we inhabited as our brains developed. For us, a cornfield will never be just a cornfield. We've been too close to the stalks. I'll tell him now: it's a farce. There is nothing in my pocket. My mother did not read Baudelaire at my bedside. She did not read at all, although she could. She sang Carly Simon in the dark. In my retelling of my mother, I fiction her a glowing cigarette at night, a father, too, for she did not smoke or have a father either. She had four fathers, and also none. It is complicated. I didn't come from long lines of educators or artists or philosophers, like my friend did. I came from water. From fields. From a fabled land between those.

It is quiet here, in the mountains. A former professor of mine told me recently that uninterrupted natural sound is endangered. It is nearing extinction, he said, at least in the United States. At my hotel, where I was staying while I visited and spoke to his students at their private all-girls school in Connecticut, I searched online for the last quiet American locales, which had a certain illogic. I discovered a nonprofit project called One Square Inch that purports to represent the one place in America where you can truly find silence, which the organization defines as the absence of any human-made noise. This place, this square inch or more, is deep in the Hoh Rain Forest at Olympic National Park. In my online search for silence, I considered silence itself. It is a whole concept. Any intrusion of sound destroys the idea entirely. In yoga and meditation, practitioners silence the body and the mind in different ways. Night is a quieter time than day so that people can rest. I had silenced my body so that I could better hear the din of my mind. If there is power and force in silence, and One Square Inch suggests that indeed there is, then it's logical that there is an equal power and force in its opposite—noise. As there is value in walking, there is value in standing still. Following Newton's third law of motion, when one body exerts a force on another body, the second body exerts an equal and opposite force on the first body. The One Square Inch project uses the same theory to present its mission: "The logic is simple; if a loud noise, such as the passing of an aircraft, can impact many square miles, then a natural place, if maintained in a 100% noise-free condition, will also impact many square miles around it. It is predicted that protecting a single square inch of land from noise pollution will benefit large areas of the park." So the silence, or the inherent purity of the silence, becomes greater than its square inch. It spreads outward, and affects everything within its range as noise affects the distance its wavelengths travel.

I believe I fear actual silence—the far edge of quietude. In Annie Dillard's essay "Total Eclipse," she describes leaving the site of an eclipse viewing before it is over because the experience is too all-consuming. She plunges into a meditation on existence, barely emerging before the eclipse's shadow sweeps her under and away for good: "It is now that the temptation is strongest to leave these regions. We have seen enough; let's go. Why burn our hands any more than we have to? But two years have passed; the price of gold had risen. I return to the same buried alluvial beds and pick through the strata again." Silence strikes me as a kind of total eclipse, and this lawn of Frost's may be just as risky. It could overtake me if I let it. Pure silence, pure freedom, would somehow reveal me to myself too starkly, too soon. The lighting would be wrong, the picture unsettling, distorted further than I expected in every direction. I want only to see a little bit more at a time, to mine very carefully through the layers of sediment below my feet. To lose water by drops and not by gushes. To fly and return. I want some sense of clarity about the buried alluvial beds, to hold as precious goods the names of its materials, to walk across them and experience the malleability of the middle, before it's pressed so hard from above and below that it metalizes.

Vermont's degenerates were identified by the state's foremost eugenicist, Professor Henry Perkins, who later became president of the American Eugenics Society. For three years, and at the exact time that Frost's school was established, Perkins would help identify "degenerates" in the state unscientifically—taking people's reputations within their communities as proof. Among them were the poor, the mentally disabled, the incarcerated, and people of Abenaki and French-Canadian descent. He charted individual families' mental failings and misfortunes on circular charts, modified from the kind used in documenting animal pedigree. He notched and lined segments of "immorality, crime, and incompetence . . . propagated through sexual reproduction." Perkins kept an incriminating file of "English Corruptions of French Names" to root them out. See the strength of words in the hands of a man with power.

Whoever we were before does not matter so much here. We bow to green knolls now. We are mountain high. We find ourselves ankle deep in streams, lost in make-believe, and choking on milkweed. We look into corners for the light from which we'll craft a day, or the next line. But even as we frolic on this mountain—I can't believe we played baseball earlier—we write ourselves backward in time. My friend revisits headlines about the collapsing coal industry from his journalism days in the Rust Belt, committed to saving Americans from themselves; I dredge my riverbed for silt, look at maps that show how the water and land have changed, and write

fiction about a boy and girl who grew up side by side along a riverbank that is barely fiction. We pick at our respective terrains for
something usable, gathering retrospective meaning where there
once was none. Headlines offer little reason, I suggest to my friend.
They reek of a senseless world. But I still know the black shape of
smoke, I tell him, and how it huddles over a small town. How it
can follow you anywhere, if you believe in symbolism. I left the
Midwest, and I could leave my whole life, too, if only he'd ask. But
if I check his pocket for the question, I won't find it. We don't live
that bravely.

There was a group of people who were neither Vermont's degenerates nor its ideal. Via a eugenic duality, Perkins noted, there existed in some lineages both "social individuals . . . those apparently
law abiding, self-supporting and doing some useful work" and
"asocial individuals . . . those who displayed the familiar repertoire
of pathologies." My family would have fallen here, neither the elite
nor the useless. But I fear that Perkins was alluding to race.
   Frost, the man, Robert. Bob. He wasn't on Perkins's list. He was
white and educated, privileged and productive. He was less gentle
than this land, but then, the land is a liar and keeps our secrets. I have
buried mine in its soil. I have screamed into gathering storms. I
have set things on fire. Bits of paper. Photographs. Frost was flawed,
like all of us, and a fire starter, too, Elder says. I find that unimpres-
sive; most everything can burn. Most everything contradicts.
   The Frost homes are empty. They have been for years. They have
their secrets, too. Elder says that the small cabin burned up once,
some townie kids with nothing to do. It was empty; so were they.
So it goes. Now there's hardly anything left inside—the damage has
been cleaned up. And once, the bigger one up higher on the mountain was ravaged by drunken teens. They hawked their bodily fluids
onto its aging surfaces and used its furniture for fire. If you could

open the chests of these youth for inspection, one by one, and distend their individual charts of misfortune, they too would reveal a study in contradictions—they were the children of doctors and professors. Because of that, I would bet these kids got off easy, which makes me wonder about Corey. If he had been the child of upper-middle-class Dutch parents, would he have ended up in prison? Those early arrests for using marijuana, joyriding, and petty theft very likely would have resulted in a police escort home and a stern warning. Being born on the other side of the river, staying out of the juvenile detention center, might have made a difference.

A line of ants pile grains of dirt near my friend's shoulder. How I want to smash the hill, a bad habit carried over from a careless childhood, but I don't because I don't want to reveal my classless impulse. I don't want him to think I'm cruel. "Do you know," I say instead, "that each ant in a colony is tasked with a role from birth, and none are expendable? Each is crucial to the survival of the colony. Even those that die of stupidity are carried home and buried." Crimes are treated equally in ant society. Lives are treated equally. He smiles at me in reply. The picnic beyond us is being carried away, though we have not eaten. The staff watches us and waits for us to want hamburgers. They think we've chosen this life, but it has chosen us. And we are tired of explaining ourselves.

The world is made of bent shapes from this view, on our backs, which is the position designed for telling lies about who we are beyond Robert Frost's lawn. I decide my friend doesn't have a mother, and John Elder may have two. My friend is a classic oil portrait and I am a watercolor picture. We could be happy here together, drying out in the sun. It's hard not to be a poet when you're sitting on Frost's lawn, especially when you are one. Together, we look for a line, a stanza, a downbeat, between the maple trees in the little wood near the lawn, because we can't help it and it's either that or suck the sap from the cut rings still raw from last season's tapping. We are that thirsty.

But the trees are not poems, never have been, do not contain poems, never have contained them. They have nothing to say about who we are. They have nothing to say about integrity or rationality or depression or the books our mothers never read. They have nothing to say about what to do next with a life. And then, and then. No. Don't look into the woods for an answer. The word *tree* is invented. We tell them what they are, not the other way around.

This is not to say that trees are not useful, that we cannot project onto them and see something reflecting back. Nature works on us this way. A walk into the woods can change you. In the *New Yorker* article "Why Walking Helps Us Think," Ferris Jabr connects the visceral ambling of characters in modernist novels such as *Mrs. Dalloway* and *Ulysses* with a mapped landscape: "Such maps clarify how much these novels depend on a curious link between mind and feet. Joyce and Woolf were writers who transformed the quicksilver of consciousness into paper and ink." I liked the idea of bodies moving across the land as common literary ground. The writer notes the way that authors sent their characters on walks to do their thinking and used these excursions as an opportunity to propel plot. "As Mrs. Dalloway walks," he writes, "she does not merely perceive the city around her. Rather, she dips in and out of her past, remolding London into a highly textured mental landscape, 'making it up, building it round one, tumbling it, creating it every moment afresh.'" I liked bodies moving across the land as common human ground, too: every moment a brief collision of past and present; every moment an instance of person and place commingling as their singular future unfolds before them. Every new view an opportunity for growth or altered perception. Ultimately, that was the essence of place to me—an ongoing reconciliation of the past, present, and future. An ongoing negotiation of memory. It was resurrection.

Eugenics was publicly promoted in rural areas of the state through Fittest Family tests at county fairs. The tests were propagandized as evidence that some families could not match up to Vermont's ideal standard of mental and physical faculties, by which they apparently meant *lineage. Race. Class.* I wonder about the ancestry of the teens who damaged the Frost properties, whether any of their aunts or uncles had been sterilized and how their destructive nature had slipped through, what with all that precaution. Maybe they'd been wait-listed, too. Or maybe they'd been wealthy enough for it not to matter.

When Elder's lecture ends, no one can stand. Our knees are gummy. Our skulls have cracked open. My brain is hemorrhaging; the acid trip has gone wonky. Make a tree a tree again. Make a bird a bird. We wait for the right words—to say, to write, to omit. To be grasshoppers would be better. Grasshoppers are never asked to explain or decide or grow up or let go. Or to make meaning of the world around them. To control themselves, or conform. *Why did they bring us here?* I wonder. They dip us into water like brushes, and then say, "Paint." Make any kind of mark on the paper, and we pass the test. None of that will work once we leave.

There are some hard rules to this suspended world—gravity, velocity, thermodynamics, genetic expression. Others are forgettable—promises, contracts, leases, vows. Entire histories came before this mountain, but they seem distant now. My husband, for example, and no one is talking about him. My friend's girlfriend, whose name I've never heard him speak. Real people have been reduced to pronouns, Saussure's semiotics run amok. My friend tells me he has three cats, and in another life, I could love him for that fact alone. This grass has always been here; before it was called grass, it was still here, existing. It will be here when we leave. We are more mutable than it is.

Before he begins the guided nature walk, which he leads each year after the lecture, Elder invites us to tour the cabin. It is open. It is empty. Go ahead.

The staff roll the last of the picnic away and give us their final fretful glances. Don't worry, I think. We belong to other, practical people who keep us from starving in our regular lives. Let us have our hunger here until night. When the sky is black we can split the stars and gather the sparks to build a fire. Let's go inside, I say, once we're alone.

We shouldn't, he says.

But we do, and I like how easily he bends for me.

It's a small place. There are two chairs, a stack of wood and kindling, and a braided rug that once may have been blue. Long planks of untreated flooring creak beneath our feet. The little windows feel bigger from the inside. I like this illusion, how it overtakes my senses. How the world is shrinking outside. It begins with wonder and takes shape.

Degenerate is also a verb.

I could build him a fire in the tiny stove, and we could sit in front of it in the rockers, holding hands. As if it were ours. As if we did it all the time. As if our imaginary children might return from playing outside at any moment. As if a pie were cooling on the counter. As if his cats would come, any minute now, to lie in our laps for an afternoon nap.

Let me do something, I could say. Let me touch your collarbone. I will get away with eccentricity. It will be expected. My moral backslides will be considered artistic. My degenerate nature, *interesting*. His collarbone will be smooth and firm, so different from the one I am used to touching, which is bonier and jagged, that I will cry. The surprise of him will be too much. The thing signified, severed from the signifier. Twice removed from bone.

He'll reach for me once I've had my fill of semiotics, and gather my hair together in his fist, gently. He'll hold it there. We'll think we hear someone, but we'll be wrong.

Go ahead, smell it, I'll say, tipping my head to his chest.

He'll bend his head over mine and inhale, still gripping my hair. He'll snuff me out this way for what I really am: an impostor who languished all day on Robert Frost's lawn, undetected. This will be somehow more intimate than fucking, which will never happen. We could do the easiest thing: undress. But we won't. We'll stand there, in Frost's house, holding these strange parts of one another as long as we want. We'll be adorned in a particular sadness, consumed by the ghosts that rise from Frost's lawn. By the trees that stalk one another into the distance, each forever gaining on the next. By the children who burned this house and trashed the other. By the children who were never born to their degenerate families. We will remember our separate pasts, whatever they are. We will fill in the stories we were never told as we drifted off to sleep. We will cast off the illusion of language itself and all the things we think we have to do. We will seek, instead, the secrets of the land, the parts we tell and retell, the histories omitted, the erasure. We will seek what hangs on after the fog lifts.

Elder never comes back from the woods, and we are the last ones to leave. We walk for a mile, our eyes fixed on the sky to keep it from falling down. A black cloud follows us. It signifies nothing but rain. For the first time, I feel no inclination to be as loud as the incoming storm. I can expand into the silence without fear of eclipse. The path below our feet is only a piece of earth that has been walked on by other feet. It needs no name, only *use*. The forest can keep its trees. The birds can keep their song.

MAP OF OUR HANDS

Out beyond ideas of wrongdoing and rightdoing,
there is a field. I'll meet you there.

—Rumi

When I returned home, I ended the long silence. I finished the letter that had sat, unsent, among the belongings I'd carted with me from place to place over the years. And Corey replied immediately. All that internal dialogue I'd generated, the fear of what would come back to me in his reply, quieted. At first I had told myself that I only needed to know that he was okay. But it was more than that. I also needed to know if my attachment to him had been one-sided, to know why it still nagged at me. I needed to know how it was possible for the lives of two people sprung from the same place to diverge in such different directions. I also felt entitled, to some extent, to some answers about what happened to him and why he'd done what he'd done. I wanted to know what facts I had missed about him. Nothing I learned in school and nothing I had learned since had given me a clear understanding of those events, and I never did like murky water. I needed to see how deep the ground beneath lay.

Before I went to see Corey for the first time since he'd been arrested sixteen years earlier, I did two things. First, using masking tape, I outlined the size of his cell, eight by twelve feet, on my living room floor. I sat down inside the rectangle. I tried to imagine his life, his body, much larger than mine when last I'd seen him, inside that space with another grown man for nearly two decades. Sitting inside the outline, I considered justice and punishment very carefully, weighed the concepts against what I had known of Corey and what function funding a potentially sixty- or seventy-year sentence fulfilled. It repaired nothing, not for the victims' family and not for the rest of the world, though, judging from the letters I received back from him, it did seem to have repaired Corey when nothing else in the past had worked. Not jail, not boys' school. Not his mother kicking him out. But perhaps, like plenty of other young men who'd been considered misguided punks as youths, he'd simply grown up. Only the mistakes he'd made had been much worse than those of the typical nineteen-year-old male. Then again, nothing about his upbringing had been typical. But I needed to see him to know for sure. I thought of my own teenaged self and the person I was now. Time was change, and judging from Corey's letters, he, like me, had changed. There was a calmness to his words, an acceptance of his past, and hope, against any promise of hope, for his future. Second, I read the rules for visiting the correctional facility, wondering what it would be like. The excitement of visiting a prison I'd experienced as a child was replaced with dread. I now had too much knowledge of that system, the people who were inside, the crimes that had landed them there.

"What does your husband think?" people asked me when I told them what I was doing. "How is that relevant?" I would reply. I would never have asked his permission to visit an old friend, but in this case I did. And he said, "Why are you asking my permission? I'm not your father." Mike supported what I was doing, and he had known about Corey for years—the basics, not all the details. Not the decades-long unrequited love angle. Saying it out loud made it sound ridiculous, even to me. He still had some questions. "I don't understand it completely," he said. "But anyone who made you who you are is all right by me." My history with Corey had tumbled out in words in its entirety while my friend Jen was visiting us in Vermont in the days leading up to my visit. Mike conceded that there were things Corey knew about me that he could never know, did not *want* to know. Jen, though, was my vault. Whatever we had been through in life—relationships, bad decisions, daddy issues—she had my back and reserved judgment. She was rooting for me, for Corey, and asked me to call her afterward to tell her how it went. This time, when I saw the gun towers and the razor-wire fences, I could barely breathe.

Rule 1. On a contact visit in prison, you may briefly embrace when the inmate enters the room.

My fingers trembled and I clenched my teeth together, wishing I could wear my nighttime mouth guard all day. I carried stress in my jaw beyond sleep. If no rest came from sleeping, how then to face the day? Brief epiphanies began to creep in as I eyed the vending machines across the room: *a thousand-dollar mouth guard to prevent headaches, what a luxury. Shower curtains. Couches. What would it be like never to shower with privacy? Never to sit down on a soft surface? Who would I become without these comforts?*

I watched the door through which at any moment Corey would emerge wearing beige prison-issued slacks and a matching shirt. Though I knew better, I still expected to see the Corey I'd known as a girl: tall and strong but not overly musclebound, tan. A smile reflecting the carelessness of his youth. I had forgotten his eyes, but not his mouth. Not his knees. Not his laugh. In our recent letters, we had compared one another to ghosts, apparitions; perhaps we had made ourselves up. We compared one another to the tiny circular photographs stuffed into a broken heirloom locket: held, kept, halved, separated. We compared one another to any number of memory devices and keepsakes: tufts of hair between the pages of yellowed books, dried flowers from formal dances, familiar refrains.

We sickly preserved and catalogued our history together, anemic though it was. It was overly commemorative and precious. But perhaps it was the effort, the act of remembering, that mattered.

When he did appear, at last, I was startled. He was a mountain of a man, solid and soaring as he walked toward me. In a word: gorgeous. I was caught abashed, wondering if I passed muster. In one letter, he had told me he saved the picture I'd sent him of me at eighteen, a freshman in college. Thin, blond. A too-eager smile. Still looking very much like the girl he had known.

He cracked a wide smile at me and scooped me up into a long hug, releasing me a moment before the guards would insist we part, as if he knew exactly how much he could get away with in the visiting room. And by now, he probably did know. We settled into our chairs at table seven and I reached across the tabletop to hold his hands. The opportunity for human touch was the only thing I could offer him, and I used it to try to bridge the years that had separated us. "Wow," we said, over and over. "Holy shit," we said, as if we'd expected to see our fourteen-year-old selves instead of adults.

As we settled into our chairs, I thought through the list of questions I wanted to ask him. *When was the last time you sat beneath the stars? Do you ever cry? How is it that you got here, exactly?* We had been writing letters to each other for almost two months this time, the third time since he'd gone to prison, but we had carefully avoided the tougher conversations that previously caused us to fall out of touch. We had avoided talking about my love and his choices, about the butterfly effect and do-overs. We had, miraculously, managed to keep the details of his transgressions gestating in the background of our letters, like unhatched chicks awaiting a birth date. But they were coming. There were things I needed to know, and the only way out was to break straight through the white, open my eyes, inhale oxygen. I still couldn't imagine my friend, a killer. Even the word felt wrong in my mouth. I had considered coming right out and saying "What the fuck?" when he sat down. Or kissing him, erasing everything that came before. Or something else equally direct that left no room for him to misunderstand what I was asking of him, what I needed him to explain to me, such as "Tell me how you killed people. No, not how. *Why.* Or how you *could.*" But what I meant was *Explain to me how I loved a person who could do this and why I didn't see it coming. Explain to me why I still feel the loss of you in my life.*

I kept thinking of *Badlands,* the 1973 Terrence Malick film starring Sissy Spacek and Martin Sheen. In the film, Spacek plays the teenaged Holly, who lives alone with her father and spends her time confined to the porch or yard, doing her homework and twirling her baton. Her solitude was all too familiar to me. When she meets Kit, played by Sheen, she warns him that her daddy won't want her to be seen with a garbage man, let alone one ten years older than she is. Nevertheless, the two become friends and lovers, stealing embraces in barns and along secluded riverbanks. But Holly doesn't fall for him because he is a "bad boy" and she is a "good girl." That trope has no place in this film. Holly seems to find Kit to be clever and surprising, nonconforming to their rural community's attitudes in a way that opens her mind a crack. He sees her as more than just a girl. But when Kit shoots Holly's father, apropos of nothing—"How'd it be if I shot you?" Kit says to him before he pulls the trigger—it happens like a dream gone bad. She becomes an immediate accomplice. You can hear it in Holly's voice-over narration of the event: she doesn't quite know what to make of it, but her life is irreparably changed. She's suddenly free to be with Kit, but her father is dead. Early on, Holly suspects that Kit's mental state is at least in part to blame. I found myself trying out snapshots of the inside of Kit's mind prior to the gun's blast. Of the inside of Corey's mind before his knife became a weapon. I wanted to know what they were thinking the moment before their lives changed forever. I wanted

Polaroids for my refrigerator that explained everything in a story-board of frozen frames.

The questions I had practiced quickly evaporated as we talked like regular people catching up over coffee or beers. Only the lives we compared couldn't have been more different, on the surface. He listened to stories about my work, my writing, my children, my husband, while I asked about his time in administrative segregation, his routines, and his general wellness, still avoiding the big question about the big crime. He told me he had spent seven years total in solitary lockup. Each time, he said, he came out a better man. Not worse, like some people who go in and don't come back entirely intact. Although, he admitted, he no longer felt altogether human. He had spent a lot of time looking at himself in the mirror. Figuring out what went wrong. Now, he was all right—altered, damaged, but all right. I saw nothing inherently *wrong* with him. He had not been diagnosed with any mental condition—I asked. He had obsessive-compulsive tendencies, but who didn't? That seemed unrelated. He sat there talking to me, and it was normal.

"I read this article about a new theory on the big bang," I began, after we had concluded general catching-up conversation.

"The one about the parallel universe?" he asked.

"Yes!" I said. The theory suggested that the cosmic beginning of time sent matter expanding in *two* directions, rather than one, due to already low entropy in the burgeoning universe as opposed to a gravitational exertion. The first direction was the one we knew—time's one-way arrow leading the charge through an ever-widening universe, thanks to Newton's second law of thermodynamics. But the second one, according to this new theory, would have expanded in the opposite direction. Theoretically, there could be, if all the same particles needed to eventually create the life we know here on Earth had been sent off in that second direction after the big bang, another world like our own.

"How did they describe it again?" he asked.

"It said that this new model 'has one past but two futures.'" It said, too, that the theory assumes the universe has an unlimited capacity for entropy, or chaos, as opposed to functioning as we know it only when entropy is low and contained. It looks more closely at the origin of the second law of thermodynamics. I paraphrased for him: gravity converts incredibly disordered systems into wonderfully ordered ones. Our universe is an example of that. "We are realizing the ancient Greek dream of order out of chaos," the article read.

"Order out of chaos," Corey said. "I like that."

"It sounds like us, doesn't it?" I said. "One past, two futures."

He nodded and squeezed my hand.

Corey told me about his weekends, his meals, and his job in the kitchen, which he was proud of and seemed to enjoy. He was doing great now, as far as life in prison goes. Like the universe, humans will shape order out of whatever material is available. He had systems for managing things like laundry and finances. He had a schedule for phone calls with the three members of his family who still talked to him. But it wasn't always that way. He told me about how, years ago, he obtained a cell phone in prison and met a woman in a chat room. He had been in a relationship with her for a few years, though they had never met in person. When I asked why a person would do that, he explained that the best the men inside could figure was that with all physical opportunities to connect rendered impossible, they became very good at talking and listening. They made good emotional partners.

Corey told me how he had sold weed and wine and LSD and heroin in a place I was afraid to sneeze in. But he had distanced himself now from the pitfalls of prison. He grew up, finally. He decided he had gone to ad-seg for the last time. He had never really wanted that kind of life, anyway—a criminal life, a thug life—though it was, in some ways, easier. Though he had changed, the opportunity to live a life of crime was ongoing. It was consistently the easier choice. Change was harder. People kept coming to him, asking him to involve himself in one hustle or another. He compared it to Alcoholics Anonymous—every day he had to decide not to "drink." He had to keep saying no in order to stay straight, which got easier with time. Now, approaching forty, he valued his visits, seeing his mom and dad. Seeing me. He wouldn't risk having it taken from him. "Please don't come back into my life and then go again," he said. "I don't think I could take it a third time."

I promised I wouldn't.

Now Corey worked, read *National Geographic* and plenty of novels, painstakingly made Japanese paper quilled crafts with makeshift tools—cards for other inmates' families and his loved ones. He grew his hair long and donated it to be made into wigs for cancer patients, cutting it himself with nail trimmers every three and a half years. "It's the little good I can do in the world, after all the damage I've done," he said. "And if I can make you smile, make you happy, and then you go out into the world and share that happiness with others, I feel like I've done something good."

Now, he tried to preserve the health and good looks he had left through yoga and exercise, healthy food choices, and adequate sleep. We were not all that different. We watched the same TV shows, read the same articles, and shared some of the same interests. "Did you read the one about the French catacombs?" I asked. "I think it was two issues ago." And he told me he had. We talked about our favorite parts of the article, and I wished we were in my living room instead of the prison's visiting room. I wished they would let me buy him out. "Couldn't you get put on house arrest for the rest of your life and live in the country somewhere? You're not dangerous. You're regular. I'd take care of you. Give the taxpayers their money back." To me, dangerous was an unmedicated uncle who had made dead-sober death threats or a three-peat violent sex offender who had a staring problem. Those men had made me feel unsafe. Corey didn't.

"Honey, I wish it were that easy," he said. "To fall asleep at night, I imagine myself in a little house or in a garage somewhere, a place away from everything where I won't bother anybody. I imagine the different things I would build, see the pieces in my mind, the way they fit together and how it would look when it's done."

"That's sweet," I said. "And a good idea, I think. To think yourself away from it all."

In Norway, the maximum prison sentence, even for murder and rape, is twenty-one years, the last five of which are spent at a special facility whose focus is relearning how to behave respectfully in the world, how to work productively, and how to live without chemical dependence. The concept is twofold: two decades without freedom gives victims a sense of justice, while the focus on rehabilitation gives society justice. Barring both the death penalty and life sentences, the approach aims to respect life on both sides of crime. Prisons in that part of the world have remarkably low recidivism rates compared with other nations. Meanwhile, the United States has 5 percent of the world's population but 25 percent of its prisoners. What would happen if we treated each "criminal" as we would want our own children treated if they committed a crime? What would happen if, as in ant colonies, each member of our communities, regardless of station and role in life, was considered indispensable?

"I think all this time I've been building it all for you."

I laughed. "So you've built me a barnful of imaginary furniture? Seventeen years' worth of chairs and hutches?"

"Something like that."

Corey had retained the best parts I remembered of him—his

humor, his sincerity. He had discarded the ones I'd never seen up close—the drugs, the poor choices, the disregard for consequences. I don't know what I thought he'd be like instead. In poor health? Incapable of communication? Closed off from me?

He revealed to me that he had used heroin, among other drugs, for quite a while leading up to the events that would end two lives and change the course of his own. And though it sickened me to hear how he was living—sleeping anywhere, sometimes even at his sister's grave—I kept listening. "I was coming off of it when it happened. Needed money, was getting sick."

"Sick from the drugs?" I asked.

"Yeah. If you can believe it, I was a hundred and fifty pounds when I was arrested."

That was seventy-five pounds less than was he was now, and he looked strong, trim, and healthy. No, I couldn't believe it. I couldn't imagine him like that. It made my skin crawl. In my head, I kept filling in the gaps, reinserting myself into his life in all the places where I should have been there, pulling him in another direction. So much of the human body rebuilds itself in a short span of time. The cells of the liver, the brain, the skeleton, the blood. We are built for survival, to begin again on the heels of physical failure. If only the social structures that govern us would give us second chances the way our DNA does. Our bodies are leaner than our laws.

"I never let you see that part of me," he told me. "You were too good for all that, and I wanted to protect you from it, from me."

"I wish you'd have come back to see me one last time. I waited for you. I called and left messages with your mom. Everything could have gone differently." If we had had cell phones—that technology was a few years beyond our time—we would have been talking. I still would have been in his life. No question.

"I never knew you called," he said. "Didn't have a phone where I was staying and I wasn't talking to Mom. I wasted every good thing

I had." His regret was like a sleeping bear. Poking it was dangerous. He had been through this all before—what went wrong. How it all happened. Slowly and then suddenly.

"I first slept outside after you kicked me out of your house," he confessed.

"Me? When did I do that?"

"You got mad at me about something and kicked me in the shins and told me the only reason I was even there was because your parents felt sorry for me."

I didn't remember it, but I didn't doubt it was true. I hated that I'd made him feel like that when all I'd ever wanted was for him to stay. To have played any part in his unraveling was unbearable.

When we talked about the past, about the horrifying act that we were still handling with conversational care, I wondered whether his criminal activity would have pulled me into its current, as he said it would have, whether it would have buried me like Kit's crimes buried Holly.

"We would have met in the middle," I told Corey. "Half-bad, half-good. Half-reckless, half-restrained. Maybe we would have saved each other."

He started to cry at that, but I watched him silently talk himself down from it. "You know, I used to watch you, too," he told me. "From my window."

"No way," I said. "Really?"

"I did. Your room was always a mess. I used to watch you brushing your hair or reading your books."

"That's all?" I asked, remembering how I'd dressed in front of the window each night after my shower.

He laughed and blushed. "No, that's not all. My mom caught me once."

"So we were doing the same thing. And it wasn't just me."

"It was always mutual," he said.

"You never said anything."

"I was an idiot. And I was afraid of your dad."

"Everyone was."

"For good reason," he said, laughing. "But I should have tried. I should have shown him I could have been good enough for you. Only I wasn't. I never figured it out until it was too late. He was right to keep me away from you, and I respect him for that. To be honest, I always looked at him as a father figure."

"What exactly did he say?"

"I was over at your house one day. Your parents were having a party. I was watching you jump on the trampoline. I was seventeen, how could I not, right?"

"I'll give you that."

"Your dad pulls me aside and says, 'You're not going to break her heart, son,' and I said I wouldn't. And then he said it again. Only that time in a way that meant he'd probably kill me if I did anything at all with you."

"You broke my heart anyway."

"I know," he said. "And I couldn't be more sorry. I can't say I didn't know what I was missing. I was painfully aware, but I didn't think I deserved it. I was always in my own way, and not only with you. It's a shame it took me coming to prison to figure that out."

I couldn't disagree with that. But he refused to consider that pursuing what we both wanted would have kept him out of trouble's way, out of his own bad decisions. It was pointless to reconstruct the past. He wouldn't admit it not because it wasn't true, because we knew it was, but instead because it was too painful for him to think about, now that his future held only more of the same: passing time as best he could in a tiny room with a locked door, no matter how sincere his regret, how sincere his remorse. Remorse is a television courtroom jury buzzword, a parole panel fairy tale, and Corey's sentence didn't have parole. But it was real. Seeing it in someone's face is the only way to know what it really means. We were both on the verge of sobbing, so we changed the subject before we were consumed by regret, before we were gripped by the white light of a tacked-on reel that held our own alternate ending—one past, one future. Not two.

Corey was fascinated by all the things that I shared with him, and his face lit up when he learned something new about me, or about the world on the outside. "Out there," he called it, as if it were a mythical land that may or may not be real. He made a joke, telling me that the only knowledge he could offer me in return was how to make hooch in prison. He joked a lot. He could tell me how to traffic drugs and six ways to hustle one dollar into ten. "I've gotten by with the only skill I have—," he said, "the ability to make something from nothing."

He told me he was waiting for the next *Game of Thrones* book to come out, like Mike; that he would bet on the upcoming Brickyard 400 to make it more interesting; that he missed the new *Deadliest Catch* the night before because he was writing me a letter. He was utterly normal, yet otherworldly. His world was completely unknown to me, yet he was more than familiar. My lost family.

"How long have we known each other?" I asked.

We counted back the time. We determined it had been thirty years. I had known him longer than anyone save for my family.

When the conversation slowed, he probed me about my life, about Vermont, and what the world looked like. He loved landscapes, so I told him about some that I'd seen. The Rocky Mountains, Joshua Tree National Park, the Gulf of Mexico. He loved to hear about simple things: the color green, for example, what airplanes were like, and whether the Blue Ridge Mountains really did look blue in the distance. "Yes," I told him. "Blue for miles."

At thirty-six, Corey had now spent more time in jails and prison than out of them. Nearly his entire life would be spent in prison. I couldn't fathom it, and, terrible as his crime had been, I didn't think anyone deserved that. People were serving less time for premeditated murders. And his wasn't that. But aside from all this, he was more focused than most people I knew. He wasn't destroyed by fear of his future. He wasn't distracted by a cell phone, like other people. He hadn't another place to be. He was there, completely present, with me.

He told me about the time he held a smartphone—one smuggled into prison. Thousands of contraband phones were discovered each year in Indiana prisons—in prisons all over the United States. It was surprising to me, but commonplace to him. "It was awesome," he said with a big grin.

I eyed the guards, and they eyed us. Corey ignored them and kept his sights set on me, though he was aware of them watching. "You're so beautiful," he said, over and over, making me blush. I wondered what the guards were thinking about our conversation. "You're the woman I always thought you would be and then some," he said. He lived his life being watched closely, he said. "But I never get used to it."

I couldn't get used to it either. I noticed everything—the ten cameras above us, the smattering of fake plants throughout the room, the metal and Plexiglas that comprised nearly every surface, the plastic children's kitchen, and the limp, naked baby dolls in the play area.

Six hours of hand-holding could not make up for sixteen years of wonder and unanswered questions, yet we persisted in believing that they could. They must. We kept trying.

Rule 2. On a contact visit in prison, you may bring up to twenty dollars in quarters in a clear plastic bag. The inmate may not touch the quarters.

I didn't realize until three hours into the visit that Corey was too polite to ask me for anything to drink or eat. I jumped up. "You must be thirsty, hungry?" One of the guards stood and took a step toward me. I sat back down quickly and then rose again, more slowly.

"A Sprite. And you pick the food. I don't care." He looked both relieved and embarrassed. "Thank you," he added.

"You must care. What do you like? Is there anything out here that you can't get in there?"

"I don't care. You pick."

We went back and forth like this, in a stalemate of manners. As it was still technically morning, I ended up choosing an egg, cheese, and sausage breakfast burrito for him and a pizza for me. I read the instructions on the burrito package, trying to determine whether to remove the wrapper or cook it with it on. A woman in a long white denim skirt and oversized red T-shirt made small talk with me. "Food's a little better up at Michigan City," she said as she ripped the ends off a small packet of pepper and sprinkled it onto a sandwich of unidentifiable meat. I looked at the vending machine and cringed. The packaging it came in read "pork-shaped sandwich."

"Keep the wrapper on and set the timer for one minute, love," she said, and I was grateful for the insider tip. I pictured myself in five years, still coming to visit Corey there. Passing down tips on using the microwave to other women, telling them which vending machines will eat their change and which are likely to jam.

I brought the food back and set it on the table. I could tell that Corey was uncomfortable when I did anything for him. He tensed and trained his gaze on the table. "Would you mind bringing me a napkin, please?" he asked without looking up, his voice so timid and soft, you'd think he was asking to borrow five thousand dollars.

I wanted to shake him and make him stop the nonsense of not

asking for what he needed—not even allowing himself to believe that he was worthy of small acts of care from someone who did in fact care very much for him. I cut him where it would most hurt on purpose. I had always been a bit mean like that and would still flip if I was provoked or wounded. "You should have asked for my help a long time ago. Come back to my house instead of sleeping in the fucking cornfield and doing drugs when things got bad." I spat the words out at him, filled with another surge of frustration. "Maybe you wouldn't be here."

"I deserve that and more," he said, offering himself up as my punching bag. "Get it all out of your system, honey, because I'm not going anywhere. Can't and won't."

He also couldn't stand up until it was time for him to return to his cell. That was another rule of the visiting room. But he turned in his chair to watch me walk to get the napkin and back.

When I got back, he was grinning. "I'm watching you because I want to savor this day. I hope you don't mind. It's been too long."

I smiled at him, warmed by his sweetness. But again, I was troubled by the vision that punctuated my thoughts. Corey with a knife. Our neighbors, stabbed. Blood everywhere. Over and over I've pictured it, unable to sequence the chain of actions that could have led to that outcome.

In one scene in *Badlands,* Holly observes Kit watching a huge, helium-filled red balloon float away against a Montana sky, knowing nothing will ever be the same. Not for him, and not for her. "My destiny now lay with Kit, for better or for worse," she says as the balloon disappears into the clouds. "Where would I be this very moment if Kit had never met me? Or killed anyone?" As she tries to imagine a different present for herself, tension fills her voice, its innocence stripped back to reveal a fragile future.

I looked up at Corey, the scene shaken away from my mind, and I opened my mouth to ask the question, the *what the fuck* question that needed to be asked, but as I did, he turned the burrito over and we saw that the tortilla was covered in a grayish film.

I pulled the plate away from him. "Let me get you something else."

Before I could stand up he pulled the burrito back, picked it up with two fingers, and gingerly took a bite. "It's fine," he said with his mouth full.

We both knew it was rotten, but he ate it anyway. It took him ten minutes to finish it. I worried that he ate it only because I gave it to him.

Rule 3. On a contact visit in prison, you may not wear any jewelry.

As we talked, we inventoried the scars on our bodies, which marked the passing of time, the way we were already wearing out, even in our thirties. Corey described the ones I couldn't see that he had acquired over the years and were hidden beneath his clothes. There was one between his ribs, from when he was shanked a few years back. Six more all over his torso, from the same stabbing. "Ice pick," he said, nonchalantly. Scars populated his arm, hand, and both wrists, where he'd had surgery to repair several breaks acquired in a fall in the prison's laundry room. Another break, knuckles that now looked flattened, from when he attacked an officer. He had had a problem with anger, he said, problems with authority, but he worked on it daily. "Every day, I can choose to deal with my life, or not deal with it." Rain was a reminder. "Arthritis already," he said. He showed me three dark specks on his fingers where he had tested potential tattooing ink. "Never get a tattoo you can't cover with a shirt," he advised, again showing his Gemini nature—being two things at once. When he was clothed, the enormous tattoos on his shoulders, back, and chest didn't show.

"Please tell me they aren't swastikas."

"They aren't. They have to do with Norse mythology." Another interest of his, about which he had read extensively. I thought it curious how, even during the years that had separated us, we had both clung to stories to make sense of our lives. We had taken an interest in the same topics—science, space, history, literature. It was uncanny the way we knew the same things, but had acquired our education so very differently. Sharing these unexpected intellectual spaces with him was, to me, extraordinary. He was thoughtful and poetic in the way he approached his limited access to the world and it endeared him to me all the more. He clung to his knowledge, and I could see that it was saving him the way it had saved me.

In turn, I showed him the age spots that were accumulating across my knuckles. I described the C-section I'd had four years earlier, the scars on my neck and back where I'd had lymph tissue biopsied. I described the cysts all over my ovaries. He flinched as he rubbed his thumb across the seemingly permanent indentation on my ring finger, where I normally wore a wedding band. He drew his mouth into a line, breathed in sharply, shook his head real slowly. The bear stirred in his sleep.

In between these inspections, we processed who we used to be (girl next door, boy next door) and who we had become (woman in the world with a husband and children, man in prison who has never used the Internet on a standard computer and refers to computers as "the machines"). We attempted to reconcile the truths against the untruths. Was it my father who kept him away from me, or was it also his mother? Was the separation carried out in concert? Was it I who said let's slow down, or Corey? I called, he called, neither of us ever got the messages. He thought I had flat-out rejected him, while I wondered why he didn't try again. We felt robbed. We cobbled together memories, rounding out our recollections into a fuller story of us: it was I who stripped in my bedroom window for him, he who turned his light off to watch. It was I who called him over one night and said now or never, he who hesitated out of respect for my age and a promise he'd made to my father. "I thought we had plenty of time," Corey said, "that we could have all that later."

I squeezed his hands in anger.

"Crush them," he told me. "Dig your nails in, let it out."

I squeezed harder and then released his hands. It felt a little better. "I'm still mad at you for leaving me there." Riverside, drowning. Broken anyway.

"I know you are," he said. "Do you think I haven't wished a thousand times I'd stayed? Done what I wanted to do with you and waited for you to graduate, then figured out a life together? Yes, I know you would have made the difference in me. You're back in my life two months now and you already have. I'm a better man with you in my life. Everyone here can see it. I walk differently, I talk differently. I don't tell them why, but that's because of you. But let me tell you from experience. You go down the what-if road, you'll drive yourself crazy." He caressed my fingers to impress his point. "We both have to live in the present."

"You and my dad had no right to negotiate around me like that. Nobody asked me what I wanted." How could I still be angry about something that had happened so long ago? When would I ever be free from what men decided for me?

"You're right, and I'm sorry about that. But what would have happened if I had? You would have started sneaking out to see me, come with me to places that would have gotten you into as much trouble as they did me. Then what? No," he said, "it's better this way."

Corey's voice was soft and tender the whole time we talked. I still couldn't imagine him hurting anyone. He was not like Kit. And I was not like Holly. This was another kind of tragedy, a loss that has never stopped taking from us, or from others. A debt that would never be paid off, though he would keep paying. It occurred to me then that Corey had come to terms as much as he could with his crime, with life in prison, with the fact that he still didn't know how he could have done what he did or how he could have gotten so lost that he lost his own head, with never having children or a woman to love and give himself to in bed. It was me who hadn't gotten over it.

"Is it?" I asked. "Is this better?" I waited a minute, then went for it. Time was running out. "Tell me what happened that night. I need to know."

He lowered his head, as if he couldn't bear going back to it. "You don't have to," I said.

But he started in. He told me most of what went on leading up to it—that he had been coming off drugs, was still rocketed by the withdrawal, needed money. He intended to rob them. He'd only brought the knife to open the door and didn't think they were home. In and out. Easy. But that wasn't what happened. He was confronted, and he panicked. He started with a few words that would have described the altercation, but I stopped him. He couldn't bear saying it, reliving it, and I couldn't bear hearing it. "I didn't want to go back to jail," he said, exasperated. His explaining cut off then. There weren't any words that could describe further what had happened or his split-second, fear-based, drug-fallout reasoning. It still didn't make sense to him; he had thought through it many times, unable to understand his own actions. He could say nothing to me that would justify why he didn't just turn and run.

"Are you telling me there is no good reason that this happened to those people?" I asked. "Are you telling me you had the opportunity to run and didn't? And that I've carried this loss with me, all this time, for it to come to this?"

We sat there with wet eyes and stunned expressions, holding each other's gazes. I hadn't expected there to be no good reason. Not that any reason was *good*. But I thought for certain there would be an explanation for what he'd done. There wasn't. Drugs themselves had not triggered his actions. There was no mental illness. There was nothing. It didn't align with my memory of him or with the narrative I'd constructed over the years.

Corey wasn't off, at least I don't think so. The psychiatrists assigned to screen him before the trial that never happened didn't think so. In my view, this was a good thing. It meant that the crime was an isolated incident, unfortunate and horrid, yes, but he wasn't a sick *person*. In some ways, he was made by where we were from and who he was from, from circumstances and repeated slips through cracks with no one to pick him back up. He was from the wrong part of town in a town where status mattered and where people of authority had little else to occupy their time. He'd been exposed to criminal life very early, and it had pulled him into its current. But he had also made bad choices. And by his word, he'd never valued his own future enough to make better ones.

"We're not much different," I said, after thinking this through a bit. "None of us. People are mostly water and thoughts."

People, especially young ones, are malleable. Like wet sediment. Guided by whatever kind of banks have lined their river, by what has held them. By what has let the liquid drain out. They try to dredge the bottom, straighten the path, widen the mouth. But the water must go somewhere.

"Thank you for sending me that picture of us," he said, changing the subject to something lighter. In it, we were laughing, sitting in the grass, the river a few hundred yards behind us. "I'd forgotten there were good parts to my childhood."

I'd gone back to see our houses before the visit. To check on our windows. It was something I did from time to time, a ritual to remember him by. I didn't want to tell him how small the place was that had warped us somehow, sending us in opposite directions, away from each other when we had always wanted to be together. I didn't want to tell him how escapable it was. How leaving didn't require extremes.

Rule 4. On a six-hour contact visit in prison, you may use the bathroom once. If the offender uses the bathroom, the visit is terminated.

Corey told me he had had nothing to drink since dinner the day before. "Dehydrating. Don't want to lose time with you."

After the burrito incident, we allowed ourselves one sip of pop each. We wiped our fingers clean as well as we could. I was happy to see him, despite the more challenging parts of our conversation, and it showed—I couldn't stop smiling. He was a lost puzzle piece finally found, the picture complete, though distorted. We posed for a photograph and smiled. I tried to make every minute count, not knowing how long it would be until I saw him again. I tried to put us both back together again, as least for the present moment.

Corey turned my right hand over—flat, open, and palm up— examining the way I was made as if I were a scientist and my skin might consist of a newly discovered element. "Can I read your palm?" This was one of the many things he had studied during his time in prison. Sixteen years down. Forever to go.

In recent conversations, via letters in the mail, we'd been considering dust and origins, the vastness of the universe compared with our tiny stakes in it. We'd been considering the stars we used to be. One thing we'd always shared: the sky. At least there was that. He wrote to me to make sure I knew when to see the super moon, the blood moon, when Saturn would be visible. There was a slim chance that we could share the sky again; the earth, too. Life sentences sometimes got overturned, but Indiana was notoriously "tough on crime," and his crime was one of the worst. The public would always consider him to be a threat. He had changed, but he would always be fragile. He had endured too much, including his own rock bottom, but I knew the world would still be better with him in it. My world was better with him in it. I had seen inside him. I knew him better than anyone else. Save for a blighted past, he was nearly whole now, as whole or good in the present as any of us could say we were. He deserved another chance, I thought. I promised to pick him up at the gates if he ever got out. I'd buy him a telescope and we'd stay worlds away from the past. We'd never drive by the river. Not even to look at our windows.

He was stoic, contemplative, as he prepared his assessment of my heart line. My fingers rested gently against his wrist in a tragic repose, an inert *come hither*. I wondered if he heard my blood rushing, or if he noticed that I was nearly breathless, but he leaned in closer, his hulking hands and shoulders striking soft poses that suggested a gentle giant of a man. A man who had learned to show great control over his capable body and his undernurtured emotions. A man who had both softened and hardened under the effects of time and punishment, who could not bring himself to kill even a fly or an ant now. A man, somehow, full of love.

My heart line resembled an aerial cartography of the river where we grew up, whooshing in one direction with various inlets and outjuttings. Corey began near the left side of my palm, running one thick finger along its rugged yet determined trajectory. "One love begins here, young and stupid but real enough," he said expertly, the corners of his mouth upturned. His finger reached a tangled breakage. "Here, midway, there's a branch that flows into the main line, only it's weaker and fades."

I nodded my encouragement at him. There was no need to name names. Instead, this was the way we would talk about deprivation and absence and regret. About entire years of nothingness. About other people we had known. This scar, a woman who wasn't me. This pale remembering, a boy who wasn't him. Here, a crescent-shaped shadow, the nick of a knife, that marked the night that we couldn't quite broach head-on in conversation.

In the final scene of *Badlands,* Kit and Holly fly in an airplane, handcuffed, above the clouds. We get only a summary of the aftermath: the details of Kit's sentence, and a report of whom Holly married instead.

I spread out my fingers as he held my wrist in place. "What else?"

He focused again as I glanced at the clock. One hour left. We sipped enough pop to keep our mouths wet but not enough to make us have to pee. We would sit there until we were forced to part.

"It picks up where it started from. The first line comes back to stay." His finger found its way to the line's farthest point, rounding the side of my hand. "What's down here?" he asked of the fleshy mess of lines there.

This was how we would talk about plenty and fortitude. This was how we would count the babies we would have had. One, two, three hashes across my right ring finger. A map of our garden in bloom between thumb and forefinger. This horizontal stroke, a clothesline like the one his mother used to have, where I would hang his jeans to dry on Saturday mornings. Everything had a different meaning now. Everything was dust. Everything was written on our hands.

"The parallel universe is there," I said. Look back and you'll see another future.

"Back to stardust."

When I started to cry, he risked everything—his visits, his good behavior, going back to solitary, being cuffed right there in front of me, who knows what all—to reach across the table to touch my face. He cupped my cheek for a moment and wiped away the tear that crested my cheek with his thumb, then put it to his mouth. We sat there, staring at each other, waiting for the guards to remove us. And though they had watched him dare to touch me, they did nothing.

· · ·

I read that a person sucked into a black hole would split in two—one self falling forever into nothing, the other a collapsed star. I left my falling self with Corey and watched it haunt the cornfields from the sky as I was leaving. A reverse explosion was alive inside my lungs. In the diorama of my airplane window, I watched the shadow of a cloud eclipse the flat, rural squares where he was incarcerated. From the sky, it wasn't that far from where we were born. I looked down and wondered whether he was sleeping, crying, daydreaming. Two people divide more readily than one does. I pressed my finger against the glass so I didn't have to witness myself leaving him behind.

No one understands black holes, those metaphors for anything—space junk incinerators, world generators, secret keepers of galaxies. There is something freeing about leaving the ground in an airplane, something that thwarts every impossibility on land. "The view never gets old," Mike always says of flying. Sometimes I look at his many airspace charts, which, unlike maps of the land, are constantly changing and becoming outdated. Maps of airspace are gibberish to me, and I find that comforting. Flight ought to remain foreign, not quite real. Like magic. When I was almost asleep in the clouds, I remembered that everything on Earth is made of stardust. Me, the plane. The seven-dollar glass of wine. It's what Corey would say to me in every letter—from stars to stars again. His own early life until his death. That's how long he would remember me, how long he would love me. How long he would be in prison.

LIFE ON THE INSTALLMENT PLAN

In 1959, Brion Gysin developed a writing method called cut-ups after accidentally cutting through layers of newspaper. When he positioned his own writing next to the newspaper, he discovered that together the cuttings created interesting combinations of words and image. He then intentionally cut up various texts and arranged them at random. Gysin taught William S. Burroughs the method and together they developed it further at the Beat Hotel in Paris. Burroughs claimed that all writing was cut-ups. "A collage of words read heard overheard. What else? Use of scissors renders the process explicit and subject to extension and variation," he says. A life, a marriage, can take the same shape.

When I returned home to Vermont, which was beginning to feel like my real home even if it lacked the more familiar landscape and grit of the Midwest, I tried to relay to Mike details of my visit to see Corey in prison: "It was emotional but natural. I can't explain."

I didn't mention that I'd been so nervous that my hands shook when I walked through the metal detector. Or that before walking down the corridor of barbed-wire fencing to get to the visiting area, I'd slipped on the wet floor and fallen. I described the food instead. "They had Tony's pizza in the vending machine. Pepperoni. I forgot how much I like junk food."

"How long were you there?"

"Hours." Forever. Not long enough. Not at all, compared with sixteen years, or time itself.

Mike just looked at me. "Are you going to be all right?"

"I don't know." My cheeks still hurt from having laughed so much during the visit. My eyes burned from crying afterward. "I don't think I'll ever get over this." But I didn't know what to do with that information. "I can't lose him again. That's all I know." But what did that mean? How would a close relationship with a prisoner housed fifteen hundred miles away fit into my life?

"I climbed a tree while you were gone," Mike said over the children's heads. "Hurt my back."

I'd never known him to do such a thing—spontaneous and blatantly youthful. To do something I would do. "Are you trying to get my attention?" I asked. Mike was almost forty. In eight years together, I'd never seen him do anything like that.

"I just wanted to climb a tree."

I understood that. But I also knew he was afraid of heights. Maybe we were both facing our fears.

The prison was a separate world from home, from anywhere, and I was a different person in it. A different person after it. Returning to my condo in Vermont was a process of acclimation. It felt too large, full of possessions I didn't really need. I didn't know what all I would feel after seeing Corey again. Some reactions were expected, but others surprised me. It was reassuring that he was still, in part, the person I remembered. I hadn't fabricated memories of him—we *had* shared important experiences together. He had been good to me. He had not forgotten me as I had not forgotten him. But although he was so readily someone I wanted in my life, there was no changing the circumstances. I wasn't used to that kind of futility. In life, when I wanted something to change, I took action. I couldn't think up an out for him using smarts; no amount of education would help me help him. I had to keep reminding myself of why he was there. When I was overcome with the lack of him,

I subverted my inclination toward sentimentality by repeating his sentence to myself: life, no parole. Felony murder. These were grave realities and justice was still paramount.

Instead of a levelheaded outpouring from that thought, I imagined his silhouette filling up my kitchen door frame or relaxing on my couch. I carried his ghost with me as if it were a worn doll, positioning him among the furniture of my life, willing him into existence all around me. My intense, decades-long physical attraction to Corey was powerful and singular. I woke in dreams of him, half-real moments of consciousness. I stayed up late watching prison-related television and documentaries: *Russia's Toughest Prisons*, MSNBC's *Lockup*, *Orange Is the New Black*. I set up a Google alert for Corey's facility. There had been two murders there in the past year—fatal stabbings. "I'm always careful," he had promised. "I avoid conflict as much as I can." But I knew that when he'd been stabbed—nearly killed ten years earlier—he hadn't told his mother because he didn't want her to worry.

In the months after our visit, I talked about Corey to near strangers, peddling the photo of us from our visit to anyone who would look at it, as if sharing it with the right person might present a magical key—one that would bring him home or make sense of it all. When I talked about Corey to Mike, it was to share something Corey had told me that added to whatever conversation we were having. By bringing him into the conversation even when he wasn't there, I was able to meld the two worlds together, which made it more bearable for me. It was a surprise to Mike to learn that they were similar in some ways. They would both tell me the same things about the same TV shows, for example. Or if I was sick, they would both remind me that my stubbornness had never served me well and insist that I see a doctor. Corey was comforted by the fact that Mike was the kind of husband Corey never got to be. Mike was glad that through Corey I had made peace with the past. They shared the same opinion about me: I could be a real handful, but I was worth the effort in the end. I hoped they were right.

Essays often veer away from their centers. A braided essay can read like the inside of a mind: digressions and associations crop up as they naturally occur in the writer's thoughts. Wandering away from the subject isn't a changing of the subject per se, but a chance for readers to compare notes with their own ideas. It's an invitation to readers to test what they have read against their own experience. It is in this associative space that the text can transform readers. In this space, readers become more than what they were before they began reading. It is an opportunity for expansion, for degrees of change.

Author and teacher Judith Kitchen advised writers to court these digressions: "Let your conversation get away from you. Let a new story take over. . . . Something may happen along the way, something to alert you to its relevance." The writer, she said, must trust herself to identify the connective tissue within the digression.

I embrace this form, this thinking. I embrace complication, trusting that the meaning will emerge with time. I would argue that this advice is not just for writers. Digressions span the life cycle of any marriage, whose shape, in my experience, resembles that of the braided essay. However, the marital adage of "growing together to stay together" implies parallelism. Two people, side by side, taking even steps along an unknowable path without divergence.

A math lesson: without the aid of technical instruments, it is impossible to construct parallel lines that do not collide at some point in the future or incrementally veer away from one another.

Perhaps a better metaphor for marriage is the patchwork quilt: the ability to add on in all directions. As individuals, people are always changing, attaching new material. But does a traditional American marriage accommodate such change? I read once that people's personalities are much more varied and inconsistent than they tend to admit. This is because our culture dictates that we must be consistent in order to be perceived as sane. In order to be taken seriously, we perform only certain aspects of the selves we "live" inside our heads. Most of us, then, are much more dynamic internally than we appear outwardly.

Some failed marriages illustrate this phenomenon. Often I'll hear that people divorced because they "didn't know each other" anymore. They grew into different people who were no longer compatible. I don't think this is an indication of a mismatched couple, but rather a failure of the expectations of marriage. In a traditional sense, marriage isn't designed to accommodate the natural change a person experiences in a lifetime. It isn't designed for the partners to court separate digressions, when the meaning and duration of the digressions cannot be known. It isn't designed to embrace the romance of mystery. For those of us who thrive on the romance of mystery, on courting digressions, this is problematic. Keeping up with the minutiae of a partner's digressions, let alone one's own personal changes, is complicated work.

Mike has been an excellent life partner. He made me a mother. He is an ideal companion, steady and grounded where I am unpredictable and haphazard. He is selfless: he paid for my failed attempt at law school, a digression I followed to an expensive halt. The list goes on. But he can't provide everything for a person who is always changing. Someday he very well may become a person who does not want to do so. No one person can provide everything to another person, not even a parent to a child. No one should have to, or be expected to. I welcome the digression that Corey offers in my life, the comfort I associate with him. With Mike, I have a solid foundation, a home, two children, a like-minded companion. With Corey, I have a long history and an intimacy that transcends passion and experience. My empathy for him shaped my life; we're linked in ways neither of us can fully explain. Mike has never known me the way that Corey does, but Corey has never seen me as a mother. He hasn't shared a home or a family with me or been with me through illnesses, deaths, or financial despair. The two people have their own separate squares on the patch quilt of my life.

Love seemed a complicated emotional action for Burroughs, as well. In a documentary about his life, *William S. Burroughs: A Man Within,* speculation and firsthand accounts of his romantic relationships cut into the story almost at random. He had a kind of sweet nesting relationship with a female friend, trading recipes with her for years. Patti Smith sang him lullabies. For a time, he slept with professional sex workers almost exclusively. Intellectual stimulation came from Allen Ginsberg, Jack Kerouac, and other Beat poets. Despite being gay, a label he rejected on principle, he married Joan Vollmer and with her had two children. He seemed to have had a lifelong romance with guns, while heroin occupied the role of the abusive boyfriend that he kept going back to. I think that perhaps Burroughs's entire life was a series of digressions. His chosen life path generated conflict in the white space surrounding each dip away from the central concern of living. I prefer my own relationships the same way, though with fewer negative consequences— with digressions, meanderings that connect us to other people and things or lead us to a more precise truth about ourselves. A life that has no map.

As my life unmaps itself, Corey's continues to stagnate. Indiana prisons have been privatized in recent years under the state's overwhelmingly Republican legislature, and because of this, new opportunities were available for prisoners while others ceased to exist. The college classes that were once offered, which Corey had been enrolled in, were no longer offered unless inmates were training to become clergy. An unlikely fit for a science-oriented atheist/spiritualist such as Corey. Rehabilitation services had dwindled. Though he no longer needed substance abuse counseling, Corey did wish he had someone to talk to about his life, the unanswered questions he had about the course of his past actions, and resisting his present temptations—continuing a life of crime in prison, the path of least resistance. (*Am I a monster?* he wrote me once. *Or was I, at least in part, a product of my childhood?*) He said the counselors who were available couldn't necessarily be trusted—talking to the wrong person could have negative consequences. It was safer to keep to yourself, protect your truths. If you cared about something, you were better off not letting anyone know so it couldn't be used against you or taken away. Mostly, he said, navigating the social dynamics of prison was the hard part. The rest was easy—just follow the routine. One day after another, like having a job you hate. Play the game, pass the time, collect the paycheck. Only in his case it was play the game, pass the time, pay your moral debt.

On the other hand, though, prison communication with the outside thrived under privatization. Third-party e-mail providers had contracted with Corey's facility, one among the "lucky" in a handful of states across the United States as the privatization of prisons gained footing. It was still relatively new, but, he explained in a letter, I could set up an account and buy "stamps," which would enable us to e-mail as much as we liked—or as much as we could afford. The rates of communication were as follows:

$0.40 per e-mail

$9.95 for a thirty-minute video visit (similar to Skype)

$5.00 for a twenty-minute phone call

$0.80 to send a digital photo

$2.00 to send a thirty-second video

Just after my first e-mail to him, Corey had sent me a video. I knew that he made only fifty dollars a month, minus taxes and a contribution to the state victims' fund, earning twenty-five cents per hour in the kitchen, and that he used most of that money for food, clothes, stamps, paper, and personal needs. When I asked him about the costs, how he could afford it, he said not to worry about it. That it was worth it and he'd find a way. But I didn't want him doing anything illegal for the privilege of almost real-time messages (the e-mails were monitored, of course) or for the simple act of him smiling at the "machine" as he sang me "Happy Birthday." So I occasionally transferred stamps and a bit of money to him when I could. How did families manage this? I wondered. You could easily spend a few hundred dollars a month to try to maintain a normal relationship with an inmate. And what about the ones who had children? Incarcerated or not, the fathers were still fathers and many of them did what they could to be present in their children's lives, even from inside. And if they couldn't, wouldn't that just set up the cycle of negative behaviors for the next generation? In many ways, these modern communication options afforded to select facilities would be a blessing to many people, allowing them to be better parents, a network of lives to be less disrupted by one person's incarceration, one person's past. It allowed the men and women inside to remain more human, less isolated, which led to less violent behavior amid the prison population, and, I believed, kept them connected to the world they would eventually return to once their sentences were served. It helped keep them sane, and that was important.

But the third-party contractors had to be getting rich, charging for services that most of us on the outside generally used for free. From the get-go, I began spending per month more than what I spend on my Netflix subscription. Meanwhile, the Indiana legislature had passed an aggressive (compared with most other states) law that required violent offenders to serve 75 percent of their time rather than the typical 50 percent (with time off for good behavior), with more and more of those inmates housed in "private sector" facilities. It added up to millions upon millions of dollars if you did the math—the taxpayer cost of housing an inmate for a day multiplied over years and thousands of inmates.

I remembered learning about privatization as an undergraduate, discussing with my classmates and professors the idea in *theory*, balking at its inherently wrong-goaled orientation. the more bodies in prison beds, the more profit the contractors make. How could such a business relationship between the state and the profiteers uphold any kind of commitment to rehabilitate inmates or, more important and certainly more effective, prevent incarceration in the first place? The arrangement, now a growing reality in the United States, shifted the focus from punishment to profit, circumventing crime prevention and rehabilitation almost entirely. The first thing you learn studying criminal justice is that deterrence—scaring people away from committing crimes through threat of punishment—is more or less a fallacy. If I called up Uncle Dave to ask him what qualities made a good cop, in his extensive experience in the field, he'd say people skills—not an imposing personality. Not muscle.

Though these privatized facilities provide jobs in poorer parts of the state where prisons are often located, keep industrial food service businesses profitable, and relieve some of the financial burden local governments face due to high incarceration rates, their existence is still a type of public corruption. Privatization is not a solution to the problem of prison overcrowding and of crime in general, especially as funding for public education and various community and entitlement programs—measures that could contribute to crime prevention—face regular budget cuts.

Corey knew many inmates who did a few years, got out, and were back in prison a few years later. He said it was easy to spot these guys who were "doing life on the installment plan." The ones who did a little time and then went back out to cook meth or revert to whatever lifestyle they'd come from ended up back in prison. He saw it all too often. Whenever he had the opportunity, he tried to counsel young offenders—the ones who could still turn their lives around, go to school or learn a trade, get out of trouble and stay out of it. "It's hard to convince young people of anything," he said. "I was probably the same way when I first came down." But that was a lifetime ago. Another person ago.

I already knew my life was somewhat unconventional. For years, I'd been caring for our kids while Mike lived in hotels nearly two hundred nights a year. When he came home, I'd go out and live my professional and social lives while he stayed home with our children. We were rarely seen together in public. Most of our communication occurred over Gmail chats at odd hours or in snapshots taken with our smartphones. I sent him a picture of our younger son's first written word, another of our older son's toothless smile. I used to keep a list of the cities where he would be staying while he was gone and phone numbers for the hotels so I knew where he'd be on any given day and how to reach him via a secondary number, but that stopped years ago. More recently, I was only vaguely aware of whether he was in the Northeast or the Southwest or the Midwest.

One night, he was in Toronto and all the smoke detectors went off. I couldn't make them stop, so I called my dad for help and ended up smashing one with a hammer because the goddamn noise just wouldn't stop even after I changed all the batteries. One day, Mike was somewhere in Louisiana and the living room ceiling was leaking. I put a bucket under it, sat on the couch, and stared. Another time, I was so sick that the kids ate an entire loaf of bread for lunch and there was nothing I could do but hope to get better fast. All the while I was consumed with guilt, worrying about the negative quantities of fruits and vegetables in their daily diet. I would miss deadlines and lose school papers and sometimes disappoint potential friends when I couldn't follow through as planned. Sometimes I gave up sleep that I really needed to avoid these traps. I tried to make everything work. There were many days that I thought, *What the hell am I doing here in Vermont? Why not just move back to Indiana, where at least I have some family and a few good friends? A support system of some kind and where I won't have to worry about overt social pressure about eating meat.* The idea I'd had that a new location would somehow simplify the logistics of my life was wrong. Certain jagged edges remained. And after bringing Corey back into my life, my mind was split, my heart was split. It became emotionally complicated, which was more than simply being unconventional.

Though I moved away for a reason, I keep going back. Three, four, five times a year. I visit Mandi, who is like a sister to me and the only person besides my brother, other cousins, and Corey who knows the whole of me. We are unbreakable, bound by blood and the unspeakable bonds that form between children who are not altogether all right. I visit a few friends—Jen and Rachel, primarily. Two more squares of the expanding quilt. As women, we have grown together well, seen each other through childbirths, postpartum depression, regular depression, divorces, and absent partners. We have never lost our wildness; under the right circumstances, we will still strip our shirts off and dance under the moon. We travel together, sometimes. Now, place is not only an escape but also a way to reconnect to our old selves. Someday, we joke, we'll buy a house somewhere that we'll all share when our kids go off to college. We won't need men at all, except for when we needed them. It isn't necessarily a joke.

I miss my old haunts, the familiar flat land, the people who know me well, even the endless corn. When I see pictures of Earth from space, the gap between memory and experience, right and wrong, past and present, closes. There is only now, only the daily choice to live the life I have the way I want to live it. I bet from space, the word *political* sounds silly. The word *anger*. *Punishment, justice, loneliness.* From that vantage point, why would you care about anything but happiness? Anything but peace? The farther away from the past, the clearer it becomes. Distance, they say, is everything. One planet closer to the sun and we'd all be dead.

My parents recently moved to a subdivision at the golf course. They wanted to live closer to their friends. Finally, our wishes aligned, albeit two decades too late. My father called me on the day they closed on their old house, the one in the cornfield, the last place I had lived with them. I asked him if he went back one last time, after the movers had come, and whether he would miss it.

"I was at work when they were there. There's nothing I needed to see. It's time to move on."

He mentioned, then, that a lot of things happened in that house. He didn't name what, exactly, and he didn't have to. We were both there. A new home hadn't changed us as people. The problems we had as a family remained. To be sure, it distracted us for a little while—another kitchen to remodel, a new lawn to tame. That is all I can really say for a change of place. It's refreshing. It can open doors, if you know where to look. But it isn't everything. It isn't a cure-all. We're still left with our complicated selves, our mixed-up past. We have our individual perspectives to reconcile and our separate futures to manage.

When Marcus was charged with battery—he'd punched a friend in the face—my mother was aghast. "I don't understand how he could have done something like that," she said. "You two didn't grow up around violence." I just laughed. There was no other response in me that remained. People see what they want to see, deny what they don't.

"When you make mistakes you can't dwell on them," said my father. "I always just move on to the next thing without thinking about it or looking back. Nobody tells you how to be a parent. You get one chance and there is no doing it over."

"I guess we all deal with things in different ways," I replied. "We do the best we can."

In a snapshot of me, Corey, Marcus, and another neighborhood friend, we are all sitting on my parents' front lawn holding kittens. Their eyes have just opened; they see the gigantic world for the first time. They cling to our shirts and our bodies. I hold mine as if it were an infant, cradling it, protecting it from falling. Corey's sits on his head and looks terrified. We are all laughing and angled toward Corey, who palms a basketball in one hand and makes a silly face. He is the sun center of our youth. The one who keeps everyone smiling, even as his own life tears away from him beyond the photographic frame.

A photograph is a living history. Like place, an old photograph is the future cutting into the present and the past ongoing. Outside the frame: Corey's home, where this beautiful boy will soon be emotionally and physically neglected, locked out and abused by his own family; where he will be left to fend for himself and propelled to places he never should have been. Outside the frame: the bar and restaurant where I will learn of Corey's crime; where I will call him even though I know he is long gone and hang up when his mother answers; where I will make money that I will save to help myself move on from this place. Outside the frame: the brown house where the people who will die when Corey is, at last, too far gone are still living their quiet lives. Outside the frame: the river that was moved a hundred years ago to make way for all of us. What happened to the

Potawatomi in their new lives on their new land? What will happen to us in ours?

Memory, it has been hypothesized, works like a compounding file system that constantly updates and pulls to the front of the file those memories that are being actively used or recalled in some way. Every memory is stored. As new experiences relate to old ones—such as hearing a new vocabulary word used in a movie, or meeting people over and over, learning more about them— the memory strengthens. Like payments made on an installment plan, new associations are added to the original memory, piling up to create a collected sense of what is remembered. On one hand, my memory of the river was romanticized. It was a place where, through countless interactions, I grew to love Corey so much that his worst actions couldn't destroy the richness of my attachment to him. On the other hand, I associated the place with negative experiences and emotions such that it made it difficult for me to return.

In Marina Abramović's performance art exhibit *The Artist Is Present* at the Museum of Modern Art, she sat a table and silently looked into strangers' eyes as they took turns sitting down in the chair across from hers. When her former lover and collaborator Ulay, whom she hadn't seen since they broke up thirty years earlier, sat down at the other end of the table, she cried and reached across the table for his hands. In the video of the performance, you can see how much he still affects her. She looks like she is surrendering, body and mind, to the memory of him. When he walked away after his sixty seconds were up, she straightened her spine and returned to normal. In 1988, the couple had split dramatically. They walked toward one another from opposite ends of the Great Wall of China, embraced, and then they went their separate ways. When I sat down with Corey, it was the same scene. I publicly surrendered myself to the memory of him—not as distant as I had convinced myself. When I got up to leave, I took care to right myself within the present reality of our separate worlds.

During the months after the prison visit, I squeezed my sons from time to time, worrying their futures like stones. The elder was intense and obsessive and had the capacity for extreme emotions. The younger one was calmer, tending to withdraw and ruminate if he was upset. They both sought love and praise. They both expected the world to be good and were shocked at anything that challenged that belief. Our worst flaws—my explosive reactions to perceived injustices, Mike's stunted emotional capacity and compulsion to verify and perfect everything—flared up among their strengths. I cupped their tiny shoulders in my hands and reminded them to be kind. It was the simplest instruction or request that I could formulate. They nodded their soft skulls in agreement. I could nearly see the synapses firing behind their blue-white eyeballs. But we have no control over that kind of thing. What sticks and what doesn't in the unseen expanse of the mind, what brief experiences get built up in memory and become the icons of a life lived. Even adults forget most of it soon enough, remembering the decades that pass only in gross summaries: the good years, the bad years, the big milestones, the few specific and vivid memories. We forget the small reasons we leave people and places, the little injustices. And we forget why, sometimes, we can't go back. We just know we can't. We know what happened but we never know why. Or we even remember it wrong, but that doesn't matter: we have our truths. We realize that newness must take not only a new shape of behavior or thoughts, but sometimes even a new landscape. Place as reboot. Eventually, I think we forgive the land and the associations we have with it. We see it for what it is, what it always was: a complex terrain with a history and a future. A place where we were, for a time, becoming what we are now.

I tried to imagine the futures my kids couldn't see coming—the boys and girls and men and women who would change my children and alter the course of their lives. I tried to imagine the kinds of people who would break their hearts and fill them with passion. What events would send them across the country in search of a place where no one knew them, where they could be someone else, anyone else. I hoped they never would feel that need. I hoped I was making enough positive associations with home, with these green mountains and this blue lake, that coming back to visit as adults wouldn't give them panic attacks.

There are no true dive bars in Vermont, not like the ones back home. You can't walk into public social settings here and expect to have a good time with people you've never met. There is no two-stepping with strangers here. I go back to Indiana to recreate the pleasurable parts of the past. To enrich my long-standing friendships with Jen and Rachel. To spend just enough time with family to remember why I love them, and why I can't stay. For now, I'm content in Vermont. It has the familiar canvas of home—water and fields—but none of the problems.

The conversation about what a life is made of, what a marriage is made of, continues in installments. We have tried to stay apace with the inevitability of change. One night, after Mike and I put the kids to bed, this challenge seemed too large. We decided to make the problem of staying on the same map smaller. We said out loud that everything was too serious; it didn't have to be difficult. Instead of more talking, we danced wildly in the living room to electronic music. It wasn't a solution per se, but rather an attitude adjustment. We chose to be free from expectations that we and other people had of our relationship, our family. When we cut away what anyone might think of us, including ourselves, life became much easier. Mike asked that night whether I'd leave him for Corey if he ever got out of prison. I shared with him Corey's "what if" advice, telling him there was no sense in our talking about a situation that wasn't realistic. But it was a relief to know that he was open to any answer I might give. We became amenable to change—that specific change or any other—simply by identifying its possibility.

Nearly a year after the prison visit, I returned to the place where I'd sat on Frost's lawn in awe of its storied past. This time, I was teaching at the annual writing conference for high school students. The inn on campus has an elevator now. Mostly I took the stairs while I was there, but that was only because I was in a Fitbit competition with Marcus, who was now living in Kentucky, running a scaffolding company owned by the same company where my dad worked. And I was losing.

Tom Paine, another instructor and writer at the conference, gave me some advice on the kids we would be teaching: "Keep in mind, no one has ever sat down with them and asked them what they think about, what they like to read as opposed to what they have to read. No adult has ever asked them what their dreams are. You get to be the one to do that."

On the morning of the day when I'd later read in the campus theater—a place I never thought I'd be, doing something I never thought I'd do—I rode the elevator downstairs for coffee. I saw, posted above the elevator buttons, the name of the company that now owns the company where my father works as a successful sales rep, and was momentarily astounded. My father was a carpenter, in the beginning. Before he was a foreman, then a superintendent of a scaffolding company. Before he was a golfer and a regional scaffolding sales rep who ended up making more money than he'd ever dreamed possible. Before all of that, he built things with his hands. He never once said to me, sit down, let me tell you about this book I'm reading. He never asked what my ideas were, or how anything at all in the world made me feel. He never asked what my dreams were. But he had paid cash for the balance of my college tuition that wasn't covered by scholarships. He had paid more into my kids' college funds than I myself would be able to contribute over the next ten years. He never thought for a moment, to my knowledge, that he'd done wrong by me in any way. Or if he did, he never said so. He taught me how to swing a hammer, how to build a wall, plumb and true, spacing the studs sixteen inches from center to dead center. He taught me how to carry on, no matter what happened. How to survive a flood, or a life. The building skills have not proved all that useful yet, but that is the knowledge he could offer me. I recognized the holding company's name in the elevator because it had, fifteen years earlier, provided four years of scholarship money for my college tuition, a ride up, a way out.

Someday, I thought, looking up at the plastic placard, *I'll build my sons a treehouse from a pile of wood and no one will know where this skill came from.* No one will know that it will be designed in the likeness of the fort I'd built with Corey and Marcus a thousand years ago with my father's tools. Our fort was an escape from our lives, a place to pretend. But theirs will be a place in the sky where they can read their books and spy their futures in the shapes of clouds.

Burroughs and Gysin thought their cut-up approach helped discover or decode the heart of a given text. It revealed what the words really meant, which of course was not exactly what they said. Burroughs thought the form might help a writer divine meaning through what he called "folding in," or inserting text from the same story in places where it would fall out of time with the narrative, creating a chaotic kind of flashback or flash-forward. He said of this method, "When you cut into the present the future leaks out." The description of how he used this approach in fiction is not unlike what creative nonfiction writers and lyric essayists today term segmentation or collage, where digressions both related and seemingly unrelated to the essay's main subject are interspersed without regard for the strict constraint of the linear narrative. These digressions begin to make sense both in the context of the surrounding white space and juxtaposition against other segments, and in the essay's future paragraphs, its central concerns, its end. I invited Corcy to cut into my present by bringing him back into my life, and a new future leaked out. A new story emerged.

Shortly after my prison visit, a friend asked if I could take her sons fishing. Our families had moved to the state around the same time, and we were all still adapting, sampling the culture. Auditioning new friends as if we were holding casting calls. "We bought all the tackle," she said, "but Adam and I don't know how to use any of it." Her husband was a professor; she was a bilingual digital strategist for nonprofits. They were both loftily educated, their young children adorable, eccentric geniuses. There was the caveat that they were vegetarians and wanted the fish to be released once they were caught. "I think we can manage that," I said, though I had wanted to show them how to clean a bluegill with a teaspoon.

We drove to a pond a few miles from Lake Champlain, where the four boys would be able to wade into the water easily. They huddled around as I sorted through their tackle box for supplies. I moved the deepwater lures aside. "Those are for boat fishing," I said. I pointed at the plastic triple-hooked lures. "You boys aren't old enough to use the jigs yet."

Their eyes widened at the foreign terminology. They protested, defending their choice of lures as *shiny* and *cool*. I loved the way they loved these objects whose functions were completely unknown to them. They loved them at face value, for their sleek shapes and colors and the pure beauty of their design, as they loved anything at that young age: found lengths of string, plastic eggs, sea glass, discarded pieces of tinfoil that could be molded into robot appendages, and a thousand other objects that would, someday, form the backdrop to their remembered childhood—holding not all, but some memories, not all, but some truth. I selected weights and bobbers for them instead, drawing the fishing line through the eyes of their poles and showing them how to knot the line to secure the clasp as my father had shown me. It would be years until they could tie the knot themselves. But they would remember, I hoped, the way my hands worked the line, the silver clasp glinting in the sun. The soggy sandwiches we had for lunch that tasted good anyway. The way we laughed when my younger son held a fistful of earthworms and named each of them Slimy. *This is Slimy, and this is Slimy. Say hello to Slimy.*

It didn't matter where we were fishing, only that we were there, doing it. Likewise, it didn't matter where Corey was—how many miles away—for me to keep him close. I wrote to him to tell him about the funny things the kids had said and done on the fishing trip. I told him about the water snake they had tried to hypnotize with a whispered charm. The way their words were magic, and, conjured in the correct order, could light fires or send snakes to sleep. The way the boys hopped like frogs and covered themselves in mud. The way they never minded mud, or noticed it as something to be washed away. Here, I can give them the best of my own childhood, an idea of what life by the river was all about, but without any of the problems.

In the letter, I asked Corey if he remembered the angelfish I'd kept as a kid and whether he remembered carrying me home that day I thought I was dying. We had added the crawdad and the bluegill to our fish tank. For each of three days, one of the fish turned up dead. Marcus and I awoke to the crime scenes: a single wrecked claw and scattered scales remained as evidence of the slaughters on the first two days. When only the two angelfish were left, the female taunted the male. Her tail hung clipped and loose as she swam toward him and away from him. On the third night, they turned on each other in a fevered and bloody fight. Only the female fish survived. Remnants of the male trailed behind her, entwined in her silky fin like a battle flag.

Acknowledgments

Versions of small portions of these essays have appeared in *Sundog Lit, Tampa Review, Hippocampus,* and *Essay Daily.* I thank the editors of these journals for publishing this work. Thanks to Lana Popovic, my brilliant agent. Thanks to Brigid Hughes, the prize judge. I am grateful to Fiona McCrae, Steve Woodward, Jeff Shotts, and the whole Graywolf Press team for their extraordinary vision and support. To my teachers and mentors, Charley Kerlin and Bill Mottolese. To those who generously read many incarnations of this work or otherwise supported and inspired me in the making of this book: Rachel Carter, Stephen Cramer, Matthew O'Connell, Shelagh Connor Shapiro, Keith S. Wilson, Brooks Rexroat, Shannon McCarthy, Kate Sykes, Christopher Castellani, and Michael Jager.

Special thanks to Amedeo D'adamo and Melissa Falcon Field. Without them, this book would have remained in a folder on my laptop.

Endless thanks and love to my parents, my aunts, and Mike, who have made writing possible for me. Thanks to Corey, for his support and consent in telling this story.

Raised in the rural Midwest, Angela Palm owns Ink + Lead Literary Services and is the editor of *Please Do Not Remove,* a book featuring work by Vermont writers. Her work has appeared in *Brevity, Paper Darts, Midwestern Gothic, Sundog Lit, Essay Daily,* and elsewhere. She teaches creative writing at Champlain College and lives in Burlington, Vermont.

The Graywolf Press Nonfiction Prize

Riverine: A Memoir from Anywhere but Here by Angela Palm is the 2014 winner of the Graywolf Press Nonfiction Prize. Graywolf awards this prize every twelve to eighteen months to a previously unpublished, full-length work of outstanding literary nonfiction by a writer who is not yet established in the genre. Previous winners include *Leaving Orbit: Notes from the Last Days of American Spaceflight* by Margaret Lazarus Dean, *The Empathy Exams: Essays* by Leslie Jamison, *The Grey Album: On the Blackness of Blackness* by Kevin Young, *Notes from No Man's Land: American Essays* by Eula Biss, *Black Glasses Like Clark Kent: A GI's Secret from Postwar Japan* by Terese Svoboda, *Neck Deep and Other Predicaments* by Ander Monson, and *Frantic Transmissions to and from Los Angeles: An Accidental Memoir* by Kate Braverman.

The Graywolf Press Nonfiction Prize seeks to acknowledge—and honor—the great traditions of literary nonfiction. Whether grounded in observation, autobiography, or research, much of the most beautiful, daring, and original writing over the past few decades can be categorized as nonfiction.

The 2014 prize judge was Brigid Hughes, founding editor of *A Public Space* and contributing editor to Graywolf Press.

From 2005 to 2012, the prize was judged by Robert Polito.

The Graywolf Press Nonfiction Prize is funded in part by endowed gifts from the Arsham Ohanessian Charitable Remainder Unitrust and the Ruth Easton Fund of the Edelstein Family Foundation.

Arsham Ohanessian, an Armenian born in Iraq who came to the United States in 1952, was an avid reader and a tireless advocate for human rights and peace. He strongly believed in the power of literature and education to make a positive impact on humanity.

Ruth Easton, born in North Branch, Minnesota, was a Broadway actress in the 1920s and 1930s. The Ruth Easton Fund of the Edelstein Family Foundation is pleased to support the work of emerging artists and writers in her honor.

Graywolf Press is grateful to Arsham Ohanessian and Ruth Easton for their generous support.

The text of *Riverine* is set in Minion Pro. Book design by Connie Kuhnz. Composition by Bookmobile Design & Digital Publisher Services, Minneapolis, Minnesota. Manufactured by Versa Press on acid-free, 30 percent postconsumer wastepaper.